Other books by PAUL L. DRESSEL
(author, coauthor, editor)

*Improving Degree Programs: A Guide to
  Curriculum Development,
  Administration, and Review* (1980)
*A Degree for College Teachers: The Doctor
  of Arts* (1977)
Handbook of Academic Evaluation (1976)
Independent Study (1973)
Return to Responsibility (1972)
The Confidence Crisis (1971)
*Institutional Research in the University: A
  Handbook* (1971)
The World of Higher Education (1971)
Undergraduate Curriculum Trends (1969)
College and University Curriculum (1968;
  2nd ed., 1971)
*The Undergraduate Curriculum in Higher
  Education* (1963)
Evaluation in Higher Education (1961)
*Evaluation in the Basic College at Michigan
  State University* (1958)
*Comprehensive Examinations in a Program
  of General Education* (1949)

Administrative Leadership

*Effective and Responsive
Decision Making
in Higher Education*

Paul L. Dressel

Administrative
Leadership

Jossey-Bass Publishers
San Francisco • Washington • London • 1981

ADMINISTRATIVE LEADERSHIP
Effective and Responsive Decision Making in Higher Education
    by Paul L. Dressel

Copyright © 1981 by: Jossey-Bass Inc., Publishers
                     433 California Street
                     San Francisco, California 94104
                          &
                     Jossey-Bass Limited
                     28 Banner Street
                     London EC1Y 8QE

Library of Congress Cataloging in Publication Data

Dressel, Paul Leroy, 1910-
        Administrative leadership.

        Bibliography: p. 221
        Includes index.
        1. Universities and colleges—United States—
Administration—Decision making. I. Title.
LB2341.D688   378.73   81-81962
ISBN 0-87589-500-X   AACR2

Manufactured in the United States of America

JACKET DESIGN BY WILLI BAUM

FIRST EDITION

Code 8114

*The Jossey-Bass
Series in Higher Education*

Preface

This volume about administration in American higher education draws upon over fifty years of experience, including a quasi-administrative role at Michigan State University for some forty years and as an observer and consultant on administrative matters in many institutions. Although I have written many books on various aspects of higher education, I long and deliberately avoided writing one on administration. An early decision on my part was that study of curricular and instructional matters combined with direct involvement with students and faculty could, in the long run, have more impact on educational quality than could study of administration. Individuals are selected as administrators rather than either trained or suited to it. Many administrators shortly become too heavily involved with external matters requiring extensive absence from the campus. Paper work and committees seem to keep some administrators so involved that they have a limited sense of faculty and student educational activities and efforts in offices, classrooms, and laboratories. Some simply preside but neither administer nor manage. A few concentrate on their own comfort and aspirations and make everyone else uncomfortable. Events in recent years, including some at Michigan State University, have convinced me that I should write about the role of administration in higher education in the hope that what I have observed and perceived will illuminate others.

Although I have provided extensive references in the bibliography and some commentary about useful materials for reading by administrators in Resource A, I have otherwise largely ignored the extensive literature on administration and management. In the first place, it is my conviction that those publications purporting to be the results of research on administration in higher education, although useful in getting some sense of the patterns and complications that exist, say very little to the administrator on the front line. Especially is this true when research publications attempt to develop theories and principles, many of which have some scholarly merit but relatively little to do with the administrator faced with a specific problem in the context of a particular institution with a distinctive faculty, student body, and clientele. In the second place, I believe that most writing on administration has not taken adequately into account the social role and responsibility of higher education and the obligation of administrators to operate within a value framework which, all too frequently, is not known to the faculty or, if known, is not accepted. Social responsibility is often at odds with faculty expectations in regard to academic freedom and autonomy and with the composite aspirations of faculty and administrators to advance the reputation of the institution and thereby enhance their own.

The chapters that follow present a series of concerns that I have developed with regard to American higher education. Chapter One offers the view that, despite faculty desires for extensive involvement in decision making, faculty members, as a group, are not able to address institutional decisions in a socially responsible manner or to recognize the obligation of an institution to relate to a system of higher education within a framework of limited resources. *Administrators are needed,* but a new type of administrator is required who can see his or her role within an institution with full awareness of the existence of other institutions and limited resources. Chapter Two continues this general theme by emphasizing the place of morals, ethics, and values in higher education and the importance of consulting value commitments in a framework of social responsibility and concern for quality. Chapter Three deals with communication, which is in itself one of the most difficult issues on a campus. One gets the impression at times that too many administrators are less than forthright and frank in communication. This is perhaps understandable in the light of the many audiences to which their communications must be addressed and the apparent inability of many of these audiences to listen carefully because of their desires to present and support their own views. Chapter Four considers various approaches to decision making and their relationship to administration. Chapter Five emphasizes the major concerns of academic administration, although pointing up that all aspects of decision making in an institution of higher education ought to be based upon academic concerns. Chapters Six and Seven focus upon internal and external factors involved in higher education and their impact upon the decision-making process. Chapter Eight emphasizes the university's obligations and the role and responsibility of the administrator in reference to these. In particular, it must be emphasized that the administrator's chore is to make evident to the faculty and student body that the institution has obligations that preclude immediate gratification of the diverse and conflicting desires of students and faculty members. Chapter Nine discusses a few of the crucial problems and issues of the previous chapters in the context of a particular problem. Chapter Ten indicates that the administrator should be evaluated. For many years, institutions of higher education have evaluated the students. In recent years, they have attempted, not very effectively, to evaluate faculty, but administration has generally not been evaluated in any forthright manner. In such circumstances, ineffectual administrators can, so long as adequate resources are available, stay with an institution for lengthy periods of time, doing neither good nor evil. Boards will tolerate them because they cause no trouble, and faculty will tolerate them because they leave the faculty alone.

Resource A suggests some of the key resources that an administrator may wish to have close at hand for quick reference or review. Obviously, Resource A is closely related to the bibliography and the suggestions for further reading at the end of each chapter. Resource B presents a glossary of some of the terminology that has proliferated in recent years in the fields of administration, management, budget making, and accountability.

Consonant with the theme of this volume, I urge administrators, in using these resources, not to do so with the expectation of immediately finding a solution. In my experience, even successful solutions of certain problems on other campuses fail when transferred because the underlying conditions are different, because key personalities are different, or simply because there was inadequate thought and preparation for introducing a new point of view, a new set of policies, or new programs. There is an unfortunate tendency when making changes, whether initiated by faculty members, administrators, or external pressures, to undertake substantial change at a given moment in time and hope that it is effective without making plans to verify that effectiveness. Review of innovations over the years demonstrates that everything (except the educational technology of the day) has been tried numerous times in the past, has disappeared, and then been rediscovered with great enthusiasm and fanfare. Although there is much talk about planning in higher education, I have not seen a great amount of it in evidence, except in those periods of time when institutions were able to assume marked increase in enrollment and income, and therefore in facilities, programs, faculty, and students. More fundamental planning with regard to educational programs and their quality and relevance to societal needs takes time because faculty members involved must lay aside old convictions and biases and acquire confidence in new ones. When an innovation deviates markedly from traditional practices, students too must be convinced that the experiences provided are sound and acceptable in the marketplace. Moreover, the maintenance of quality is never assured by a program change made at a point in time that is followed rigidly thereafter. The lines by James Russell Lowell are profound (*The Present Crisis,* Stanza 18):

> *New occasions teach new duties; Time*
> *makes ancient good uncouth;*
> *They must upward still, and onward,*
> *who would keep abreast of Truth.*

By demonstrating a rational approach to defining, understanding, and analyzing problems faced by an institution or unit thereof, an administrator can gain trust and support. By involving faculty members in analyzing problems and defining the values implicit in various solutions, an administrator can provide the faculty with an in-service continuing education far more significant than that embraced in most of the so-called programs of faculty development. With careful planning, over a period of time, the faculty can be brought to understand the need to look at traditional and sacrosanct practices that have been difficult to change. Innovations fail when they are not well understood, endorsed, or enthusiastically embraced.

The fundamental problems that beset American higher education today are due to the failure of faculty, administrators, and institutions as a whole to consult continually their obligations to the society that supports them. In responding to social expectations, institutions of higher education must engage in planning and institutional development in a responsible and professional manner. This requires that they make a continuing and determined effort to assess the values prevalent in society, the role of the institution in adjusting to, supporting, or modifying these values, and the manner in which the programs and processes of the institution relate to institutional and societal value commitments.

Acknowledgments

Numerous people have contributed in various ways to this volume. First of all, I would acknowledge the opportunity, over more than twenty-five years, to observe and work with John Hannah, who was president of Michigan State University from 1941 to 1969.

I am also greatly obligated to Stanley Ikenberry, president

of the University of Illinois. Years ago, Ikenberry served an apprenticeship under me in the Office of Institutional Research. Over the years, his writings and my interactions with him from time to time have influenced my own thinking. He generously read the entire manuscript and made very insightful comments and useful suggestions. Cassandra Book, from our College of Communication Arts, read parts of the manuscript and was particularly helpful with her comments on Chapter Three on communication.

Although not directly involved in this particular task, Laura Bornholdt, vice-president of the Lilly Endowment, and Frederick deW. Bolman, formerly director of the Exxon Education Foundation, have long been stimulating to me because of their interest in my studies and writing and have helped to obtain funding for my various projects.

Finally, I wish to acknowledge the efforts of my longtime assistant, Ruth Frye, whose invaluable work in typing, editing, and bibliographical search has helped bring this and other publications to fruition.

East Lansing, Michigan   Paul L. Dressel
July 1981

Contents

The Author

Paul L. Dressel is professor of university research at Michigan State University in East Lansing. He received his bachelor's degree in mathematics from Wittenberg College (1931), his master's degree in mathematics and physics from Michigan State (1934), and his doctoral degree in mathematics from the University of Michigan (1939).

Since 1932, when he first joined the mathematics faculty at Michigan State University, Dressel has served in various capacities and was often the first person assigned to a particular responsibility. In 1936 he began coordinating the orientation program for new students, which led gradually to developing a testing program, remedial services for students, and a counseling center that he directed for over a decade. For several years he was chairman of the Board of Examiners, which was empowered to grant, by any appropriate means, credit in any course offered in the institution. The Board eventually became the Office of Evaluation Services and was charged with designing and carrying out numerous studies on educational issues. From 1949 through 1952, Dressel was director of the Cooperative Study of Evaluation in General Education sponsored by the American Council on Education; results of the study were reported in *General*

Education: Explorations in Evaluation, coauthored by Dressel and Lewis B. Mayhew. In subsequent years, Dressel's staff was expanded to conduct educational research and related studies at Michigan State, and in 1959 he became the first person to head the newly created Office of Institutional Research.

Dressel has served as a consultant to numerous colleges and universities. He was long active in accreditation with the North Central Association of Colleges and Universities and served on the executive board of the Commission of Institutions of Higher Education, 1966-1970. For over ten years he has been chairman of the Illinois Commission of Scholars, which reviews and recommends or denies all new doctoral proposals from Illinois state-assisted higher education institutions. He was president of the American Association of Higher Education, 1970-71, and has been involved in studying Doctor of Arts programs, resulting in the publication of *The New Colleges: Toward an Appraisal* (1971); *Blueprint for Change* (with Frances DeLisle, 1972); *College Teaching: Improvement by Degrees* (with Mary Magdala Thompson, 1974). He also was involved in critiquing nontraditional graduate programs as reported in *A Review of Nontraditional Graduate Degrees* (1978) and *Problems and Principles in the Recognition or Accreditation of Graduate Programs* (1978).

Dressel has received awards for research from the American Personnel and Guidance Association (with Ross Matteson, 1950) and from the American Educational Research Association (the E. F. Lindquist Award, 1980). He was granted an honorary Doctor of Laws degree by Wittenberg University in 1966.

Administrative Leadership

Effective and Responsive
Decision Making
in Higher Education

ONE

⮑⮑⮑⮑⮑⮑⮑⮑⮑⮑⮑⮑⮑⮑⮑⮑⮑⮑⮑⮑⮑⮑⮑⮑⮑⮑⮑⮑⮑⮑⮑⮑⮑⮑⮑⮑⮑

The Need
for Administrators

Compared with business, industry, and government, higher education is a distinctive enterprise. In business and industry, purposes, goals, and policies are formulated at the apex of a pyramidal structure and subsequently interpreted to and carried out by individuals operating within relatively inflexible rules and limitations. Although some management theorists have expounded extensively on employee involvement in decisions and on the significance of humanitarian concerns in achieving both high morale and production efficiency, the necessity of maintaining a profit margin, combined with insatiable individual expectations and union demands, ensures that administration and directive management must be present.

Democratic government theoretically draws its directions and policies from the people through elected representatives who enact laws and formulate policies that are interpreted and applied or enforced by an ever-expanding bureaucracy nurtured by routine, red tape, and a general reluctance to abolish any budgeted agency or policy. The elected representatives tend to become career oriented in governance and therefore endorse those policies and make those decisions that appear most likely

1

to achieve reelection. In this circumstance, special-interest expectations and demands take precedence over rational policies based upon democratic, humanitarian, and practical values embodying optimal benefits for all. The ideal of the democratic society becomes unattainable because there is no accord on values and little willingness to accept an indefinable optimization for all as more desirable than a definable maximization of benefits desired by various groups.

Higher education differs from business, industry, and government in several respects. The first difference is in the nature of the outcomes. Higher education uses tangible resources to produce intangible outcomes and does so by processes that are not well defined, that are highly idiosyncratic to the units and individuals involved in the processes, and that appear exceedingly inefficient and wasteful to those inured to directive and controlled procedures more obviously related to outcomes desired. Higher education is more like the church from which it sprang than any other modern social organization. The professoriate, the higher education priesthood, would prefer that their lay brethren exhibit faith in higher education and buttress this by good works demonstrated by generous support. In the prevailing modern mood, church membership and commitment to religious beliefs and good works are no longer widely regarded as ensuring salvation and life everlasting. Similarly, college degrees are not regarded as the keys to either a good life or a successful one. Fundamentally, both education and religion depend upon deferred gratitude. Reverence for past glories no longer provides relief from the exigencies of the present and certainly no insurance of a desirable future. For most people in the present day, the guiding philosophy is that of living a reasonably pleasant and satisfying life in the face of complete uncertainty. Immediate gratification is the order of the day, but this is made unattainable by the realities of infinite expectations, decreasing resources, and human fallibility and venality. Hence the motivations and performance of all individuals and organizations come under review. The professoriate is not immune to fallibility and venality, and sheer incompetency is not uncommon. Fragmented by specialization, egotism, and idiosyncrasies, a college or university faculty is unable to agree on purposes, goals, and policies and to demonstrate accountability in the use of resources unless some form of central administration succeeds in bringing harmony and unity out of the prevailing discord and fragmentation. The supporting agencies and ultimately the public require and deserve honesty, frankness, responsible performance, and accountability in the use of educational resources. Unwillingness or incapability in these regards casts doubt on the validity of the entire enterprise. Coordination and management of higher education by individuals and organizational structures committed to directing higher education institutions and their resources to meeting individual and social needs and to long-term improvement of society are essential if the university is to regain and maintain the prestige and respect once readily accorded to it.

Motivations of Administrators

These reflections on administration suggest that any individual who seeks or who has been offered an administrative position in a college or university should seriously consider the question: "Why do I want to be an administrator?" The individual will also do well to look into the implications of becoming an administrator and talk with his or her family about the implications for them. If there are friends sufficiently close to ensure complete, even brutal, frankness, he or she should enter into a discussion with them also. Another appropriate chore is to consider and review with some care the actions and decisions of administrators with whom the administrative aspirant has worked or whom he or she has had the opportunity to observe. Occasionally, deans and presidents are hired who have had no prior administrative or faculty experience in higher education. Such individuals will almost certainly err if they make judgments about administration in higher education in relationship to administrative experiences elsewhere. They should probably reflect back to their own experiences as students and think about some of the administrative decisions that were made and the reactions of students and faculty members to them. They will also do well to talk with some administrators in colleges and universities, if they number such among their friends, and perhaps even with some students at the graduate level who will have had a period of insight into administration in one or more institutions. An individual who is strongly interested in an administrative post at a college or university and is being seriously considered ought also to have the opportunity to talk with a number of persons on the faculty other than those on a selection committee and to review the recent governance issues on the campus. Some of these suggested and desirable activities are not feasible today. There tends to be a hush-hush situation surrounding the employment of administrators which, on the one hand, prevents the institution from thoroughly examining the characteristics of an individual being considered and, on the other hand, deprives the individual of the opportunity to explore in considerable depth the precise nature of the institution and the extent to which affiliation with it would be congenial and productive. Nevertheless, the aspirant administrator will benefit markedly from a searching and completely honest self-examination. Indeed, one may be sure that the individual who is unable to do this should probably avoid an administrative assignment.

There are those who are attracted by the salary and perquisites. This is apt to be more of an attraction to persons who are serving on faculties of institutions than to individuals from outside. The individual who has already achieved an administrative role in business or industry has far better salary expectations there than in higher education. However, there are many state universities in which the salary of the president and perhaps of one or two other individuals may be significantly higher than that of the governor and other political officeholders. The salary can be an attraction, but it should be noted that, in most cases, both husband and wife become essentially full-time employees of the institution and the salary alone, in relationship to the demands and responsibilities, is misleading.

There are those who are attracted very strongly by social status, and here the spouse may be involved as well as the administrator. A president is one of a kind in an institution and naturally receives recognition and attention not coming to others. There is a certain status involved in an administrative title, but the social obligations that go along with top-level administrative positions place heavy demands on personal interests, family life, and, for an academic, any continuation of scholarly effort. One must ask the question whether knowing prominent and influential people in a community by their first names and being invited to a wide range of social affairs is a real benefit or a liability.

Some religious denominations regard any position in connection with education as a calling essentially equal in status and urgency to the calling to the ministry. I recall a story told to me by the president of a liberal arts college. When he was first asked to the college to be considered for the presidency, he had very little interest. As he was driving back to his home after the interview, he was struck by a powerful emotional surge. He stopped his car, got out on the road beside it and prayed, asking God to tell him whether he should accept the call. He said that the positive response came through immediately and he accepted the position. Considering that he was acting on the authority of the Almighty, it is not surprising that he operated in an almost dictatorial way, but he did accomplish significant things for the institution. Occasionally, one finds individuals who are second- or third-generation college presidents. Their assumption of that role may not be a calling in the sense of the previous one. In talking with several of these people, however, I have come to the conclusion that not infrequently the possession of a prestigious name coupled with the status as offspring of a president causes the individual, as well as members of some boards of trustees, to regard the presidency as a matter of expectation and heritage. In my view, this is a dubious basis for entering into administration—especially in the same institution. The individual so called tends to regard the call as coming from outside the institution and from a source even beyond the board, so that the preferred role may be one of telling less-favored individuals what has to be done.

I have known several persons who moved into an administrative position subsequent to extensive study of higher education with the hope that their insights would enable them to restore integrity to an institution or, in some small measure, to higher education generally. Such individuals come to an administrative position with a mission and too frequently with a lack of understanding of the realities of institutional governance. The result may well be the imposition of a number of new patterns upon an institution and a sweeping elimination of past practices and even of people. The motivation is excellent and can be very productive. Provided they are kept under control, board members, faculty members, and possibly influential alumni in the community must become involved and accept the new ideas. Some people are quite comfortable with a lack of integrity, and what is seen by one individual as a lack of integrity may be seen by others as forthright and appropriate performance.

Another motivation that has brought a number of administrators into higher education at any level from department chairman to president has been the founding of a new institution or the addition of a new unit to an existing institution with the expectation that this new unit will develop a theme and a pattern of operation distinctly different from and, it is hoped, superior to the traditional. Thus new colleges and universities have attracted as chancellors or presidents individuals who have long harbored ideas about revolutionizing undergraduate education and who find this an opportunity—prior to the appointment of any faculty members, the arrival of students, or even final determination of structures—to do educational planning in depth. Frequently, these plans turn out to be idealistic and begin to crumble the first day that faculty members arrive on the campus to organize their disciplinary courses. Some of these pet ideas, such as emphasizing personal and social development of individuals, run counter to the long-time commitments of faculty members oriented to intellectual development and to their disciplines. The development within a university of a residential college having all the significant aspects of a small liberal arts college but providing immediate access to the resources of the university has been an attractive concept to numerous individuals who shortly found that neither students nor faculty were as enchanted with the concept as was the founder.

Still another motivation that has brought some persons into administration is that of accepting a post on an interim basis as a holding operation. One has only to review the history of departments, colleges, and universities to find in the list of administrators a number of persons designated as "acting" and holding the assignment for anywhere from a few months to many years. There are some individuals who would never, in the ordinary course of affairs, accept an administrative assignment but who, when asked to take on the interim or holding operation, feel an obligation to do so for the sake of the unit and the others in it. In one sense, this mode of entry into administration is a very appropriate one if one takes the view that anyone who strongly desires an administrative position is immediately suspect. The role of an acting administrator is often very simple— taking care of the day-by-day chores and avoiding any major issues as something for the next administrator to handle. When the acting administrator is appointed by a superior without much involvement by the faculty, that may be the only possibility. In other cases, acting administrators selected with faculty participation have turned out to be very effective, all the more because faculty members recognized that these individuals were not out to make a name by energetic administration. The pattern of inaugurating a president only after he or she has been in office for a year reflects something of this same view that an individual should be in an acting role for a period of time before full acceptance.

A variety of other minor and somewhat humorous factors operate in the decision to become an administrator or to remain as one. A friend who reluctantly accepted the post of acting dean agreed, after a year, to remain as dean because the position carried an assigned parking place and the individual simply could not face a return to hunting for a parking place each day.

The various motivations that have just been discussed reinforce the earlier contention that an individual considering an administrative post should enter into a period of honest self-evaluation. It is not necessarily bad to crave some power and authority, although any administrator in higher education will find that there is far less of this than appears from an external point of view. Nor is it necessarily bad that an individual is attracted by social status or by salary and perquisites. However, unless an individual has some basic commitment to the achievement and maintenance of quality in higher education and is particularly willing to face up to the question of what a particular institution and its various constituencies want and need, he does the institution and its adherents and himself an injustice by accepting the position. The individual who takes on an administrative position with the intent to take full advantage of all of its perquisites without generating any activity or change that would arouse dissent or animosity is simply using the institution to his or her own ends. One can find many instances of administrators who deliberately avoid any action or change that would provoke difficulty and generate publicity that might interfere with movement to an equal or higher level in a more prestigious institution.

A new administrator, whether department chairman, dean, vice-president, or president, if remaining on the campus on which he or she has been located for a time, will soon find that his or her relationships have undergone a subtle change. Continuing maintenance of close friendships will be endangered by the attempt on the part of some of these friends to utilize their intimacy with the administrator for their own ends or for the advancement of the ideas of some group with which they are affiliated. Even those friends who carefully avoid any use of the friendship may become suspect by other faculty members who view these individuals as having special privilege and suspect that any recognition for them is the result of favoritism rather than merit. The new administrator, too, will find that what had been regarded as an endearing or humorous personal characteristic may now be seen in an entirely different light. I recall a close friend, an excellent researcher, who in his contacts with people was given to humorous, sarcastic, and sometimes withering comments. Yet, knowing the person and the lack of any mean intent, people regarded these characteristics as endearing rather than otherwise. After being appointed as a dean, the individual continued to act in a perfectly natural way but, in so doing, generated, both internally and externally, such complaints and repercussions that retreat from the deanship became a necessity. An effective administrator must learn to listen to others, and not only to listen but try to understand and reflect upon what they propose. Frequently, the administrator's best ideas are put into effect only after they have been assimilated by a few others who present them in their own names. Administrators who are always proposing new ideas that they expect to be immediately accepted are likely not only to be unsuccessful but also to develop a resistance that will undermine any attempts to bring about change. The administrator, too, must pursue a rather narrow path between great enthusiasm for new ideas and abrupt rejection of them. However, a smiling, courteous, and complimentary reception of every idea presented is likely to be misinterpreted. Some faculty members will be certain that the president has enthusiastically accepted an idea and others will be disgusted that the apparently cordial reception was a false front betraying indifference.

Some administrators are pleased and even delighted because their new-found position requires their presence at many campus meetings. For top-level administrators there will be added a number of boards, committees, public service groups, and even state and federal meetings, conferences, and advisory groups. In the financial exigencies of the day, an administrator at almost any level is likely, too, to find it incumbent upon him or her to seek additional funding from a variety of sources. Thereby the administrator can find a multiplicity of excuses for avoiding both the major issues with which he or she should be concerned and the mundane paperwork activities that increasingly load the desk of every administrator.

Institutional Autonomy and Academic Freedom

One of the major responsibilities of an administrator in an institution of higher education is to interpret the nature of the institution to the public and to expound upon and clarify circumstances and factors that are essential if the institution is to perform its various functions. One aspect of this, little understood by individuals outside the institution who are offended by remarks or writings of faculty members, is academic freedom. There have been times in the past in which attacks on academic freedom were carried through with vigor and vengeance. In my perception, this has been much less of a problem in recent years, although one still hears or reads of the attack upon or the firing of faculty members because of expressed views contrary to the beliefs or convictions of some group having an interest in the institution. It is difficult in many of these cases to decide whether the individual concerned has expressed a serious and well-considered view, has deliberately placed himself in the limelight with a controversial statement, or is seeking to bring about a confrontation on a termination of appointment by making the case one of a violation of academic freedom rather than of incompetence. There are individuals and organizations who so overinterpret academic freedom that it has indeed come, in some respects, to be interpreted by some faculty members as freedom to do poorly or well whatever they want to do. A recent critical review by the American Association of University Professors of the discharge of a female professor emphasized the fact that the termination was almost certainly based upon life-style rather than upon competency. But it seemed to me, upon reading it, that any individual indulging in the unusual life-style there described on a small campus in a small town and in a college house next door to the president is evidently lacking in both good judgment and a sincere concern for the institution served.

Institutional autonomy has, in the past, been viewed by many individuals as a necessary concomitant of academic freedom. I view this as an unsound argument. Autonomy, in the usually discussed sense of complete freedom on the part of an institution to handle its own internal affairs, does not and has never existed. It has been limited by law, by the organization (for example, the church) with which the institution is affiliated, and by a variety of controls and the exercise of influence and power that go with financial support. Autonomy is simply an extension to an individual or an organization of a considerable degree of freedom in determining what is done and how it is accomplished. The extension of autonomy is based not only on trust but also on the regular proffering of data information and documentation showing that the resources allocated to the institution are being reliably and responsibly used and that, in considerable measure, the anticipated results are being obtained. Some of the most appalling abridgments of academic freedom have been brought about by administrators and boards of institutions rather than by interventions from external sources. And likewise some of the most serious abrogations of the autonomy of an institution have occurred when administrators and faculty have sought funds almost without regard for the strictures accompanying the receipt of the funds. Thus autonomy, in great part, rests upon the integrity of the institution and compliance with those values that are widely accepted in the society it serves. Basically, academic freedom refers to the freedom, indeed the responsibility, of the scholar to seek for truth and report it accurately and responsibly. Individuals in business, industry, and governance may, by the confidence they have achieved, have essentially the equivalent of academic freedom. Likewise, autonomy is extended to an institution because of a conviction that autonomy should be used by the institution in its academic units and in its administrative and financial operations to promote the search for knowledge, the organization and preservation of knowledge, and the application of that knowledge to the benefit of mankind. The last few words give a hint of those interventions into academic freedom that occur when the university takes on highly restricted projects with strict governmental limitations upon publication of results. In a sense, this action by the institution makes it a compliant and possibly even a cooperative and enthusiastic partner in the assault upon academic freedom.

The claimed advantages of autonomy lie in the independence of the institution to define areas of instruction, research, and service in reference to both its own strengths and public needs. Autonomy is presumed to enable greater diversity and innovation on the part of an institution. In fact, the evidence on this point is clearly drawn from those institutions where resources have been found to expand and to emulate the major public and private universities with a great range of programs, services, and research activities. Inevitably, some institutions have displayed irresponsibility in overexpanding.

Autonomy, as already noted, is urged as a means of pre-

serving academic freedom and recognizing the professional expertise of professors trained to an advanced level in their particular fields. Yet, repeatedly, one finds professors straying
from their areas of competence to make pronouncements in
other areas or to develop levels and types of programs for which
they are relatively untrained. Autonomy supports the separation of the university from the political spoils system, although
presidents and board members sometimes become victors or
victims of that process in ways that are not always open to public review. Autonomy presumably aids the institution in its obligation to engage in some societal criticism, but doing this in a
tactful and helpful way is difficult. Private institutions supported by particular individuals or groups find some difficulty
with the occasional faculty member who makes direct attacks
on sources of support and are occasionally driven back to confront the problem of an individual who is untactful, implacable,
and a threat to the continuing support of the institution.
Autonomy does serve to avoid many crises—or at least it has in
the past. Many a critic of an educational institution has found
that his charges and demands were of little interest and were ignored or ridiculed. Undoubtedly this has, in part, occurred because of a general recognition that no organization, especially
not an educational institution, can be effective if it must respond and adjust to every outside criticism. However, the protection of internal operations by this autonomy has resulted in
too many instances in which boards and administrators have refused to take action or have delayed action on critical situations
within the institution. It is precisely this unwillingness of some
institutions to deal with their own incompetencies and inappropriate uses of sources that has been brought to light and serves
as the major basis on the current scene for interventions into
institutional operations.

A primary contention with regard to autonomy is that its
existence supports quality. The truth of this convention depends largely upon the integrity and social responsibility of the
faculty, the administrators, and the board of an institution.
Various surveys (see the bibliography) demonstrate that too
many faculty members give low priority to undergraduate edu-

cation and prefer to engage in graduate instruction, research, and pursuit of their own interests. In visiting institutions during the summer or holiday periods, I have heard repeatedly that a college or university is a fine place when the students are gone. This is intended as a wry joke, but as frequent repetition suggests, the priorities of faculty members are not always in accord with the expectations of the supporting public. Indeed, in the last few years, the criticisms of college graduates in regard to their inadequacies in communication and other competencies bear witness to the fact that external review often must become the basis for stimulating a thoroughgoing internal review.

The proper balancing of institutional autonomy and academic freedom with social expectations and responsibilities constitutes a major continuing concern and obligation of administrators. Individuals who are uninterested or who regard these concepts as abstractions devoid of practical significance have no place in higher education administration.

Administrative Problems and Priorities

Faculty members, as presumed scholars, engrossed in one or more of the several responsibilities of the institution (instruction, research, and public service), are considered to be largely self-directed and busily engaged in the tasks appropriate to the particular assignments that they have defined. To a considerable extent this is true. The forty-hour week or less, which has become so common in many fields of work, is half or less of the total time spent in relevant activity by many academics that I have known. Many, indeed, have gone so far in expending all of their waking hours on academic tasks that spouses and children have been ignored. In a sense, this pattern of self-direction, with a heavy personal commitment that results in a combination of work with pleasure, provides the grounds for arguing that the extension of academic freedom and full autonomy to individuals will result in the best possible performance for individuals and for the institution. There are two deficiencies in this pattern of reasoning. The first is that a few lazy or incompetent faculty members will do little or nothing. The second is that

many of the academics I have observed who have indeed put in
many hours beyond the call of duty have done so in ways not
consonant with the public responsibilities and obligations of
the institution. They have instead regarded the institution as a
means of supporting them to pursue their own interests without regard to any administrative or external expectations. Some
private universities may be able to support this. But as these institutions have accepted funds from public sources, they have
found that acceptance of support demands accountability. Public institutions have never really had the prerogative of letting
individual staff members do as they please. Yet some have done
so, and it is the revelation of that, as data have been collected
and operational patterns reviewed, that has raised such widespread concerns about the management of universities. Without
strong leadership and a definite plan of action, departmental
and college programs degenerate over time, if only because continuing repetition of the same courses and patterns of teaching sap the enthusiasm of professors, breed indifference and disgust on the part of students, and result in a state of boredom
and ennui incompatible with the essential motivation and
enthusiasm required for effective teaching and study. A program review is seldom proposed by those within the unit responsible for the program. Likewise, institutions tend to be
ineffective in dealing with personnel matters. The conception of
tenure conjoined with a continuing review of individuals both
prior to and after achieving tenure has been applied carefully in
some of our better institutions as a means for maintaining excellence. In many others, achieving an initial appointment has created an expectancy of lifelong tenure. In one state in which I
reviewed the impact of a state governing board upon institutions, I was told repeatedly by faculty members and administrators that the immediate insistence upon a critical review of
young academics prior to granting tenure was particularly disturbing and unfair. In recent years, the patterns of operation
with regard to clerical and technical personnel, buttressed by
the presence of a union or the threat of one, has brought into
academe the concept of job security which, in some ways, is
even stronger than tenure.

Another area in which institutions have frequently been remiss is that of environmental deficiencies. I recall visiting one campus on which the facilities generally were run down. In response to my comment, the president remarked that he did not want a college such that students or faculty were attracted to it by the quality and attractiveness of the campus or its buildings. Other presidents, however, have quite evidently attempted to make their reputation on the basis of the new structures they have brought to the campus—sometimes at needless expense and, on occasion, not even well adapted to the programs assigned to them. In the matter of facilities, not infrequently lack of integrity is made evident. I recently read some remarks by a president to the effect that academic facilities on his campus were not very effectively used and that one of his major problems was to try to bring about some change on the part of the faculty without having his remarks get back to the legislature because he was placing before them a major request for new facilities.

Another reason why institutions of higher education need responsible administrators and managers is that the pluralistic nature of the university makes it almost impossible for faculties to resolve priority issues. Administrators cannot force priorities on a faculty, but they can enter into discussions that will achieve a reasonable degree of consensus when the responsibility of the institution to its public and its particular role in serving that public are made clear. Moreover, the administrators at each level have the responsibility to present to their superiors, and ultimately to the board, a coherent statement of responsibilities and priorities for adoption as institutional policy. In preparing this statement the administrators and the board must have an eye to the demonstration of integrity in meeting these responsibilities. Once this has been accomplished, most faculty members and academic units can be expected to assent and to perform responsibly within that framework.

I shall give here a few of the priority issues, deferring until later more intensive discussion of these and others. An initial question upon which there are diverse opinions is: Whom does the university serve? I recall some years ago being brought to task by a professor for my emphasis on our responsibility to students and society. His comments, unduly extended, simply made the point that the responsibility of the university was to serve the faculty, for in providing an effective faculty and letting them do as their individual and collective motivations directed, the institution provided the maximum contribution to students and to society. But as a part of this same issue, there is the question of whether the institution must direct its energies and resources to meet the immediate needs of society or whether its obligation may not be, in greater part, to provide the knowledge, the applications, directions, and value commitments that might support and improve society in the future. Since students of the present day will be part of a future extending beyond the present faculty, the focus on students would automatically receive a higher priority than my professorial critic admitted.

A second priority conflict surrounds the intellectual heritage, the concern being whether to give priority to the preservation and dissemination of the past accumulated heritage or to the expansion of it as a basis for further development. In a sense, this concern reflects basic conflicts between the humanities and the sciences. These are easily resolved by the view that one needs to understand something of the past development of knowledge in order to understand the present state of our heritage and provide a base for the future. But that view is countered by the many humanists who insist that the accumulated heritage must be assimilated for its own worth. This argument leads to the concept of the liberally educated person as one who has assimilated the cultural heritage and is also convinced that attaining a liberal education is impossible if primary concerns are focused upon the utility of knowledge. This issue is one that will likely never be fully resolved. However, I personally doubt that the society of this age supports higher education to produce classical scholars who may become ministers or professors of literature. Implicit in this immediate issue is the problem of priority between research and instruction. An ancient argument exists that there is no incompatibility between emphases on research and instruction, and that indeed only research scholars can engage in effective instruction because this is the way teachers expand their knowledge and maintain their enthusiasm. But universities and colleges that have placed heavy emphasis on research, and have accordingly reduced teaching loads and recognized faculty members primarily for their research, have invariably found some difficulties in maintaining the quality of undergraduate teaching. And there is a still further extension of this basic issue into consideration of general and liberal education versus special or professional education. General education has been variously defined but, for the purpose of the moment, it may be regarded as the breadth component of a liberal education, dealt with primarily within the first two years of the undergraduate program. Liberal education equally has been used with various meanings, and too often derogated to mean little more than the coverage of a certain amount of the so-called liberal arts. Unless liberal education is interpreted in respect to possession of some organized worthwhile body of knowledge and the ability to apply this in the context of social problems and concerns and in reference to some generally accepted set of values, the concept of liberal education becomes meaningless. No one has defined or can define the liberal arts by specifying the kinds and amounts of knowledge that characterize a liberally educated individual. Nevertheless, that concept still appears in many institutions as a basis for contending that any special technical or professional education is inevitably at the expense of a liberal education. Quite frankly, that argument seems to me to reflect that the person who makes it lacks a liberal education. Any college or university that offers a baccalaureate degree in technical, professional, or preprofessional programs has certain social obligations. These are to educate individuals in those programs to a reasonable level of skill in communication in all its forms, and to foster development of value sensitivity, social responsibility, and the ability to relate knowledge to the analysis and resolution of problems in their chosen careers.

The issues just mentioned and the priorities involved have been before us for many years, and they will be for many years ahead. In the past, the major developments in regard to these issues have come through administrators. In my experience in the last forty years of working with institutions of higher education, it has invariably been administrative leadership that has brought faculties to look at these issues. And many times, in turn, it has been as the result of external questions and demands that administrators have considered and moved on the issues involved. There is a true need for administrators, and active ones, but not necessarily for administrators who would turn a second- or third-rate institution into a competitor of Harvard, Michigan, or other internationally known institutions. The need is for leaders who will so manage an institution as to direct the attention of the faculty to the obligation of the institution to serve effectively in those missions particularly appropriate to it and to refrain from wasteful duplication of efforts and programs of quality already available elsewhere.

Suggestions for Further Reading

Balderston, F. E. *Managing Today's University.* San Francisco: Jossey-Bass, 1974.

Caws, P., Ripley, S. D., and Ritterbush, P. C. (Eds.). *The Bankruptcy of Academic Policy.* Washington, D.C.: Acropolis Books, 1972.

Cheit, E. F. *The New Depression in Higher Education: Two Years Later.* Berkeley, Calif.: Carnegie Commission on Higher Education, 1973.

Corson, J. J. *Governance of Colleges and Universities.* (Rev. ed.) New York: McGraw-Hill, 1975.

Hostrop, R. W. *Managing Education for Results.* Homewood, Ill.: ETC Publications, 1973.

Schmidt, G. P. *The Old Time College President.* New York: Columbia University Press, 1930.

Thwing, C. F. *The College President.* New York: Macmillan, 1926.

~~~~~~

TWO

Morals, Ethics, and Values in Higher Education

Value issues in higher education are seldom resolved because of the existing confusions, conflicts, and competition among values. They may not even be clearly identified. Perhaps one of the values operative in some institutions of higher education is the avoidance of decision making unless all parties agree on the precise nature of an issue and on the principles or rules by which it is to be resolved. Like the society in which it is embedded, the American college or university is pluralistic. The faculty is generally conservative and does not welcome innovations in curriculum, course content, and instructional practice. Such changes usually are the results of gradual modification over time rather than a complete restructuring of an educational program to adjust to new demands.

The very existence of an institution of higher education is evidence of a value commitment. At some time and place some persons decided to establish the institution and found the resources to do so. In all likelihood, the founders and the initial administrative and faculty appointees wrote a statement of pur-

poses and goals for the institution. Implicit in this statement
was surely a commitment to certain values. Such a statement is
subject to change or to complete replacement. It is unlikely
that the founding commitments determine the present character
and operations of any institution. For example, many of the
church-related colleges, founded to provide an appropriate education for church leaders, have long since abandoned any close
denominational connection. Some colleges are still attempting
to resolve the difficulties and ill feeling generated by a weakening association with the church and the subsequent difficulty of
establishing a unique role, mission, and clientele. Nevertheless,
one can list values to which almost every institution of higher
education was and is presumed to be committed. These values
include truth, beauty, integrity, moral-spiritual values, and belief in the worth and dignity of the individual. Even so, the
statement of these values is likely to be quite different currently
than it was two or three hundred years ago. Today universities
seek the truth whereas many a college earlier was confident that
the truth had been found and that the task was to pass it on to
the next generation. The shift from emphasis on the humanities,
largely focused upon the past, to technology and science as a
means of ushering in a better future has also modified convictions as to the nature of truth.

Similarly, many colleges and their faculties were once certain that beauty in its fullest sense was found in the creations of
artists, writers, sculptors, and composers of earlier centuries.
Today new conceptions of artistic and literary worth, coupled
with respect for the views of individuals, make beauty a relative rather than absolute concept. Indeed, we have moved far
toward acceptance of the view that beauty is in the mind of the
beholder. Beauty may also be sacrificed to attain other more
pragmatic values. Yet the modification of a building entrance to
accommodate handicapped individuals may reflect more in
beauty of spirit than was lost by compromise of the original
architectural design. Originally, integrity referred to a composite of qualities involving honesty, trustworthiness, forthrightness, and responsibility. It expanded to involve the concept
of scholarship, a deep commitment to search for the truth, and

a stalwart resistance to pressures in a contrary direction. In the past, this has meant to the professor that the essence of a discipline must not be sacrificed by adjusting it to the interests or incompetence of students. Today's emphasis on equity, practicality, and relevance causes us regularly to make such adjustments. Some scholars have even asserted that any idea can be presented with integrity and mastered by individuals at almost any age or ability level.

The conception of moral-spiritual values in the modern college or university is far different from that of an earlier day. The classics provided the moral values, and the tutors (usually recent graduates themselves) were only mediators between the students and the classics. The president furnished the character model and, in chapel and possibly a senior seminar, he presented moral and spiritual truths. Respect for the worth and dignity of the individual went little further than acceptance of fellow Christians, so long as they were northern European stock and adherents of one of the relatively small number of accepted Christian sects. Our current operable conception of individual worth and dignity extends far beyond this to include equality of ability, opportunity, and reward. Thus our pragmatic social commitments also differ from the earlier ideal. The search for truth is regarded often as the development of a technology providing a more complex and comfortable (though not necessarily better) life. Knowledge is seen as of little value except as it meets a need or solves a problem. Even humanities professors seem at times to be more concerned with pursuing specialized studies and acquiring a paycheck than with providing a relevant liberal or humanistic education for students. The voiced concern for integrity and for moral-spiritual values has been modified or sacrificed by the demand that education be made available to all who want it. Respect for the worth and dignity of an individual once admitted the possibility of recognizing individual deficiencies. Today's colleges are expected to accommodate to physical, educational, mental, and social deficiencies that once would have ruled out college attendance. These demands are reinforced by a federal bureaucracy run wild which seeks to enforce upon the institution an always increasing list of demands regarding personnel practices, developmental services, and improvement of facilities and equipment, and to impose rules and policies with regard to use of federal money for financing research. Thus institutions attempting to maintain quality are cast in the role of resisting progress, misusing funds, or being incompetent in administration and management. Unfortunately, there is some justification for this view. Numerous institutions have exhibited nonfeasance, misfeasance, and malfeasance in the use of funds.

The availability of federal funds for research, in many respects, has pulled the universities away from their role as an instrument for achieving social justice. Since the Ph.D. degree has become the union card for university and college faculty members, a high value and priority have been set on research for the faculty member. The reputation of an institution has become equated to its research output and to the offering of graduate and professional programs based upon it. In the search for external funds, the appropriateness and worth of particular projects to an institution or faculty member are ignored. Acquisition of these funds has resulted in diversions and disallocations of resources, thereby weakening the traditional value commitments of the university. As enrollments taper off and funds are further reduced, the conflicts between traditional roles and unjustified aspirations become even more apparent.

Much has been written about this situation from many viewpoints. Administrators and faculty members criticize the politicians for shortsightedness and for failing to provide the money that is obviously needed. Those who so contend are apparently sure that all problems would be resolved by more money. The history of federal support of research, however, shows that support has always led to demands from an increasing number of institutions ambitious for recognition as national research resources. Even the community colleges have sought a piece of the research support pie. A carefully written history of the last twenty years may find that it was fortunate that expansion in federal funding of research was discontinued not only to reduce fund wastage but also to retain some measure of integrity in the institutions.

Other faculties and administrators are certain that if new student sources could be found, the well-established principle of funding institutions on the basis of enrollment would resolve their problems. Such overly simplified solutions ignore the fact that the American economy and society are in deep trouble. People are disillusioned on many counts. Government and political leadership is everywhere suspect as incompetent and opportunistic. Higher education has suffered a severe loss of prestige and confidence. Its insatiable demands for more money, accompanied by obvious misuse in many institutions and mismanagement in others, cause the public to wonder, with some justification, whether the institutions of higher education any longer recognize that they were brought into being to serve the needs of society rather than to become a self-righteous and self-seeking group responsible only to itself for performance of those things it chooses to do. Instead of providing a model of what man and society might be, higher education imitates the behavior of other groups that seek status and funds with little apparent concern as to the means used so long as the desired ends are achieved.

American higher education today can be viewed as an astounding success or as an abject failure. On the positive side, the increase in the number of institutions of higher education and of people seeking to acquire a degree, the extent to which other countries have based modifications in their programs upon the models provided in the United States, and the many and obvious contributions that universities and colleges have made to the development and enhancement of American society provide some evidence of success. On the negative side, the competition among institutions for programs and projects and the seeming desire of administration and faculty in each institution that it become nationally and even internationally renowned for its programs of research, service, and instruction, regardless of their need or cost, suggest that institutions are altogether self-serving. Yet this judgment is somewhat unfair, for, in a certain sense, the institutions were only responding to expectations. Indeed, the expectations of those supporting higher education, including governmental agencies, have been confusing and conflicting. They have taken little account of the nature of the university, either in its organization and operation or in its distinctiveness from business and industry. In short, society and its various agencies speak incoherently and in several different voices with regard to what they expect of institutions of higher education. In this confused situation, then, one could take the point of view that the faculty and administration generally will move in those directions that promise the greatest benefits to them and also the greatest satisfaction in the day-to-day activities. Outsiders observe the confusion and make critical observations about lack of management and direction and the resulting poor performance—especially in teaching. Some administrators join the external critics and comment that the faculty is not interested in teaching and does not know how to teach. To that refrain may be added the further comment that many faculty members do poorly in the service role and that there is a great deal of waste in research funds because of incompetency in identifying research topics and in carrying out research activities. The faculty may argue, in turn, that too many students now admitted to institutions are not really interested in or capable of learning. They only seek credentials or certification leading to a good job and are inclined to think that the university should guarantee this at the time of admission. And on the research side, faculty may argue, with some reason, that support of research is inadequate and that the constraints and the monitoring imposed not only take a significant share of the funds allocated but also make good research difficult to carry out.

Thus, in many respects, the confusions and value conflicts within the institution result from and reflect similar problems in our society. Indeed, it is difficult to decide just what the major commitments of American society are in the present day. Verbally, there is apparently a commitment to pluralism—socially, philosophically, religiously, and morally. There is a commitment to a political, liberal democracy, to economic capitalism, to individual responsibility and equality of opportunity. Despite the almost completely relativistic orientation involved in these views, there is a sense that there must be something on which we can all agree—some basic moral principles that we all accept and a security and mutual trust and respect emerging from this that assure the continuation of a productive, pleasant, and prosperous society. However, there runs through all this a developing conviction that social pluralism and economic capitalism, through misinterpretation or misuse, have placed us on the road to ruin; that governmental intervention to attain equity, equality, security, and integrity has made a mockery of individual responsibility, completely confused what is meant by equality of opportunity, and, to a large extent, ignored or controverted the desires and values of the majority by overresponse to the demands of persistent and noisy groups asserting (often with attendant threats) the necessity of immediate response. The very nature and worth of the political liberal democracy ideal is brought into question by the obvious inability of many politicians to place national, humanistic, and social priorities ahead of those of the majority of voters in their immediate constituencies. Again, a great part of the difficulty lies with the ideals involved in each of the major commitments. What are the tenets of economic capitalism? What is meant by equality of opportunity? What are the basic moral principles? And, once statements are made which in themselves do not come easily, the next question is, What do these statements really mean? How are they to be applied and by whom? What constraints, if any, are to be imposed upon individual responsibility? And what punitive measures are available to deal with those who misuse or fail to respond to the expectations of individual responsibility? Individual responsibility extended indefinitely implies complete individual freedom, and complete freedom extended to individuals means surely that differences in power and in the exercise of it will result in destruction of the freedom of some individuals. This brings us back full circle to the need for placing limits on individual responsibility or for defining it in more precise terms, as well as for specifying sanctions as to appropriate and inappropriate responses in the name of responsibility.

Efforts to resolve these continuing problems by elaboration of rules, regulations, policies, and laws run afoul both of the difficulties in deciding precisely what is involved and in expressing them in such manner as to have immediate and direct relevance to the behavior of individuals and groups. For example, the attempt to provide equality of opportunity immediately causes difficulties in an attempt to determine the exact meaning of equality. Is unequal treatment justified to restore equality? If that unequal treatment is unduly expensive, and perhaps even then leads to the provision of inferior service because initial disadvantages cannot be fully overcome, has the attempt to provide equal opportunity not actually resulted in unfairness to others because of the disparity in allocation of resources? How far is unique treatment truly appropriate for unequals? There is an unwillingness to admit that there is ultimately some standoff in the full realization of any particular value because of limits on the resources available to meet all values. Even if resources were limitless, the problem would not be resolved, for the advantaged, having limitless resources available, would be able to move farther in reference to their personal goals than the disadvantaged, who must first use resources and time to overcome their handicaps.

With limited resources, there can be no fully satisfactory answer to resource allocation, either in programs or in funds. If weights could be assigned to diverse values and the available resources allocated in proportion to these weights, there would still be problems. This is demonstrated in respect to the social legislation of the last decade. Appropriations for this or that service program are jealously regarded by those who preferred a different approach or program. Truthful evaluations of any major social service activity have become virtually impossible because those involved know full well that critical comments will be seized upon by others to weaken or destroy the program. It is difficult to argue against allocation of funds to the arts, yet one can well wonder, recognizing the dire needs in food, clothing, shelter, and education in our large urban areas, whether these allocations to monuments are not, in some subtle way, a placement of priority on art rather than on humanity. Our increasing national debt, national frustration, and malaise are all indications of this vain and impossible attempt to do everything that a significant number of individuals deem worthwhile. We return to consider the significance and impact of these problems in regard to institutions of higher education.

Professional Ethics and Values

The major work of the university is done by the faculty, assisted by a wide variety of service personnel and coordinated by administrative sources. Faculty members share a commitment to objectivity in engaging in study and research in their respective disciplines. As faculty members move into the governance area, one might assume that their scholarly qualifications and objectivity would make them equally competent in decisions about their institutions. It is readily apparent at any committee or faculty meeting, however, that scholarly objectivity can quickly disappear when issues involving personal preferences and advantages are under discussion. The values operable in scholarship and in governance are by no means identical. The same scholar who may be making major breakthroughs in research is likely to view with suspicion any major change in the structure, mode of operation, or priorities of the institution. There is, too, a commitment to accuracy and detail in measurement and reporting that is not possible or appropriate in institutional data reporting and policy statements. There is a commitment to sharing accumulated scholarship with others, which ideally imposes the obligation to publish. There is a commitment to a high order of specialization, which results from the conviction that a scholar should become preeminent in some field and that the only way of accomplishing this is to dig more deeply than anyone else has into a particular aspect of that field. There is a deep commitment to academic freedom, although it somehow has become perverted into a concept of complete personal autonomy permitting each professor to do as he or she prefers with the expectation of praise and payment for it. Those values include, if they do not generate, an aversion to rules and a general abhorrence of administration and its costs.

There is also a conviction on the part of many academics that it is somehow indecent, unethical, and perhaps even immoral to attempt to influence others. Thus faculty efforts at decision making tend to be interminable, with a high toleration for the presentation of varying views, many of which may be completely irrelevant to the situation under discussion. Rules and policy statements resulting from compromise are frequently so ambiguous as to admit of a variety of interpretations, justifying individual faculty members in their convictions that there should be no limitations on their activities except those that are self-imposed. Faculty statements on professional ethics and obligations, like those of other professions, place great emphasis upon personal responsibility and personal freedom but are very lax in spelling out any means of dealing with those circumstances in which individuals fail to meet their obligations. Faculty members, on the whole, would rather tolerate incompetence on the part of their associates and even on the part of administrators than take forthright action to resolve the situation, partly on the basis of humanitarian concerns, but largely on the grounds that action in such cases would set precedents that might ultimately endanger their own autonomy. The extension of the same concerns leads faculty to avoid involvement in decisions on fund reductions, program elimination, or personnel terminations. My own observation is that a faculty member or department would rather argue with a single administrator about the issue than submit the matter to the decision of colleagues. Those cases in which the faculty have been asked to participate in funding reductions and staff elimination indicate plainly the inability and unwillingness of faculty members to face up to such decisions. In a real sense, the desire of the faculty to run a self-governing institution presents an impossibility. If resources were infinite, so that each person and each department could have all it desired, and if truly the interests of the academic corresponded to the concerns and needs of society, there would be no problem; but, in all likelihood, there would be no university either. For the faculty member, the university comes close to being an end in itself. It furnishes the salary, the place to work, the materials and resources necessary to accomplish that work, and a relatively high degree of self-determination on the part of the individual as to how time is spent. It is not unnatural for many faculty members to view the university as an institution created by society to provide a place for the elite to get together, to extend the range of knowledge, to examine the implications of knowledge for improvement of society, and even perhaps to map out the directions required for improvement. Administrators caught between governing boards and the faculty frequently find themselves playing up to faculty to assure continuing support, knowing full well that a determined attempt to move in directions, no matter how appropriate, that are resisted by a major segment of the faculty is quite likely to lead to departure of the administrator and subsequent difficulties in locating another position of equal or better stature. Thus, with the administrator, as with the faculty member, security and survival weigh heavily.

In this milieu, the needs of the student may be lost. Though the students can bring the institution to a screeching halt, the majority of the students do not view their college years as ones in which they can or should make major decisions for themselves or for their institution. They see the university as an interlude between adolescence and assumption of full responsibility as a worker, a citizen, and perhaps as a family member. They seek good records in school as a means of acquiring a good recommendation and a job and they are inclined to trust in the faculty judgment as to the ingredients and processes that define the education that provides direction and security. The students have a right to know why the faculty recommend or require certain courses. They have a right to know why the courses cover certain materials and specify certain expectations. They have a right to know why these courses are scheduled in a particular order, how they are related, and what the consequences are of following through the sequence laid out by the faculty. Recognizing the reality that no one course in itself is the difference between competence in a given field and incompetence, students should have some right to choose their programs and adapt them to their own hopes and aspirations. This requires that they be provided with much more detailed information about the content of courses, the conduct of courses, and the relationship of a course to other courses and to various fields of endeavor. Students have a right to fairness and forthrightness on the part of instructors, of administrators, and of all personnel within the institution. Yet, on the whole, students who, by written institutional commitments, are supposed to learn to think for themselves, make value judgments, and become responsible participants in society are given little opportunity to do so. The typical pattern of the American college and university has been to encourage students to engage in student government, having first deprived the student government of any responsibility or authority in regard to what faculty members and administrators construe to be the main business of the institution. To a great extent, this view applies even to graduate students and professional students. The graduate-professional school typically admits students in an initial convocation in which the dean and others welcome the new students as professional associates but soon move into the explanation of rules, regulations, and requirements with regard to courses, sequences, examinations, and even perhaps appropriate dress. Again, there seems to be implicit a conviction on the part of the faculty that a rigorous and rigid program is the best way to develop a responsible autonomous and competent professional.

Stability and Change

Some segments of the faculty of a university back slowly and reluctantly into the future, meanwhile disparaging most changes as mistaken deviations from past glories. There are a few who argue that a sound educational program based upon fundamental principles, concepts, and values should be the same everywhere and at all times. Other segments of the faculty are so concerned with current issues and with their research activities that they view the present as largely separated from the past rather than as a continuing interlude between the past and a future the nature of which hinges on the values underlying our activities of the moment. And there also exists in most faculties a group of activist-oriented and frequently noisy persons who are discontent with present patterns and with what they regard as policies or practices inconsistent with the true nature and role of the institution. They demand instant change without recognizing that instant change threatens the very foundations of the university, for it involves taking positions on vital issues that have not been fully analyzed and upon which marked differences of opinion exist.

In some ways, the university is one of the more rapidly changing phenomena in our society. There is a continuing student flow through the institution and a continuing change (though less rapidly than in the years preceding 1970) in the faculty. New courses are added, new programs are introduced, new research areas are opened, and the service programs of the university continually expand to meet newly identified needs and demands. Yet it is difficult to change certain aspects of the university. It is true that the basic objectives or values of education for the individual do not change greatly over time if one interprets those objectives or values in the broad sense of developing such abilities as thinking and making wide judgments, communicating effectively and cooperating with others in the activities of society and its governing agencies, and understanding and accepting the basic values upon which any democratic society must be based. But the interpretation of these objectives or values does change. As pointed out earlier, the conception of equality and equity has been undergoing a change in recent years. The means of attaining these objectives or of developing awareness and understanding of basic values certainly will be changed by the accumulating knowledge and insights in new disciplines and by the use of new technologies for communication. Another crucial factor is the recognition that the resources of this world are finite, that continuing competition among nations, combined with the expectations of an increasingly high and wasteful standard of living, imposes limits that interfere with, if they do not actually deny, the full attainment of other values. In recent years, demands for added safety in automobiles and for reduction in contamination of the environment have added materially to the cost of living. Even if our basic values remain unchanged, our past misuse of resources forces reconsideration of priorities.

Despite these pressures that make change inevitable, universities and their faculties cling to outmoded programs, policies, and structures because the barriers to change are numerous and formidable. The departmental disciplinary structure has, in institution after institution, voided any attempt to redefine undergraduate education as anything more than a collection of courses acceptable for a degree. I personally have experienced, over the last fifty years, a marked change in priorities in respect to undergraduate education both in universities and in liberal arts colleges. I first entered college teaching in a mathematics department. There was at that time a rule that classes should not exceed fifteen students—a class of sixteen students was divided into two sections. The first obligation of a teacher was to check the background of students and see that everyone was properly assigned. It was expected (and the department head checked) that instructors make regular assignments, collect papers, and give examinations regularly. In multiple-section courses, although relatively few of them existed at that time, reasonable uniformity was expected in the examinations and in the grading process, and an instructor was expected to account for excessive failures. I particularly recall that the standard teaching load was fourteen, fifteen, or sixteen credit hours, with occasional loads exceeding that. Only a few of the faculty members were seriously engaged in research (with little or no reduction in teaching requirements). Little time was taken up by faculty committees and governance processes as they exist in the present day. Today emphasis on graduate work and research has resulted in a low priority for undergraduate teaching. Classes are large, faculty loads of six to eight credit hours are common, assignments are made but seldom checked, and two or three examinations provide the only incentive for study. One might reasonably describe the change over a span of roughly fifty years as a shift from a faculty committed to and taking some satisfaction in undergraduate teaching to a faculty that places emphasis on scholarly work, enjoys interaction with graduate students, begrudgingly gives time to undergraduate education, and wastes endless hours participating in institutional governance.

The Problem of Priorities

Much of the shift in priorities can be defended. The federal government, by making available extensive funding for research programs and graduate education, sanctioned such emphasis, and the reputation of a developing institution obviously depended more upon research activity than on teaching. One mathematics department in a nationally known university announced that it would no longer teach undergraduate mathematics other than for selected majors committed to graduate study. It speaks well of the administration that the department was quickly brought back to reality. But one is left to wonder about the quality of the instruction once a department has registered such a point of view.

Priorities generate conflicts in periods of rapid growth, but stability and decline generate even more difficulty. State-supported institutions continue to present unrealistic budget requests generated from the twin assumptions that the relatively light teaching loads of the last decade must be continued and that graduate programs should continue to expand despite the apparent lack of need. One professor of English bluntly told me that the state had an obligation to support an individual in attaining a Ph.D. in English whether or not that degree offered any immediate career outlet. A graduate school dean, presenting the case for a new Ph.D. program, admitted that no more Ph.D.s were needed in that field at the moment but added that unless a Ph.D. program were approved some of the best people in the department would defect at the first opportunity. Moreover, he argued that the institution needed the degree to enhance its status whether or not society needed it. Here again we have the assumption that if something is good for somebody there ought to be sufficient resources to provide it. There is a continual complaint in universities that the paring of unrealistic budget requests indicates lack of appreciation of the efforts of over-worked faculty members. Morale slips several notches and it becomes more difficult to arouse faculty members to engage in serious review and improvement or elimination of out-of-date and weak programs. Presidents reinforce this stance with dire warnings that quality is being seriously threatened by the lack of adequate support. In the face of that charge, a faculty may reasonably reject any efforts to improve quality, for to do so would make the president a liar. After five or ten years of the refrain that low budgets threaten quality, legislators may be excused for wondering how many more years will have to go by before some programs are terminated because of a lack of quality.

The feeling that higher education is not fully valued and is generally misunderstood is easily pushed to a belief that honesty is a questionable policy because it would deprive the institution and students of the opportunity for a sound education and the maintenance of quality programs. Thus many institutions of higher education have come to operate upon the principle that the magnificent and unquestionable ends they pursue justify the use of deceitful means. So widespread has this practice become that a number of legislators with whom I have spoken and one governor agreed that university administrators are not to be believed in budget presentations. The most serious aspect of this situation is that the university pursuing this pattern evades the more profound question of whether it is indeed performing those functions, meeting those needs, and supporting those values for which society has created and supports the institution. Activist students, minority groups, women, and others, in viewing the university as a means of correcting inequity and as a source of jobs and status, have placed heavy financial demands on the institution. Thus it appears that many competing groups seek control of the university to direct it to the achievement of their own ends rather than those for which the institution was created. If the university is to return to and maintain its mission, it must reassess the ethics and values that justify its existence and must define itself and operate in such a way as to demonstrate to the public that the institution indeed fulfills its societal obligations in a sound and superior manner and at reasonable cost. Faculty members, by virtue of the limited purview provided by departmental disciplinary settings and the mixed signals that come to them from various sources, will not (and indeed they cannot), because of the many value differences existing within a faculty, resolve these difficulties. Administration and management must take responsibility for assuring its various constituencies that the university functions in an effective and accountable manner.

After reading an early draft of this chapter, Stanley Ikenberry, president of the University of Illinois, wrote to me as follows (July 9, 1980):

> A . . . thought that occurred to me as I read this chapter . . . relates to the definition of success in higher education in the 1980s. What is it that we value? To what do we strive? How do we know when we have succeeded? Very frankly, I think the overriding value commitment of higher education during the 1960s and 1970s was to access and growth. Decline in size during those years was viewed as a sign of failure. Growth during those years had a foundation in the value system of our democratic society: namely, the commitment of a democratic society to access to education, to the improvement of the quality of life, and to equality of opportunity through education. It was from this fundamental value commitment of our society that we proceeded to embark on an unprecedented era of growth in higher education.
>
> Now the 1980s confront us with a very different value dilemma. Does our commitment to equality of opportunity and to access require further expansion in the size of higher education institutions? Quite obviously, the answer to that question is no. While our earlier commitment to equality and to access must continue, it will not manifest itself in growth.
>
> One then asks the question, What value commitments will be preeminent for higher education during the next twenty years? In my judgment, those of us in higher education have yet to fashion a satisfactory answer to that question. We are adrift. My own personal answer is that our commit-

ment during the next two decades should be to preserve and enhance quality.

These comments affirm the central role that values and statements about them play in the activities and public pronouncements of administrators.

Suggestions for Further Reading

Banfield, E. C. "Ends and Means in Planning." In S. Mailick (Ed.), *Concepts and Issues in Administrative Behavior.* Englewood Cliffs, N.J.: Prentice-Hall, 1962.
Brubacher, J. S. *Bases for Policy in Higher Education.* New York: McGraw-Hill, 1965.
Cohen, M. D., and March, J. G. *Leadership and Ambiguity.* New York: McGraw-Hill, 1974.
Downs, A. *Inside Bureaucracy.* Boston: Little, Brown, 1967.
Leys, W. A. R. "The Value Framework of Decision-Making." In S. Mailick (Ed.), *Concepts and Issues in Administrative Behavior.* Englewood Cliffs, N.J.: Prentice-Hall, 1962.

THREE

~~~~~~

Improving Administrative Communication

Communication is a process whereby two or more entities engage in an exchange, interaction, or transaction by means of symbols that have a common meaning. These symbols include words (spoken and written), signs, gestures, tone of voice, colors (red for *stop* or *danger*), facial expressions, body movements, and clothing. Many of these, including words, have more than one meaning. The juxtaposition of words and their ordering can make meaning more specific or introduce additional meanings and consequent ambiguity. Meaning depends upon context—environment, culture, and the specific groups and individuals involved.

Communication permits establishment of contact among individuals and groups for exchange of information, cooperation in achieving shared goals, and reinforcement or alteration of attitudes and values. However, the fact that communication can be ambiguous by intent, by lack of verbal or symbolic sophistication of sender or receiver, or by erroneous inference in sending or receiving a message can make the process difficult and hazardous.

The ends of communication are not always the common good, and the methods used to influence the attitudes, values, and behavior of individuals range from affection, praise, and justifiable rewards through indifference to threats, bribery, punishment, or extinction. The difference between a reward and a threat or actual punishment is not always obvious. Denial of affection or of an expected reward can be a punishment. The purposes of communication and the intents of individual communicators are often loaded with moral and ethical issues. An appeal for action on an issue is quite different from an attempt to persuade people to support a projected view or take a specific action. Yet even the simple appeal for action may arise out of a commitment to unity, accord, security, or order that is inconsistent with individual freedom.

Communication holds the possibility of ambiguity both in sending and receiving. In addition, the sender may, by unconscious emphases or movements and by insensitive choice of words, unintentionally communicate to an audience personal views, values, or attitudes. The potential receiver may ignore or be completely unaware of an attempt to communicate, but awareness of and attention to a communication almost certainly lead to an inference and judgment about the meaning of the communication and the underlying intent of the communicator, as well as to some degree of understanding and acceptance or rejection of the substance. If it be accepted that any intentional communication can and usually does include some unconscious, and hence unintended, aspects and that reception always involves some inference, then it is appropriate to include as part of the communication process the inferences generated in others by unintended and/or unconscious behavior of an individual. One consequence of this addition is the recognition that an individual (in the presence of others) can scarcely avoid communication, fragmentary and ambiguous though it be.

Communication is a problem on every campus. I recall visiting a new and very small college that, in one year, had doubled its enrollment from 75 to 150. In my discussions with staff and students, everyone agreed that communication had become their most serious problem! The expectation that the newcomers would accept practices and policies determined by their predecessors explained some of the difficulty, especially since the newcomers (both in students and faculty) outnumbered the old hands. Former means of communication were no longer adequate. Unwritten, once commonly understood, views and policies needed to be made explicit, reviewed and rejected, or accepted. Oral and informal means of communication had obviously become inadequate and a new pattern developed. Adjusting communications in extent, frequency, content, and mode so as to meet needs without overwhelming channels and recipients is ever a problem.

An administrator at any level within an institution who becomes concerned about communication should accumulate in a special file every memorandum, newsletter, committee report, and similar item issued on campus for two or three months. Added to this should be the student newspaper and any regular institutional bulletins published on a recurring or occasional basis. A summary of the notices and other materials displayed on various campus bulletin boards will further expand the accumulation. In recent years, ease of duplication has encouraged a deluge of duplicated memoranda, letters, and news or journal articles. The amount and nature of material thus collected will vary greatly over the academic year. Most administrators, even though they have seen items day by day, will be surprised at the accumulation over two or three months. My own experience in viewing such accumulated materials on several campuses suggests that much more than the administrator has previously recognized is communicated by these various means. Reviewing this mass of material, one is likely to find repetitions, elaborations, errors, corrections, and irrelevancies. If to this accumulation of written communications one adds phone calls, meetings, interviews, and other oral exchanges, the composite is even more disconcerting.

Campuses suffer from an overflow of materials that attempt to communicate but fail to do so. This failure results from many factors, as will be discussed later in this chapter, but there are four points to be made about communication from the immediate context. First, the sheer amount of communication encourages people to ignore much of it. Much of what passes for communication is really not focused and serves no purpose other than to call attention to a particular person, office, or organization. Second, the total volume of material circulated involves expenditures that are probably not justified by the results. Third, the sheer volume of the presumably communicatory materials is used by some offices and administrators to present a facade of openness while, at the same time, refraining from communication on some of the most significant issues—a snow job, in short. Fourth, attending to communication demands provides the reluctant administrator with an excuse for postponing decisions.

Reasons for Ineffective Communication

Communication may create crises rather than avoid or alleviate them. Hastily conceived statements may be in error or may convey something very different than intended. Hence individuals acquire differing views of the issue, the factors involved, and the available alternatives. When confidence and security are disturbed and mutual trust has disappeared, the restoration of open, forthright, and honest communication is likely to be both difficult and delayed. Recently I saw a memorandum on a highly controversial change in policy affecting many members of the faculty. The memorandum, which called for reactions and comments, elicited numerous replies questioning the wisdom of the change. Thereupon, another communiqué announced that the decision had been made and that only the implementation procedures were open to discussion. The blunt tone even suggested retribution to the objectors for their audacity in questioning the decision.

Each stage in the communication process includes numerous potentialities for ineffective communication. The communication source may be unclear about message substance or purpose or both. Lack of understanding, of intelligence, of information, or of sensitivity may lead to vague, uninformative messages. Naiveté in dealing with the situation involved or lack of an audience sense can lead to irritation having little to do with the real issue. For example, many failures of communication that I have observed within colleges resulted from lack of understanding and rapport between an administrator and students or faculty. Even a generally well-accepted decision may disturb individuals who did not know that the matter was under consideration and were thereby denied input. The communicator may be under such pressure or stress with regard to the issue that the communication takes on more the character of a reprimand than of a statement of future policy or a plea for elaboration, clarification, and modification essential to reach understanding and perhaps agreement.

Oral communication is fleeting and the communicators may have markedly different recollections. Writing is more time consuming but it presents both parties with a record and the possibility of consultation and modification. Even then, individuals of good will and high principle may find it difficult to attain a definitive statement acceptable to everyone.

Individuals who have studied communication problems in business and industry, and are also acquainted with the situation on college and university campuses, generally express the opinion that communication on the campus is superior to that in business and industry. Whether or not that view is correct, there are certain conditions present on the campus that make the communication problem there rather distinctive. The *first* factor is that the departments and faculty are the primary agencies in planning and providing the services of the institution. Departmental and college units are dominated by specialized interests holding a diversity of views, which results in different emphases and policies and their interpretation. Upward communication becomes important to convey these unique factors and concerns. Downward communication needs to be predicated on awareness of unit differences and necessary autonomy, but administrators find it difficult to maintain adequate familiarity with the unique problems and concerns of each college and department. Inevitably, decisions from central administration must allow for some flexibility in interpretation. There are complications in formulating communications so as to convey a definite and uniform message to persons who differ in views, are differentially affected by the message, and may require some flexibility in adapting it to their circumstance.

A *second* factor in communication problems on campus is that the employees of a college or university are well above the average in formal education and therefore relatively sophisticated in vocabulary and in communication processes. One might expect that communication would be eased by this circumstance and by the fact that communication itself plays a major role in the educational process. However, these characteristics produce a situation in which communications are scrutinized with particular care and with the possibility that a wide variety of meanings and inferences may be attached to words, phrases, and sentences. The story of the two psychiatrists passing each other on the street with the exchange of a quick "hello" and a subsequent question in each one's mind as to the other's meaning is not inappropriate.

Communication among the various sectors of an institution of higher education is complicated by the differences in orientation of students, faculty members, administrators, and service personnel. Some communications pertain to all and go to all; some pertain primarily to one group but have disturbing implications for another. It is tempting to find reasons (if one is so inclined) for arguing that some communications to faculty should not go to students or to the general public, but it is futile and therefore dangerous to assume that such selectivity is possible.

The presentation of ideas in various ways to different audiences is understandable and, at times, necessary. For example, reports of scientific research findings in newspapers and in a scientific journal must be distinctive. But when communication relates to policies that may immediately affect individuals and groups, variation in phrasing and emphasis can lead to a suspicion of underlying motives and possibly duplicity. Complete openness and honesty bring other problems arising out of the motivations of those who select and interpret ideas to achieve their own respective ends. Attempts to achieve full cooperation of journals and newspapers in communicating the strengths of the institution are likely to be ineffective. Stories about athletic scandals, federal investigations of fund utilization, and charges of unfairness or inequity by students or faculty members carry the day. "Those seeking their own ends" include reporters, editors, politicians, and (regrettably) representatives of other universities. To paraphrase Gresham's law—bad information drives out good. One who insists upon openness and honesty in communication may be victimized by others who distort or select items to achieve their own ends.

The extent of on-campus communication, coupled with the special interests of the various communicators, virtually ensures that some topics will be reported inadequately or inaccurately. Student newspapers naturally highlight those aspects of an issue that directly concern students. In so doing, student reporters may ignore or unfairly treat aspects of a situation in order to assert that students are being unfairly treated. For example, student newspaper treatment of a rise in tuition and fees is unlikely to recognize inflation or the expectation implicit in a legislative appropriation that such action will be taken.

Colleges, departments, centers, institutes, student and faculty organizations, and offices attempt to interpret their programs so as to attract more members. Persuasion and self-glorification, rather than factual reporting, quite naturally become primary motives and tend to distort the message. Supporters of unionization sometimes stretch the truth and make or imply accusations that administrators are devious and self-serving, failing to recogize that the accusations are self-serving for those who make them. Minutes and agenda for various committees and faculty councils flood the campus mail and move across desks into the wastebasket—the circular file. An excess of communication can be as harmful as a lack of it. Moreover, the communication process becomes expensive in use of supplies and in time of communicators and receivers when carried to an excess. Accordingly, the costs and results of communication also deserve attention, but they must be dealt with in the context of the nature, problems, and purposes of communication.

Nature of the Communication Process

The following discussion of the communication process draws upon the views of individuals who have written extensively about the subject. The attempt here is to clarify the nature of the communication process, the problems involved in it, and the role that it plays in the conduct of any enterprise. Subsequent to that discussion, I shall return to a discussion of communication on the campus and undertake to lay out some principles and policies that might become the basis for recurrent review and improvement of communication of a college or university with its several audiences.

Communication is a process whereby the source or communicator undertakes to send a message to one or more receivers. The communication process involves ideally a full cycle of processes in that the receiver of a message transmits reactions back to the source. The source can repeat or modify the message because this feedback is both a confirmation of receipt and an effort to improve communication. Communication is not necessarily intentional. An individual may unconsciously communicate to others satisfaction, rejection, or disgust by involuntary facial expressions, gestures, body movements, or choice of words. The communication process does not necessarily require two or more individuals. One individual can serve as both communicator and receiver as, for example, by taping and playback of ideas. By means of writing and self-critique, an individual can achieve insight into the adequacy and clarity of both an idea and the statement of it. The expression, revision, and polishing of a communication is often a highly desirable step before attempting to communicate it to others. The comments, criticisms, and suggestions of receivers are most helpful to the communicator who has already, by critical self-appraisal, clarified the idea he or she has undertaken to express. The purposeful communicator also needs to define his or her audience and specify the purpose of the communication. Informal conversasation frequently lacks purpose and achieves none. I recall the tale of the woman who talked unceasingly and incoherently. When a friend suggested that some prior thought might be desirable, the immediate question was, "How do I know what I think until I hear what I have to say?"

Even in more formal circumstances, both the communicator and the receiver may be unclear regarding purpose. For example, the communicator provides the information on the pretense that it will be of interest to all who receive it. The primary intent may well be that of establishing the reputation of the communicator both as a data resource and as a knowledgeable individual desirous of extending assistance to others. As with many letters to the editor, the communicator may be simply expressing personal concerns about issues by questioning facts, denying statements, or remonstrating at the character and expression of an idea. Some communications, perhaps unwittingly, communicate by inference more about the source than about the information or message presented. Obviously, the purposes of a communication are manifold, and they may be either manifest or latent, depending upon the knowledge and sensitivity of the receiver. The communicator may be seeking attention, habituating others to the receipt of ideas and suggestions from a would-be influential source, undertaking to shock and arouse individuals on a particular issue, or sincerely and honestly informing others as to the issues. Unfortunately, even in a college or university, some communication is intended to deceive, although the underlying motives (attracting students, for example) may be, in some respects, commendable.

Communication takes place in some context, and that immediate context will usually be more obvious to the initiator of a communication than to its receiver. It may also be different for the receiver than for the initiator. Ideally, the communicator has determined on the message, the reasons for sending it, and the context(s) making the message important to both communicator and receiver. Next in the communication cycle comes what is called "encoding." This process puts the message into a form for transmission to the receiver. The means of encoding and transmission chosen obviously depends upon circumstances and upon the relationship between the communicator and receiver. By prior agreement with the auctioneer, the bidder at an auction may use the wink of an eye, a gesture, or other inconspicuous mode of communicating a bid. Other nonverbal means of expression include symbols, graphs, charts, pictures, facial expression, eye contact, physical movements, dress, the decor of a room, and the dynamism or passiveness of an individual.

Face-to-face oral communication between two or more individuals involves (perhaps unwittingly) use of certain nonverbal factors to clarify, amplify, or emphasize parts of the communication. These nonverbal components may suggest disagreement between the words used and the feelings or views held, thereby casting doubt on sincerity or truthfulness. The voice alone is capable of variations that communicate effectively between individuals well acquainted with each other. A telephonic exchange, although lacking visual elements, may nevertheless be more effective and frank than a written one. An oral exchange, with or without visual contact, permits continuing feedback, repetition, and cooperation. Vocabulary is often a problem. Words have a range of meaning and connotation that may be distinctive for persons of different age groups and backgrounds. The individual who seeks precisely the right word and meaning to express concisely a point of view may well find that this is far less effective than repetition using different words and examples. Redundancy is a common characteristic of conversational exchanges, especially on the phone—perhaps, in that case, because of the lack of a visual component conveying intent, conviction, and sincerity.

The communicator may tend to oversimplify a presentation, thereby raising doubts about his motives and hidden agenda. However, total lack of inhibition or restraint in presentation of any idea may destroy the purpose of the communication. I recall a president engaged in the presentation of a program for evaluation of faculty who, in response to a critical but unanticipated question concerning the use of the appraisal results in promotion and tenure, destroyed the whole program by saying that obviously this should be a major purpose of the effort. The credibility of the communicator is always a concern. The receivers of a message must trust the communicator if they are to receive and act on that message. They must also have confidence that the communicator can carry out whatever responsibilities or steps devolve upon him in following through with the communication.

The encoding process (like card punching or typewriting) has possibilities of error embraced in the mechanical aspects of encoding. Mispronunciation or misspelling can become the basis for attack by those in disagreement with the ideas presented. In the extreme, such incidental errors can be used to discredit an entire communication on the basis that its progenitors are illiterate incompetents who do not even understand the issues about which they would communicate. Inflection, stress, emphasis, and volume in oral communications can influence the acceptance of the message. Overuse of these devices, however, does not usually prove effective on a college or university campus as most faculty members, despite conflicting values and a considerable degree of emotionality, hold to the view that any attempt to influence others by means other than the presentation of factual information and its logical consequences is inappropriate.

The choice of the transmission process or the means of communication should be based upon the nature of the communication, the purposes, and the audience to be reached. In turn, the structure and content of the communication should be related to the means to be used. Static or noise may be introduced not only in the sense of telephone or radio communication but also in the sense of additional conflicting issues or demands that distract attention from the message conveyed or create complications not foreseen by the communicator. Loss, delay, and even interception by individuals other than the intended receiver may pose problems. If messages are transmitted through third parties who may add, modify, or garble a message, the transmission process itself may become the major factor in ineffective communication. Few people can relay a message accurately, and many individuals simply do not want to do so because they dislike the message, do not want to be held in any way responsible for it, or are simply unable to assimilate fully the real message because of their own conflicts and values. The rewording by deans of presidential statements or requests prior to communicating them to faculty makes an interesting study of this point. Serial reproduction and transmission of messages in a hierarchical pattern actually set up a conflict between a bureaucratic form of governance and a collegial one. In so doing, it incites on the part of faculty and students an increasing expectation for direct involvement in the governance of the institution. Both faculty members and students have long known that upward communication through the administrative hierarchy is ineffective in that the successive transmitters tend to divorce themselves carefully from a demand or complaint and, in so doing, to soften it or somehow imply a lack of justification for it. There are also two forms of horizontal communication that are frequently defective. Vice presidents, deans, and chairpersons may make decisions affecting other sections of the institution without consulting their counterparts at the same level. Cancellation or revision of a course taken by students in another department is an example. Some administrators are delinquent in keeping their immediate staff informed of actions or pending decisions, so that the unavailability of the administrator creates embarrassment and unnecessary delay.

The decoding of a message for or by the receiver includes all the factors involved in the encoding process but also depends on the interest, attention, and concentration of the receiver as well as his or her attitude toward the communicator. In the face of a flood of communication, many faculty members and students give superficial attention to messages judged as of peripheral import, often finding later that the communication was deemed peripheral only because its context and full meaning were not grasped. Despite the recognition that it is at times difficult to get the attention of individuals, there is a tendency in universities to assume that a statement appearing in official publications communicates to those involved. In fact, the communication process is so important in the total education of faculty and students that the communicator has the obligation to assure himself that the message has been received and understood by at least a reasonable proportion of the intended audience. There is no better indication of this than feedback from the receiver. Certainly a major part of the difficulties associated with communication in institutions of higher education lies in the fact that some communicators do not seek and seemingly neither desire nor receive responses. Others delight in favorable responses and praise but ignore or react vindictively to pointed questions or criticism. The receiver of the message tends then to assume that his or her views are of no interest or will have no impact and may, as many faculty members do, dismiss the whole matter as irrelevant—especially to his or her own case. However, the individual originating the communication tends to assume that the message is complete and that closure has been attained. The ultimate end of the communication process—a new level of understanding, a better basis for cooperation, or a change in behavior—may not be reached. This is the reason why communication is deemed so inadequate on most campuses.

Another problem in communication occasionally arises when individuals communicate messages that have had no prior discussion and no common background or context for understanding. This occurs especially as a result of external pressures. The implications are that a hidden agenda and a secret communication flow exist. This is seldom the most serious problem. Most issues discussed by student and faculty committees are threshed around so extensively over time that many other issues become involved. Consensus, if any is achieved, is so limited as to be little more than a pious hope that university personnel will be aware of certain concerns and operate accordingly. Vague pronouncements permit those who think otherwise to do otherwise. Ambiguity and laissez-faire practices ably abet each other.

Credibility and Trust in Communication

Lack of credibility is a major hurdle both in the initiation and in the reception of communication. Aside from obvious incompetence and lack of status or influence, most credibility gaps arise from doubts that what is said is true or that it unambiguously reflects the underlying purposes or motives. No credence is given to the statements of one who is not trusted. Many communications are seen as simply overlays having little to do with the underlying reality. The concealment of actual motives is often attended by an insistence that the concerns are generated out of a desire to serve the needs of students or of a specific clientele. I have found that it is commonplace in proposing new doctoral graduate programs to provide extensive data and numerous letters from influential individuals. Both sources imply that the program is needed, that it does not over-lap or duplicate existing programs, and that, in the course of time, the program will generate benefits far beyond those re-quired for initiation and support. Frequently the evidence amounts to little more than opinions of paid consultants, state-ments of program uniqueness (usually denied by institutions offering like programs), and supporting letters from individuals who respond out of good will without any real knowledge of or interest in the program proposed. Carefully selected data and views may appear persuasive but they are not convincing once the bias is established.

As another example of communication under circum-stances raising doubts about credibility, consider those institu-tions that, faced with the possibility of falling enrollment, sud-denly become interested in serving a new clientele. When that clientele was previously ignored, the credibility of the an-nouncement is naturally in question. This is one of many rea-sons why such new clienteles turn out to be less numerous than initially assumed. They see self-interest rather than service as the motivation.

Many of the confrontations regarding resources that take place on the university campus are generated on rather different grounds than is evident in the verbal exchanges that take place. Resources or the lack of them is always a major factor from ad-ministrative points of view, whereas lack of resources seldom enters into student or faculty deliberations. The latter groups tend to dismiss such declarations as irrelevant or untrue, or as temporary states that could be readily overcome if administra-tors accepted their obligation to reorder their priorities and raise funds to support faculty and student desired programs. Administrators tend to consider inefficiency, ineffectiveness, and external pressures as bases for reduction of unneeded and duplicating programs. Self-interest, the apparent needs and de-mands of even a small number of people, and pervasive doubts as to the validity of administrative concerns yield a very differ-ent point of view on the part of affected faculty members. It is not surprising that at times administrators have communicated a policy decision without prior discussion or without explanation, knowing that prior discussion may only complicate the issues and that explanations will be attacked as misrepresentations or as invalid.

One contention in the communications process is that some groups or individuals fail to listen to others. It happens, and there are numerous explanations for it. One who has heard the same thing many times inevitably becomes somewhat indifferent. If what is said does not correspond to others' perceptions or judgments of the intent or to their ideals, communication can be completely balked. When a communication makes demands regarded by individuals as unreasonable, there is a natural tendency to be irritated or simply to ignore the communication. Many sermons possess that character. There is little point in talking endlessly or recurrently about a problem unless a plan of attack leading to resolution can be developed. Some problems are chronic and irresolvable—for example, class size. Some are chronic and precious—for example, the role of the humanities in liberal education. Attempts at resolution simply drive some individuals to add further complications or seek another problem of equal perplexity. In fact, most problems of major concern in higher education and in society are never solved. Promotion of a solution to a problem often reveals a gross oversimplification of the problem and generates one or more other problems. The development of a new problem may appear to solve an existing one only because the attention and efforts of individuals are diverted to other matters. Communication deficiencies only reflect human deficiencies in the face of irresolvable complexity. Ready solutions to complex problems strain and ultimately destroy the credibility of the proponent.

Purposeful communication is an attempt to provide individuals with information in a manner that will influence their thinking, actions, and points of view. This can happen only when communicator and receiver develop credibility for each other and when they accept at least a few common values and hold similar convictions with regard to the purpose and mission of the institution. Achievement of credibility requires that the communicator be clear in his own mind about what is to be communicated and what results are expected from it. He should seek to identify his own purposes and values and separate them from the controlling purposes, values, and missions of the institution itself. He should be frank in expressing this view to all audiences and should regard early communications on an issue as a basis for encouraging thought and promoting discussion and feedback. At the same time, when communication is undertaken to resolve an issue, both the external and internal implications of a problem and its resolution should be dealt with and emphasis should be given to the point that continuing communication is to be directed to achieving a satisfactory decision rather than indefinitely postponing it.

In an institution, decision making at times tends to become a confrontation or continuing negotiation between the administrators or managers, who are expected to control wisely the allocation of resources, and the units or individuals within the institution who are, from their point of view, injured by a change. It is not to be expected that negotiation, however long extended, will be effective in achieving full acceptance and cooperation by those adversely affected by a decision. Those adversely affected can, and often do, enlist the support of others within the institution who fear that they might be next in line for similar action. To avoid this possibility, communication should be carried through on a broad front involving all individuals who are concerned with the role of the institution and the quality of its services. Open communication and full records of it are essential to establish accountability and to support actions of an institution when, as seems to be increasingly the case, decisions made within an institution are taken into the public forum. Carrying this public forum pattern to an extreme will deny to an educational institution the informal interactions among individuals and units that are essential to learning, organizing, and applying ideas. Many of the failures of communication directed to both the needs and concerns of individuals and the formal operations and purposes of the institution result when discussions become heated and even violent because of the hesitation of individuals to speak frankly with one another about behavior, beliefs, and relationships. Some of these behaviors and beliefs that interfere with quality and productivity are too sensitive for public discussion and come to light only when a crisis develops that requires immediate action. Some never come to light and remain as a hidden agenda that complicates the predictability of the behavior, and hence the credibility, of some individuals. When communication becomes complicated by choler, by unrevealed and perhaps unrecognized assumptions, and by actions prejudicial to one or more of the parties concerned, maintenance of a character of communication appropriate to an educational institution may no longer be possible. Numerous such cases have reached the newspapers in recent years and have been resolved only by judicial decisions.

Some Advice to Administrators

Faculty members and students must have opportunity to communicate their concerns to administrators. They should be able to leave the administrator's office with confidence that their views have been heard and understood, whether or not the views are heeded or their requests granted. To accomplish this, an administrator will do well, just before parting, to attempt to synthesize and report back to the individual or group the essence of what they had to say and, having achieved that understanding, should make clear that other factors also have to be taken into account and that no assurance can be given that the results requested will actually be achieved. Because communication on these matters is so important, a wise administrator, even the one adept in words and language, will avoid making extensive comments on any issue or request unless or until such time as he or she has had the opportunity to consider the matter in some depth and arrive at a reasonable and feasible way of dealing with it. In interactions with individuals or groups that are both pleasant and persuasive, it is all too easy to make or imply assurances that are unwise or insupportable. But having made some commitment, even if only to study the request further, the administrator who attains and deserves the confidence of his or her associates will make a memorandum on the matter, follow through on it, and ultimately provide a response, with an attached commendation for calling the matter to his or her attention. Such a response is desirable altogether apart from whether the request itself was granted in whole, in part, or completely denied. Accessibility and willingness to listen to individuals, combined with an apparent concern with equity for individuals while achieving and maintaining quality, are strong points in any administrator and will be recognized and appreciated by students and faculty.

Committees dominated by students and faculty pose special problems for administrators. Advisory committees can be chaired or directed to an administrator-devised agenda without undue fear of accusation of dictatorship. Even so, adequate provision should be made for committee members to propose agenda items and to develop a synthesis of opinion rather than simply an expression of individual opinions. The administrator need feel no compulsion to disseminate reports of advisory committee meetings. They have no authority, take no actions, and exist and meet at the pleasure of the administrator. Committees (whatever their designation) that are part of the formal governance structure are very different. In the present day, such committees expect that the chairperson will be a faculty member and, in many cases, the committee will elect the chairperson. An administrator sitting with such a committee is in an anomalous position in several respects. A few committee members may expect administrative direction or hesitate to express personal views that may disagree with administrative convictions or existing policy. Other committee members may take the opportunity to express dislikes and concerns proceeding out of administrative actions that may have little to do with the committee charge. And still others will tend to push the committee into an executive role not appropriate to the charge and generally inappropriate for committees. In such circumstances, an administrator can waste many hours in meetings without tangible accomplishment and meanwhile lack time either to analyze current issues or formulate statements or policies regarding them. The incumbent committee may become somewhat educated as to administrative problems, but that task in the face of rotation is never ending.

The preceding remarks clearly indicate the importance of communication in providing direction to deliberations as well as to the reporting of their results. To improve both the process and the results, I suggest the following:

1. When possible, an administrator should delegate to an assistant the responsibility for attending committee meetings.
2. The assistant should be an individual of sufficient stature to assure respect and be known as having the confidence of and influence on the administrator represented but not possessing delegated power to make commitments.
3. From time to time, the administrator should, through the delegated representative, direct attention to issues and raise questions upon which advice is desired.
4. The administrator should meet with committee chairpersons and clarify the relations suggested earlier and explain the rationale for them.
5. The administrator or assigned representative should offer services to the committee in collecting data and other materials, in preparing reports, and in providing agenda and minutes, thereby assisting discreetly in maintaining close contact with the committee and providing some direction to it.

In my judgment, administrators report to superior administrators, to the president, to the governing board, and, through the governing board, to the public or other supporters of the institution. Thus they are not bound by committee reports but ultimately by their responsibilities, obligations, and personal values and integrity.

Another level of communication faced by the administrator is that in which, either orally or in writing, the entire staff of his or her area of responsibility is addressed. I have sat through many oral presentations and have been amazed and disturbed at the number of administrators who addressed their audience with no apparent indication of purpose and no clear statement of expected results. A few seemed unable to distinguish between chairing or coordinating a meeting and completely dominating it, much like a professor lecturing to a class with no opportunity for questions or discussion. For the administrator who wishes to avoid such pitfalls in either oral or written communication to an organizational unit, the following suggestions should prove helpful:

1. Decide whether the purpose of the communication is informational, motivational, or instructional. If the purpose is informational, written communication is frequently better than oral. This would not be true, however, when the material presented is on a problem and policy level at which the dynamism, persuasiveness, and presence of the communicator is contributory to understanding and acceptance. Motivational presentations demonstrating the need for deliberation and action, encouraging both, and depicting some of the possible alternatives can be either oral or written. Instructional communications ("do this") can also be either oral or written but, with reasonably autonomous and self-directed faculty, a tactful and rational oral statement, accompanied by the institutional problems, obligations, and social responsibility involved, may be better received and provide a degree of receptivity for the written statement which, in such circumstances, must surely follow.
2. Consider the nature of the audience and its range of contrasting views and values. Select language, information, organization, examples, and circumstances and mode of communication so as to avoid emotion-laden crises, confrontations, or chaos. Except in cases wherein an institution is forced by external demands, the initial communication on any topic should be the initiation of continuing dialogue.
3. Avoid oversimplification by not insisting upon dealing with an issue in isolation from others directly related, and likewise avoid undue complications by not encouraging or permitting the introduction of largely extraneous alternatives.
4. Present a balanced analysis of the issues involved and an overview of the available alternatives, with a reasonably adequate but not necessarily exhaustive consideration of reasons supporting each of the alternatives. If a particular alternative is advocated, the values and priorities supporting this alterna-

tive should be emphasized while recognizing also that some compromises or sacrifices are involved.

5. Recognize that the formulation of any communication other than a factual observation will usually have a significant impact upon the communicator as well as upon the receptor and that discussions or other interchanges will also affect both. Willingness to approach communication in this manner is a sine qua non for satisfying and productive communication.

Suggestions for Further Reading

Berlo, D. K. *The Process of Communication.* New York: Holt, Rinehart and Winston, 1960.

Blake, R. H., and Haroldsen, E. O. *Taxonomy of Concepts in Communication.* New York: Hastings House, 1975.

Haney, W. V. "Serial Communication of Information in Organizations." In J. A. DeVito, *Communication Concepts and Processes.* Englewood Cliffs, N.J.: Prentice-Hall, 1971.

Mailick, S. (Ed.). *Concepts and Issues in Administrative Behavior.* Englewood Cliffs, N.J.: Prentice-Hall, 1962.

Rockey, E. H. *Communicating in Organizations.* Cambridge, Mass.: Winthrop, 1977.

Schramm, W. "How Communication Works." In J. A. DeVito, *Communication Concepts and Processes.* Englewood Cliffs, N.J.: Prentice-Hall, 1971.

FOUR

〰〰〰〰〰〰〰〰〰〰〰〰〰〰〰〰〰〰〰〰〰〰〰〰〰〰

Conceptions
of Decision Making

The term *decision* conveys a note of finality more clearly indicated by the adjective *decisive*. Avoidance of a decision can be decisive, for it is a decision not to alter or even enter into an issue of current concern. Decisions in higher education are seldom decisive, either in time or in application. By probing records, most institutions will reveal the existence of decisions, rules, regulations, and policies never altered or revoked but long since forgotten. A review of them usually brings out inconsistencies, ambiguities, and contradictions. Many decisions arise out of a series of choices and commitments made over time; they are cumulative rather than climactic. It is likely and appropriate that decisions will be modified from time to time and that the rules, policies, or actions based upon them will recurrently require review and evaluation. However, all too many of the changes result from whims or pressures of the moment rather than from examination of the basic values, considerations, and context that originally engendered the prior decisions. Since those prior decisions may also have originated from administrative whims or momentary pressures, the operative values, considerations, and context may not be determinable.

Indeed, meeting minutes and records generally do not well reflect the underlying rationale for actions taken and policies stated, perhaps because the compromises involved in achieving a decision are neither readily explained nor phraseable in words entirely acceptable to the parties concerned.

Areas of Decision Making

A brief discussion of some types of decisions facing a manager or administrator will clarify the nature of the process. There are perhaps six reasonably distinctive areas of decision making, varying from the routine with little or no significance beyond the immediate specific to those effecting major changes in institutional character and individual careers. The *first* area concerns routine decisions. If the process of registration generates, as it frequently does, criticism from students and faculty, the administrator must make a decision either to ignore the matter or investigate it. The existence of full confidence in the registrar would suggest no interference other than perhaps an expression of interest in measures taken to alleviate the complaints. Routine processes and attendant circumstances tend to generate appeals by persons who claim an exception or exemption from a rule. Intervention by an administrator and a directed individual deviation from strict rule or policy raise the issue of fairness and may generate further demands destructive of the whole system and of the morale of those immediately responsible for it. Extended listing of exceptions encourages individuals not only to take undue advantage of them but to seek further exceptions. Decisions are required, but an administrator cannot afford to waste time on such matters other than to see that those more directly responsible promulgate means (possibly formal appeal procedures) for resolving the problems. Routine decisions should generally be made routinely.

A *second* area of decision making involves administrative or managerial responsibility for monitoring and correcting deficient performance. The immediate decision to interfere can be overly long delayed or rashly entered into in the initial rush of irritation. The decision to interfere should include both a date and a plan of action. For example, complaints from parents, legislators, or others about admissions policies and practices are inevitable. At some minimal level they may be regarded as routine, although they should receive courteous treatment and should never be totally ignored or brusquely treated. Even a small intensification of criticism, because of both the potential for creating ill will and its implications of a new factor, may be a signal for a quick appraisal of the admissions operations and personnel to determine whether some recent change in practice or personnel lies at the root of the increase in criticism. It is usually better to raise issues at an early precritical stage and to take action than to let the matter become critical and public. Long delay may generate external demands that require resolving the difficulty under pressure with attendant emotional involvements beneficial to neither the institution nor the persons involved.

A *third* area of decision making is that of innovation. Individuals often settle comfortably into habitual ways of doing things, follow tradition, and reject any innovation simply because it requires effort or the surrender of some prestige or initiative to others. The call for change also implies criticism of existing performance, policies, and personnel in any unit to which the call is directed. Some segments of the faculty in a university are oriented to the past and regard innovative suggestions as attacks on standards and quality. Innovation in procedures can be as difficult as innovation in substance. I recall suggesting to a registrar a more efficient way of handling certain matters. The answer, given with a smile and a thank you, was that the procedure was convenient and so it remained unchanged. Change is disturbing, especially when existing procedures and forms possess an aura of respectability and provide a sense of satisfaction.

A *fourth* area of decision making involves personnel policies and practices in appointment, promotion, reward, fringe benefits, and retirement. The labor-intensive nature of a college makes staff morale and satisfaction major concerns in all personnel decisions. Unionization has moved many of these decisions to a bargaining table over which academic administrators neither preside nor have much direct influence. Nevertheless, administrators should be sensitive to conflicts among individuals, staff groupings, and segments of the institution and should seek resolution before they become critical. If the conflicts relate to major institutional policies or operations, these policies probably require review. One of the problems of administration in maintaining morale and satisfaction is to combine an appropriate degree of certainty with a necessary component of ambiguity and uncertainty. When policies and practices become rigid, there is little room for either individualism or innovation, but lack of clear policy can result in chaos. Individuals require some guidance and direction to decide whether their activities are appropriate and will be rewarded when done well.

A *fifth* area of decision making has to do with institutional mission, role, purpose, and scope. Statements made at the founding of the institution have almost certainly been revised or replaced by successive boards and administrative officers. Today the mission, role, and scope of each state university are usually reviewed or defined and imposed by some state agency. Nevertheless, these statements require review and reinterpretation with changing circumstances and demands. Conflicts between internal demands generated by the faculty and external limitations imposed by coordinating agencies frequently become a source of conflict. A statement placing reasonable limits upon an institution, while permitting and perhaps even encouraging new ventures consistent with the accepted role and mission, is difficult to write, for it must thread a perilous path between insipid and unrestrictive vagueness, on the one hand, and an undesirable and unduly limiting specificity, on the other.

Finally, in the *sixth* area are the personal decisions, including the weighing of the implications of personal involvement in and responsibility for other decisions. An administrator may appropriately consider whether a decision is consistent with personal values and aspirations, as well as whether the decision will be generally accepted or generate a storm that threatens peace of mind and future career. Too many presidents have ignored, countenanced, or even encouraged practices in the recruiting and eligibility maintenance of athletes which have ultimately brought criticism to them and retribution to their institutions. Administrators are responsible for whatever goes on under their area of responsibility. They should be discharged for incompetence or malfeasance when they are ignorant of or fail to control inappropriate activity. Since most decisions involve a value commitment, careful examination should be made of the various factors or bases upon which a decision is to be based as well as of the ends to be achieved by it. Inconsistencies and conflicts between personal values of administrators and the values supported by an institution or sectors of it are inevitable and some accommodation becomes essential. Administrators should feel comfortable in their task or depart. They have no right to rebuild an institution in their own image, but if they impose no standards (that is, stand for anything) they clearly stand for nothing. That, unfortunately, describes the careers of many academic administrators who wander into administration with neither insight nor convictions and ultimately leave in the same vacuous state of mind.

Dimensions of Decision Making

The preceding six areas of decision making (routine, monitoring, innovation, personnel policies, institutional mission, and personal involvement) are by no means independent. They do provide one way of looking at the range and complexity of decisions faced. Another and, in many respects, more helpful perspective on decision making is provided by a second set of factors or dimensions, seven in number, each of which may be used in considering the nature and implication of *any* decision from the most trivial to the exceedingly complex.

The *first* dimension is the awareness or consciousness that a decision is expected and is being made. The administrator who lightly dismisses as interesting or amusing the comment or suggestions of a faculty member or student has, for that individual, made the decision to ignore the matter, although the administrator may not even recall the incident. By unavailability, by ignoring correspondence and phone calls, and by their modes of response, administrators are often seen as making decisions when they are not conscious of having made them. It is relatively easy to ignore issues so long as they are viewed as individual and incidental comments or complaints.

A *second* decision dimension is the importance or interest attached to an issue and a decision regarding it. What will be the possible impact of various results? What conflicts may be engendered or resolved? What precedents may be set that have disturbing implications for other issues? Who will be affected and in what ways? What are the probable costs and benefits (and not solely in dollars)?

This second dimension has immediate implications with regard to a *third*—the process by which the decision is to be made. In some cases, the decision can be made directly and immediately by the administrator. Usually, this will involve situations in which the impact is limited and the number of people affected small. If a moment's reflection suggests that the decision involves particular areas and problems that are best understood by another individual or group, delegation of the decision making with the expectation of discussion and endorsement may be appropriate. A decision affecting the whole area of responsibility of the administrator might be made a coordinated decision involving one or more special committees or task forces. In some cases, the individual identified as the decision maker may actually be only the direct instigator of the process by which the decision is reached.

A *fourth* dimension of decision making is the identification of exactly what is involved in making the decision. Some decisions are simply application and interpretation of policies or decisions already in existence. Special cases may arise that are not covered by any rule or precedent, and the decision may then be highly specific. In other cases, the decision takes the form of a rule or policy having no significant impact until sometime in the future. For example, the realization that the student number system used in an institution will, at some future date, require an expansion of the number of digits used may generate an immediate decision that has little or no immediate impact.

A *fifth* decision dimension is the amount of flexibility or rigidity that exists both in directing the nature of the decision and in the decision itself. The statistician speaks of degrees of freedom. Here we might speak of the number of available options and include the possible reversibility of a particular decision in the light of unanticipated consequences. Many decisions, of necessity, involve a high level of ambiguity. This is not necessarily bad, for a long-term commitment to excellence could very well result in the opposite if it attempted to specify for all time what is meant by excellence in respect to both process and results.

A *sixth* decision dimension is the identification of whether the decision deals with structural, procedural, or substantive matters. Structural matters, like the calendar, present a framework within which various procedures take place. These procedures have many degrees of freedom that can be chosen in terms of the purposes and quality commitments of the institution. Registration, instruction, and counseling exemplify processes that can be carried out in many ways. Decisions on substantive matters are much more complicated and inevitably involve a degree of ambiguity. Academic freedom is an example of a concept of great significance but one so difficult to define in particular circumstances that a great deal of attention has been turned to spelling out procedures that provide reasonable guarantee of academic freedom. Quality is ultimately dependent upon the processes and structures used to define and maintain it.

Finally, the *seventh* dimension of decision making is implementation and evaluation. Review of the records of most institutions will produce a large number of rules and policies that have been completely forgotten or simply ignored and never enforced. The making of a decision should include the designation of one or more individuals responsible for carrying out that decision or monitoring its application. There should be well-defined procedures and a delegation of responsibility for monitoring and evaluating the effectiveness of the interpretation and application of the decisions. There has been a tendency in recent years toward overuse of faculty committees in carrying out such responsibilities. Committees are ineffective unless related to an individual office responsible for carrying out stated policies. Furthermore, committees cannot be effectively held accountable for performance; they can only be discharged. Implementation of a decision and the monitoring or evaluation of the impact of a decision and its enforcement are separable functions. Evaluation may lead to altered procedures or to substantive change. Committees or task forces can be useful ways to review and evaluate impact and performance.

Bases for Decisions

Although most decisions are based, in part, upon facts, they are also based upon values. Even a fact may involve a value judgment. A bruised apple may be called rotten and discarded. Others may regard a partially rotten apple as partially salvageable. Both maintenance of quality and prevention of waste involve values. Obviously, varying interpretations can generate conflicts. Many institutions added black studies or women's studies so rapidly that quality was sacrificed. Flexibility becomes a value when the need for individualization is recognized, but flexibility is frequently regarded as destructive of rigor. Accountability, efficiency, and cost-benefit comparisons become value concerns to those who seek to improve the management of higher education institutions. Acceptability becomes a major operational value when contemplated changes may generate either applause or criticism from an important clientele. A possible increase in tuition fees is surely accompanied by a discussion of its anticipated impact on enrollment. Those who extend freedom or autonomy to students, faculty members, or departments are concerned with responsible use of that autonomy and would incorporate accountability procedures. Individuals accorded autonomy resent imputation of possible irresponsibility and may argue that autonomy should not be conditional or subject to withdrawal. The conflict of ideals and absolutes, on the one hand, with the realities of mean intentions and ineptness, on the other, are as evident in the university as elsewhere.

As suggested earlier, the probable effects of any decision should be carefully examined. Who benefits from this decision? Presumably, both the institution and the faculty benefit when salary raises are based upon merit. The raise provides an incentive for meritorious work from which the institution ultimately profits. However, I recall a president who asserted that college salaries should be kept modest to maintain a spirit of sacrifice and altruism. Many church congregations still support this view in respect to the pastor's salary.

The reinstitution of a discarded foreign language requirement may benefit the entire faculty because it leads to a more balanced load. It can also be argued that students benefit from studying a foreign language because it is part of a liberal education. Society also benefits when more individuals possess foreign language competency. However, many educators feel that the liberal education benefits of foreign language study are exaggerated. In our culture, relatively few people find much use for a smattering of a foreign language acquired by exposure in a one-year course. Perhaps students should study a more *useful* field. The value conflict is clearly indicated. It is also evident that value commitments are hardly separable from personal biases and benefits. I have heard foreign language professors argue for a requirement on the grounds that their jobs were at stake. Educational decisions almost always involve conflicts of interest in which the needs and desires of students may be ignored.

This observation brings us to another aspect of the role of values in decisions. Justice, wisdom, courage, honesty, integrity, and loyalty are generally recognized as desirable virtues. Whether they result from a college education is uncertain. As with all values, there are dubious extreme positions and differences of opinion as to desirable or appropriate positions in varying circumstances. Meeting the demands for equity made by some individuals and groups creates inequity for others. Wisdom surely requires recognition that everyone (including oneself) is at times lacking in wisdom. Courage must include occasional hesitancy or even timidity, else it becomes rashness. Honesty carried to an extreme results in untactful behavior in social interactions. Institutional loyalty does not justify hiding institutional errors and inadequacies from the public eye. Virtues themselves may become means of attaining power, achieving happiness, or merely surviving. Hence the motivations underlying decisions are difficult to determine and are interpreted in various ways by individuals holding contrasting views. The decision maker does not always correctly identify or fully understand his or her own values. One who claims objectivity will find that others reject that judgment.

The achievement of consensus in regard to an issue or problem involved is commonly regarded as desirable. In contrast, compromise is often decried as undesirable and as indicative of a lack of commitment to any fundamental values. Consensus itself is often achieved only by defining and resolving an issue at a superficial level that avoids or glosses over value differences. Consensus does not assure that a decision is right. Compromise does not mean that the resulting decision lacks clarity or validity. Since values interact and may conflict with or support each other, a compromise may approach an ideal so far as that is achievable in the real world. The most difficult individuals to woo in attaining either consensus or compromise are those with strong commitments to a set of value priorities that dictate (for them) a unique and rigid decision. Idealism, dogmatism, and academic status melded together are very difficult to handle. The professor who always thinks otherwise does exist.

The obligations of institutions of higher education to their students and to society require integrity in isolating and considering the various values that are and should be involved in decision making. There are, however, other bases for decisions. The collection and interpretation of factual data are usually presented as an alternative, but this approach also has value overtones. The relevance, accuracy, and interpretation of data are value laden, and the decision as to the appropriate action is even more so. A professor regularly fails 25 percent of the students in a course, whereas other professors in the same course fail no more than 5 to 10 percent. Does this indicate unfair grades, inappropriate standards, poor teaching, or an inferior group of students? It is evident that views as to the appropriate data to collect and the interpretation of that data will differ. Is comparability in grading standards of two different teachers even desirable?

Policy decisions may only reflect practice rather than determine it. Indeed, some individuals studying decision making in business have tried to develop complex computer programs that will yield the same decisions as were recorded for the accumulated cases. This approach makes several possibly unrecognized assumptions. One is that past practice has been fair and wise. Presumably, the inability of the computer to reproduce past decisions could be interpreted as indicative of a high degree of variability in judgment resulting either from use of unidentified factors or from variations and errors in judgment. Most policy decisions originate out of specific cases conjoined with a desire for continuity, uniformity, and equitability in dealing with similar circumstances. Establishment of equity and continuity, on the one hand, and maintenance of flexibility and individuality, on the other, are in continuing conflict. An individual responsible for specific case resolution may develop a high level of sensitivity and expertise or may simply make a series of snap judgments. Consistency in decisions sets precedents that become embedded as customs or traditions. However, precedent or tradition is an unsatisfactory basis for decision making in an academic institution committed to the development of new ideas and procedures.

Policy formulation can lead to humorous results. One university faculty committee, trying to resolve the relationship of course credit hours and the amount of work required, produced a rule that a student shall receive one credit hour for three hours of effort, however expended. The student personnel officers of a small women's college, concerned with the amorous partings between the young women and men as they returned to the residence halls, developed a rule permitting a goodnight kiss or an "I love you" kiss but debarring anything more expressive. These rules dramatize a concern but leave much to individual judgment. Other rules are highly explicit. Many institutions once had a rule that excessive absenteeism from class sessions resulted in a failing grade. The origins of this rule probably lie in the inadequacies of lectures as much as in the indifference or irresponsibility of students. A policy statement that students are expected to attend class regularly and to fulfill all course requirements is probably more appropriate. It has implications for both students and faculty in that the expectation that students attend class implies that the faculty provide a significant education experience.

A policy statement provides a guide for actions of individuals; it also provides for some flexibility and adaptation in a range of situations that may differ markedly in nature and purpose. Policy statements and principles seem more appropriate to educational institutions than specific rules and penalties. Nevertheless, some rigid rules ensure uniformity in dealing with certain recurring problems. For example, what proportion of fees should be refunded to a student withdrawing from college? Some rules attempt to impose desired patterns of behavior. The assumption is made that requiring certain behaviors will develop desirable and permanent habit patterns. It is also true that the enforcement of rigid rules makes it impossible to ascertain whether individuals are developing desirable traits and responsibility in those matters to which the rules relate.

Decisions, especially as they pertain to practices, are often unclear because they result from the gradual accretion of discrete choices and commitments over time. The ultimate formulation of a rule or regulation is a double decision. The first decision simply recognizes the importance of the substantive issue or problem. The second decision specifies either a resolution or a procedure for attaining it. Any policy statement is a decision and an official commitment to certain goals and values. General principles and policies imply, by their very nature, a degree of flexibility and adaptation and the extension of some prerogative of decision making on the part of the individual interpreting and enforcing the policy. Thus policies, rules, and laws are forms of decisions that direct or guide more specific decisions. If consideration of a certain problem with a high frequency level results in a decision to continue case-by-case resolution, the maximum of individualization and flexibility has been achieved at the expense of continuing conflict resulting from difficulty in rendering equitable decisions. Most specific rules and regulations were originally developed as recommendations or guides with full realization that exercise of judgment in specific cases would be desirable. However, rules tend to be rigidly construed in a bureaucracy, for a bureaucrat who makes adaptations may incur reprimands from or appeals to higher levels. In recent years, it is inevitable that some procedure for exceptions to particular rules or policies and appeals from the decisions made with regard to them be established; and it is entirely likely that these routes of appeal will be increasingly used. To some extent, then, decisions take on a procedural character as well as a substantive one. Decisions have to be made as to how rules or policies are interpreted, enforced, and appealed.

Effects of Decisions

Small groups of individuals, out of mutual respect, similar values, commitments, and tolerance of ambiguity, may operate quite effectively when rules or policies are ambiguous or nonexistent. As organizations grow and differentiate, individuals use the ambiguity for personal advantage. Thereby a demand arises for rules or policies to establish equity for all. I recall one university in which the administrators and faculty had operated for years with no specific travel policy. All requests were honored. A new department head, taking advantage of the situation, soon had himself and members of his faculty traveling to diverse parts of the world at university expense—but only for a year! The existence of decisions does not ensure that they will be effective. Many faculty members see themselves as self-directed and autonomous so long as they make significant contributions. Thus rules or policies with regard to consultation time and stipends are notoriously difficult to enforce. Individuals who have developed a reputation by consultation closely related to their teaching and research find limitations unacceptable and unreasonable. When a sufficient number of people (including some administrators) accept this view, the policies are ignored. As earlier noted, there is often no formal assignment of responsibility for enforcing the decision. Furthermore, if no punitive measures are available, it is not clear just what enforcement means.

Professors who support a decision may still regard themselves as exempted from it. A few individuals or departments may even engage in a planned evasion. In one such instance, a department threatened by a new university policy relating budget to departmental credit hour productivity moved immediately to increase all course credit hours without increasing the class hours.

Such examples suggest that decisions involving specific rules or regulations are unlikely to be effective unless a significant proportion of the staff of an institution accepts both the necessity of the decision and the essence of it. Even so, as with parking regulations, unless there is a procedure for enforcement and a penalty for violation, the rules will be ignored. When decisions involve general policy (for example, teaching responsibilities wherein flexibility must be allowed for professional judgment), the policy will have little impact unless unit administrators are charged with auditing performance and students are provided with routes for reporting and appeal. Unless a list of specific examples of violations of the general policy is provided, judgments are difficult. If exceptions to a policy are permitted, the exceptions may soon destroy the policy. The exceptions indicate that someone is regarded as exceptional; but almost all faculty persons so regard themselves.

Those academics who dislike a decision can make changes that void it. For example, a review of course offerings in a university indicated considerable duplication in content across departments. The recommendation was made to eliminate certain courses. What, in fact, happened was that the course titles and descriptions were completely rewritten and the courses continued. Over time, the preferences, biases, and values that are embedded in rules or policies do change. For many years, the convenience of residence hall dining services dictated that no classes would be scheduled during the noon hour. Students were expected to return to their place of residence for meals. Increasing campus size and class scheduling problems have forced changes, usually over the objections of a few individuals who preferred tradition, social formalities, and personal convenience to increased efficiency.

Decisions do not resolve problems unless they are enforced, and the enforcement may generate more problems. Thus

decisions beget decisions, and decisions must regularly be reviewed to determine whether they are indeed being followed
and also whether they in themselves may be causing more problems than they resolve.

Patterns of Decision Making

Should an institution of higher education be administered
or managed? Administration seems to be the preferred term in
organizations that are input oriented and that lack specific goals
and measurable outputs. In such organizations, it is apparently
not possible to "manage" the operation by finding and imposing the most effective processes. The organization tends to follow predetermined policies, procedures, and regulations, and
permits wide variation resulting from personal preferences.
Some direction is given by developing an appropriate organization for executing the assigned tasks, but since the execution is
remote from the central administration and requires individual
expertise, administration tends to be more adaptive, passive,
and less reactive than management, which is as concerned with
how a task is accomplished as with directing or assigning the
task. An administrator is expected to be more of an expediter
and a servant than a leader. Faculties are generally seen as pre-
ferring it this way, although my own observation is that this is
generally true only of a minority of the faculty. The most productive segments of a faculty are likely to prefer direction and
control that expedites faculty activities. Faculty involvement in
policy determination and administration encroaches upon scholarly work by heavy demands made upon faculty for participation in governance and decision making.

If a university functions as a group of highly competent
specialists loosely coordinated by administrators operating in
the context of several sets of rules, regulations, and policies
coming variously from government, boards of trustees, and the
faculty, there will be confusion and ambiguity as to how all of
these various rules and policies are related and how they apply
in particular cases. There has long been an awareness that the
rigid application of rules, either to faculty members or to stu-

dents, is likely to be unfair to some individuals. Such rigidity is also inconsistent with the nature of a university that purports to value and cultivate individual differences. Thus each administrator, from department chairperson to the president, finds excessive time required to assimilate (and heed or ignore) rules, regulations, and policies while also sitting with many committees, subcommittees, and task forces that undertake to deal with both the routine and the crucial. Hence chairpersons seek for and acquire associate and assistant chairpersons and assistants. Deans and presidents likewise acquire assistants and associates, leading ultimately to such extended titles as assistant to the assistant vice-president. Paper work multiplies, confusion increases, and judgment wanes. Ultimately, common goals and a sense of unity are lost in the maze of committees, confusing administrative connections, and the isolation and ultimate dominance of subunits.

The university actually requires more management. Management is output oriented. The facilities, resources, and manpower of the institution are provided to achieve specified goals and objectives. The university finds difficulty in stating these goals and objectives because of internal disagreement over whether its major obligations are to provide benefits to its students and to society or whether, indeed, the obligation rests with society to provide an environment conducive to scholarly activities and research. The root of the problem lies with the nature and purpose of research. Much of academic research has no significance except in maintaining the vitality of the researcher as a scholar. But to demand that all research have relevance and practical consequences would so restrain research that some of the most significant issues would never be investigated. The faculty understandably argues that individual faculty members should decide on the worth of research activity, although the avidity with which individuals seek research funds allocated to particular types of research suggests that individual commitments are largely adventitious.

This internal quandary with regard to faculty goals and social obligations is heightened because most funding (private or public) available to institutions is associated with expectations as to how the funds will be used and what will result. As these expectations become clearer and more specific, the university is pushed in the direction of management, responsible not only for management of resources but for planning and acquiring resources. This movement toward management has brought into the university many management aids originally developed for use in government or industry. These management aids include budgeting procedures, means for attaining accord on objectives and goals, and ways of reaching those goals. Many of these procedures are quantitatively based and involve, explicitly or implicitly, a series of debatable assumptions that are not always recognized in their academic adaptations. (Many of these management aids are briefly described in a glossary of administrative and management terms in Resource B.)

Several management theories have been developed. These theories emerge from a combination of actual experience in consulting with organizations and institutions and the development of some superstructure or theory buttressed by assumptions and procedures for introduction and application. Thus, management by objectives emphasizes the use of facilities, resources, and manpower to achieve goals and objectives. Management by directives (the pattern in many organizations) is characterized by issuance of orders followed by varying amounts of insight into their rationales. Much of the discussion of management theory in recent years has emphasized participation of the workers in decision making, both in reference to objectives and to procedures for reaching them. Implicit in this development has been a shift in view about people and their motivations. The view that most individuals dislike work, avoid responsibilities, and have no strong desire for advancement is being rejected. The present tendency is to assume that most individuals seek competency, advancement, and consequent satisfaction in their work. If this assumption is correct, worker involvement in decisions should improve production. There should be a shift from a directive and exploitative management to one concerned with improving working conditions and developing a consultative and participatory relationship with employees. Increased productivity provides benefits for both management and employees.

Lacking a satisfactory objective measure of productivity, the university is faced with a somewhat different problem. Is the primary goal of education to improve society or to benefit the individual? The issue cannot be resolved by arguing that the maximum development of individuals will produce the best society. What individuals are benefited—students or faculty? Obviously, the answer must be both, but it does not follow that faculty preferences in use of resources will be the best for students or society. Management is a necessity. The objective of maximal development gives place to optimal development for all. What is optimum and who decides?

Power, Influence, and Authority

Power, simply defined, is the ability, by any means, to control or determine the formulation, interpretation, or application of policy. *Authority* is recognized power—that is, power formally vested in an office or person. *Influence* is informal power achievable in a variety of ways. An individual who is an "authority" in a particular area may, through consultation, suggestion, or personal statements of views and of their implications and impacts, markedly influence the exertion of power by others. An individual who is persuasive and possessed of social graces and patience may acquire consensus support that determines how and for what ends power is exercised. Public opinion polls or the views of a selected group may influence decisions. Such means of influence are generally viewed as appropriate. Undesirable and possibly illegal means of influence are represented by bribery, threats, and promises.

An individual's position is interrelated with the authority, power, and influence exercised. By election or appointment to a managerial position and title, an individual acquires an area of responsibility and some delegated authority. This authority is supported by two considerations. The need for recognition and assignment of responsibility and authority is acknowledged and some deference to authority is a natural consequence. Deference to authority because of position and title varies with country and culture. In a democracy, deference depends, in part, on the quality of the individual as well as the title. A second source of power for an individual with conferred authority is through the inducements, rewards, and sanctions intrinsic to the exercise of that power.

A position and title do not always carry authority, although the individual holding them may exercise considerable influence through a recognition of status and by various inducements, intimacies, privileges, suggestions, and directions that are frequently extrinsic to the immediate situation. These may also involve public recognition or the use of covert incentives such as bribes and threats. Thus a dean of one college on a campus may influence, by indirect means, decisions in other colleges or in departments not under his immediate supervision, especially if these units are highly dependent upon that college for their students. An assistant to the president will find that presumed ready access and influence confer power where none has actually been delegated. A person with no position or title may still exercise considerable power or influence through contacts or through external inducements, rewards, or sanctions unrelated to the institution. Influence is also exercised through a rational approach buttressed by expertise and status as an authority on the issues in question.

In summary, there appear to be four reasonably distinctive bases for attainment of power and a decision-making role. One is the recognition of authority—that is, of delegated power. A second is the formal role of authority in controlling a system of rewards and sanctions that enforce that authority. A third basis is the use of external inducements, rewards, or sanctions by individuals not directly involved in the organizational structure. This is an informal but effective route to power. A fourth basis is the expertise of the individual and the recognition by others of this expertise. The individual becomes an authority because of respect for his competency and he thereby exercises influence. There are personable individuals whose judgment and experience are respected and who have ready rapport with many persons. Such individuals may markedly influence events without even intending to do so.

Motivations Underlying Decisions

Those possessing the power to make decisions should attempt to be critical and frank with themselves as to factors underlying their decisions. Assuming that the ends in themselves are not disreputable or criminal, what is there about a particular purpose or goal that justifies a decision to seek it? The university in which I have long been located has, for years, annually proposed a new law school. There is one in the nearby community of Lansing, one at the University of Michigan, and one in Detroit. There is no good evidence that either the state or nation needs another law school, although some data to that effect have been generated. Why, then, should effort and resources be used for a new law school? One reason given is that no university is really complete without one. Another is that law graduates from other institutions play major roles in the state legislature. Another is that the particular nature of the institution provides the opportunity for a unique and critically needed approach to law. Several presidents have held office during the period of time in which the idea has been advanced. Whether their support of the idea was motivated by a desire for personal recognition for attaining a major new program, an expectation of institutional advancement, or a sincere belief that a unique law program would result is unknown. No doubt the individuals involved would have had difficulty in assessing their own motives. The presence in many states of coordinating or governing boards empowered to authorize the development of new programs is a clear indication that the motivations of single institutions in the addition of programs relate more to the institutional advantages than to the actual need. The motivations of individuals outside of an institution in supporting a program addition are not necessarily pure and unalloyed. At one time, a number of legislators who supported the addition of a law school to a nearby university indicated a desire to achieve a law degree while fulfilling their legislative obligations. Governors and presidents have been suspected of making some decisions in reference to their impact on the next election rather than because of national need or personal convictions. Likewise, faculty members seek power through participation in governance and tend to place their interests ahead of those of the students and the public. The various models of university governance present a variety of issues, difficulties, and advantages in assuring that the institution fulfills its designated role.

Models of University Governance

A professor at Columbia University once characterized the governance there as a "benevolent anarchy," indicating that individuals and units went their diverse ways with only a few common policies and rules. That characterization was made in a period long before universities ran into difficulties with students, federal support programs, rapid inflation, and general suspicion of the integrity and quality of universities. Many faculty members and some administrators still conceive of a university as a loosely coordinated group of essentially autonomous units. In its fullest blooming, this autonomy requires each unit to accept responsibility for acquiring its own resources. Each unit may offer all instruction required for its various programs or contract with other units to provide certain services. Each unit gains from the presence of certain common resource units, from the prestige conferred by the university association, and from interactions with other units of the institution. This organizational pattern requires faculty members and administrators who act as independent entrepreneurs in developing programs and finding resources to support them. It is, in a sense, the epitome of the laissez-faire approach to governance. In a few institutions, benevolent anarchy seems to have worked reasonably well.

A second model of university governance is the autocracy. Reading the history of American higher education, it comes as somewhat of a surprise to those who have visualized colleges and universities as run by the faculty to learn that faculty involvement is a relatively recent phenomenon and that most of the significant advances in higher education came about through dominant and dynamic leaders. Persuasive and influential administrators, board members, and donors with well-organized proposals often have brought about major changes within institutions, although the permanency of these changes after the departure of the founder has been uncertain. In a few cases, such as the University of Chicago and Stanford University, new universities have been brought into being in relatively short periods of time. An autocracy is advantageous in defining the institution, in presenting an unambiguous program for development, and in making rapid moves. In a new or rapidly growing institution, most everyone is preoccupied with his or her own problems. Administrators and new faculty can be imported to support the view of the autocrat. There are still numerous institutions (mostly small liberal arts colleges) that are run in an autocratic way. But there comes a time in maturation when even the most respected autocrat finds board members, faculty, alumni, students, and others asking for some voice in planning and in selecting administrators. The efforts of the American Association of University Professors, the advance or threat of unionization, and the widespread difficulties in acquiring adequate resources make autocracy a pattern of the past.

The often discussed ideal model of university governance is the collegial or shared government pattern. The collegium is often described as a community of scholars. Each faculty member is regarded as having a high level of competence by virtue of training and ability. Competence for the office held results from experience, stature, and the respect of colleagues rather than particular training. Academic and professional freedom are highly valued. Decisions are to be achieved by consultation and consensus, with the expectation that they will be more appropriate and more humane because the faculty has a major input into all decisions. Unfortunately, as institutions become larger and more complex, the interests and needs of various faculty units differ. Consensus seldom exists or is achieved only after conflict or compromise. Fatigue, disgust, and the pressure of other matters often play a major role in acquiring the votes needed for majority acceptance of some policy. In large institutions, attempts to maintain collegiality have led to innumerable committees at various levels, with excessive involvement of time by administrators and faculty sitting with the various committees. Despite the fact that the college or university, by its nature, has a flat or horizontal plan of organization with only about three or four levels involved, the advent of associates, assistants, and assistants to assistants in administrative offices has led to development of a hierarchical bureaucracy rather rigid in nature and frequently with specific status, authority, and finely divided responsibilities assigned to each bureaucrat. The typical bureaucrat's most obvious exercise of authority is found in negation of ideas, proposals, or deviations from existing rules. Authorization of an extraordinary proposal, be it an innovation or a deviation, will surely be carried to higher levels of the bureaucracy, with each level hesitating to acquiesce without the approval of a superior.

Another view of university governance (see particularly Baldridge) is that it is, in large part, a series of political maneuvers growing out of a succession of conflict situations. Internal power blocks seek conflicting ends and values, and influential external groups attempt to influence both processes and procedures in the university. In this model, decisions are negotiated compromises, with eyes variously focused on what will be at once acceptable internally by the faculty, president, and governing board and externally by the various agencies that provide resources. The political model captures something of the conflict and competition going on in committees and academic senates of universities. It is deficient in that there exist no parties with clear sets of goals and basic differences in view. A faculty in a particular unit may unite in defense of the prerogatives of that unit, but rarely does there exist a well-organized cross-sectional group supporting a particular view. Academics are inclined to think otherwise, and at times they appear more concerned about making explicit why they differ from a colleague who supports the common policy than about getting the policy itself approved.

I find no one of the various models of university governance adequate to explain what goes on in most institutions that I have observed. The governance scene in the immediate period is more difficult to characterize than earlier ones. When institutions were growing rapidly and new resources were available, faculty members were very anxious to be involved in the decision-making process. Now that institutions are facing the necessity of some reduction in activities (perhaps the elimination of some programs and units), faculty members are not much inclined to take a major role. Given the opportunity to determine in what areas reductions can be made, they find many reasons why the decision should be deferred. This is not surprising. The view of faculty members with regard to the larger institution is somewhat limited. Their own status and their future depend primarily upon the immediate unit in which they operate. They are naturally inclined to ward off any harm to that unit, but equally they do not wish to be on record as favoring the elimination or weakening of another unit. This reluctance is based upon three considerations. First, faculty members recognize that they lack an overview of the institution and its total role in the educational system of the state or area. Second, they fear that a unit taking a negative position on another may incur enmity prejudicial to their own. Administrators are expected to make the nasty decisions and take the blame. It is also recognized that program deletions will ultimately have to be approved by higher levels and perhaps even by sources external to the institution. In short, the typical faculty member recognizes that authority within the university is ultimately related to funding sources and factors over which the faculty committees have little influence and often even less knowledge.

Delegation of Authority

In seeking more influence and power in institutions of higher education, faculties generally have emphasized their expertise in the various functions carried on within the institution. Their contention is that the several major institutional purposes and the associated functions are all vitally interrelated with the major fields of knowledge represented by the departmental disciplines and professional schools. Therefore, the operation and budget allocation for these programs should have major faculty input, if not complete determination. To some extent, I think, faculties have confused authority arising out of competency in a field with authority for making decisions where that field or discipline is involved. In fact, the two conceptions of authority are very different. Faculty members well trained in research in a discipline often lack competency in developing undergraduate curricula or in teaching undergraduate courses. Indeed, graduate schools have so thoroughly ignored the problems of teaching and curriculum that the individual faculty member's knowledge of those matters is largely based on personal experience as an undergraduate or on experience in planning and teaching courses to undergraduates. Decisions with regard to undergraduate courses are often made by relatively inexperienced individuals who lack insight into the broader curriculum problems. Thus it happens that deans, counselors, and other staff members in close contact with undergraduates are sometimes in a better position than departmental faculties to make recommendations about course planning and the sequence of courses for a degree program.

In truth, then, the "authority" of the faculty has little to do with self-governance. There is no collective faculty fully aware of the problems of the institution and of the exigencies and limitations under which these problems must be resolved. In a sense, the autonomy of the disciplines, departments, and the individual faculty effectively prevents the university from becoming a collegium, even if the faculty express that intent. It is no surprise that faculty senates, representing the total faculty constituency, or augmented senates, including students and representatives of service aspects of the institutional operation, are ineffective in understanding and resolving major issues. The resulting extensive committee structure is productive of untold meetings in which the time is largely taken up by expressions of differences of views of individuals and units and by editing documents that are seldom improved thereby. The search for a decision, in a sense, turns out to be that of finding the least common multiple without actually resolving whether the resulting statement is sound and justifiable on educational grounds. Nevertheless, a segment of the faculty committed to faculty dominance in decision making expects that the authority for most decisions will be delegated to the faculty, and that the president, dean, or department chairperson will be elected by the particular group to preside and to assist in communicating faculty-developed policies to higher levels, including finally the board of trustees. There is, in fact, no justification for this view in the history of American higher education and precious little support in the earlier history of the universities of Europe in which students played the major role.

In the United States, both public and private institutions are operated by a board of trustees. Since state institutions are owned by the state, the board of trustees is an operating board. Most private colleges and universities are owned by their boards, although a few private institutions have also had a separate operations board. The board of the public institution is responsible to the people through the legislature and the executive and judicial branches of governance for effective operation. Although in industry the chairman of the board is often the chief administrator of the corporation, the pattern in boards of institutions of higher education is that all board members serve on a part-time basis. They employ one or more persons in whom they vest the responsibility for the operation of the institution. In some cases, the president also becomes the presiding officer, although a chairman exists who can and may convene the board at certain times in the absence of its appointed officers. The president, as an officer of the board, deals directly with many of the funding sources. The president formulates a budget for board approval and administers and manages the budget and the institution by board authority. This is not so much a delegation of specific authority from the board as a statement that, as the officer of the board, the president (within certain defined policy limits) makes decisions for the board. When issues arise beyond this, the president must discuss them with the board, perhaps making recommendations as to the resolution. As the president acts in the name of the board, the board has shared responsibility with him and can hold him directly responsible for improper action. There can be no delegation of authority from the board to the faculty because there is no satisfactory way whereby the faculty or groups of faculty can be held responsible for improper performance. What does happen is that a board, by implication or by some usually ambiguous statement, provides courtesy delegation of authority and contingent conditions to the faculty, subject to coordination and management by the president as an officer of the board. A reasonable expectation is that improper and irresponsible performance must and will result in immediate abrogation of the courtesy delegation.

The government of the United States is based upon a separation of the executive, legislative, and judicial powers and an elaborate system of checks and balances by which each has significant influence and even power over the other two. Many persons have observed that this separation of powers has never been completely realistic. Courts, to some extent, have taken on administrative or executive roles; investigative committees, commissions, and other federal agencies have moved into quasi-judicial activities. The university pattern of governance never really accepted this separation of powers, and any attempt to analyze university governance on this basis is fraught with difficulty. Faculty senates and committees in many institutions are regarded only as advisory. Generally, neither faculty nor students are satisfied with the assignment of legislative powers because they are as concerned with policy administration as they are with the policies themselves. Generally, the professional role of the faculty has resulted in their formulating or recommending academic policies and also dealing with any appeals. The expectation has been that appeals to higher levels in an institution would be based more upon a review of procedures than upon the substantive aspects of an issue. Increasingly, however, institutions have had to insert various routes of appeal at various levels with the expectation, always, that some appeals will be carried outside the university to state and federal courts. Thus, in still another sense, external agencies have come to have considerable impact on internal matters within institutions, and some decisions are certainly made as much with an eye to the ultimate implications in terms of appeals as to the essential academic considerations. Thus any apparent delegation of authority, whether contingent, conditioned, or otherwise, becomes uncertain. On the one hand, authority may be withdrawn if improperly used; on the other hand, it may be appealed even to agencies outside the university, always with the possibility of reversal. Judgments and decisions made in this situation inevitably become pragmatic. No one likes to be reversed, and academics in particular begrudge the time given to the appeal process because it subtracts time from academic pursuits and it also generates a state of mind inimical to these pursuits.

Administrative Responsibilities

This chapter has dealt at some length with various conceptions of decision making, has discussed the distinctions between administration and management, and has pointed up some of the problems in the university decision-making organization. By way of summary, it is appropriate to suggest the nature of administrative responsibilities in an institution of higher education, a subject that will be explored in greater detail in the following chapter.

In the nature of the university organization, with its various semiautonomous units, a major responsibility is that of determination of priorities. Priorities, in turn, involve the purposes and the long-term goals and objectives of the institution. The purposes, goals, and objectives cannot be stated with the specificity of business or industry. Frequently, they are difficult items upon which to get agreement since each of the units within the university has its own goals and its own priorities growing out of those. Yet determination of priorities is meaningless unless there is wide involvement of faculty, clientele, board, and influential fund sources. Thus the administrative responsibility for determination of priorities must be a shared one, and it must, in great part, be related to the governance pattern. Administrators prepare statements of policy; they design programs; and they are concerned with communication strategies, with the development of control systems, and with the designation and recognition of reappraisal signals and procedures. But it is essential that this phase of policy preparation be shared with and modified by the views of those affected. Only when there is general acceptance can the administrator move to the management of resources, involving people, money, materials, time, and authority to support the policies agreed upon. And as the administrator moves to the execution of policy, acceptance and some degree of enthusiasm on the part of those involved are also important. In the execution of policy, administration involves more detailed planning and resource allocation. It requires placement of programs and activities in the context of past experiences and a recognition that differences within the university require an extensive amount of coordination of the total enterprise. Any major policy of the institution involves interaction with the environment, with external agencies, and with individuals. The administrator, with an overall institutional point of view and with a composite external-internal orientation, must carry major responsibility for these interactions. The administrator also must be aware of any developing conflicts within the institution or between segments of the institution and externalities and must seek suggestions or make suggestions for modification and adaptation. In this whole process, communication becomes a vital aspect of the enterprise, with great importance attached to clarifying the rationale for programs and policies, delineating the value elements involved, and generating cooperation in policy and program performance. Recognizing that continuing interaction with others is essential, and that this imposes some limitations, the appropriate administrative actions are decision making, programming to carry through a decision, continuing communication to interpret policy and derive from those concerned their reactions to and problems with the policy, establishment of some controls to ensure that intent is reinforced by action, and recurrent, if not continual, reappraisal of the effectiveness of decisions and operations based upon them.

Suggestions for Further Reading

Baldridge, J. V., and Tierney, M. L. *New Approaches to Management: Creating Practical Systems of Management Information and Management by Objectives.* San Francisco: Jossey-Bass, 1979.

Dill, W. R. "Administrative Decision-Making." In S. Mailick (Ed.), *Concepts and Issues in Administrative Behavior.* Englewood Cliffs, N.J.: Prentice-Hall, 1962.

Dykes, A. R. *Faculty Participation in Academic Decision Making.* Washington, D.C.: American Council on Education, 1968.

Landau, M. "The Concept of Decision-Making in the 'Field' of Public Administration." In S. Mailick (Ed.), *Concepts and Issues in Administrative Behavior.* Englewood Cliffs, N.J.: Prentice-Hall, 1962.

Millett, J. D. *New Structures of Campus Power: Success and Failures of Emerging Forms of Institutional Governance.* San Francisco: Jossey-Bass, 1978.

Palola, E. G., Lehmann, T., and Bleschke, W. R. *Higher Education by Design: The Sociology of Planning.* Berkeley: Center for Research and Development in Higher Education, University of California, 1970.

Simon, H. A. "The Decision Maker as Innovator." In S. Mailick (Ed.), *Concepts and Issues in Administrative Behavior.* Englewood Cliffs, N.J.: Prentice-Hall, 1962.

FIVE

∼∼∼

Focusing
Administration on
Academic Goals

The word *academic* in the title of this chapter does not limit the discussion to academic vice-presidents, deans, and departmental chairpersons. A college or university is an academic institution because it is committed to one or more of the three major academic functions: instruction, research, and public service. Performance of these functions generates need for extensive supporting services. It is vital that all activities, essential and supportive, be so directed and coordinated as to strengthen the institution's academic character. This requires understanding and cooperation within the several segments of the service operation and between these services and the instructional, research, and service personnel that constitute the faculty. I recall a vice-president for business, imported from industry, who began his tour of duty by insisting that every unit make specific the services and materials that it expected to buy on next year's budget. Budget approval was granted in specific terms and any attempt to purchase an unlisted item was rejected. This approach was inappropriate and was shortly altered. Faculty members do need to realize that units must live within budgets and that budgets must be subjected to some constraints to ensure that the university demonstrates responsibility and accountability in its use of funds. This concept of accountability applies in all offices and units of the institution. Funds are to be so used as to contribute constructively to the academic purposes of the institution.

In its more restricted sense, academic administration, for many persons, includes departments, college units, special institutes and centers, support units directly related to the instructional, research, and public service activities, and the academic vice-president or provost. In large universities in which departmental units may involve 50 to 150 or more individuals, departmental chairpersons may be assisted by several associate and assistant chairpersons. Deans' offices similarly have assistants and assistant and associate deans. A divisional pattern introduced between the college and the department may be headed by a director or by assistant or associate deans. My study (Dressel, 1980a) of the divisional unit in a number of colleges and universities indicates that it serves little purpose in most institutions. Only when divisional directors have authority supported by powers of budget development or control does it have significance. A sure sign of the impotence of divisional units is the appointment as directors of junior faculty members who must continue to be responsive to departmental chairpersons.

Vice-presidential titles also tend to expand into executive, senior, associate, and assistant vice-presidents, and assistants are added to these functionaries. In some well-established hierarchies, a vice-provost is the equivalent of a vice-president, thereby ensuring that the provost is clearly a notch above what traditionally has been regarded as the second line of authority. Although some presidents have remained aloof from academic matters except as they are presented by the chief academic officer, my personal view, buttressed by visits to many colleges, is that the president should demonstrate an active concern with academic matters. He or she should be chosen, in considerable part, because of anticipated leadership in the development of academic programs, research, and public service. Presidential statements and public appearances should provide to the general public and other agencies a sound and realistic picture of the academic enterprise. Even faculty members are more profoundly affected than they readily admit by presidential pronouncements or requests on academic issues.

All of the administrators named share some common responsibilities in giving direction to the educational activities of the institution. In so doing, they must be attentive to changing needs both within and external to the institution. They must be sensitive to and encourage suggestions for improvement by individuals and faculty groups. They should encourage and supervise the formulation and reformulation of educational policies and present them to faculty, administration, and board for consideration and approval. They may arrange for appropriate external groups to review plans and proposals before they are finally adopted. The responsibilities require that administrators direct faculty attention to changing educational thought and practice in higher education and to changing demands and expectations for employment. It is a truism that the budget of any unit should reflect its academic commitments and goals, but a program budget relating educational programs and expenditures is not easily achieved. Budgets tend to reflect organization and expenditure categories rather than programs, although budgets inevitably provide limitations on programs. Yet the most difficult conflicts arise when budgets are constructed on a set of assumptions that ignore or deny the validity of the policies and procedures that direct the conduct of the various academic programs. Discussions about curriculum, new teaching practices, and other aspects of the academic program should always consider the fiscal commitments involved.

Academic officers must be concerned not only with the curricula, courses, modes of instruction, and the way in which these are arranged into programs but also with admission requirements and processes and with interpretation of these to the faculty. Academic units should and usually do control the classification and the assignment of their students to classes. To do so effectively, they require full knowledge of the background of the students. Housing, residence halls, food services, student activities, counseling, health service, library, and other service programs have great potential for supporting or undermining academic programs. Therefore, each of these is a concern of academic officers. Each administrator should seek to find out from students, faculty members, and others whether and how these several services advance or impede the involvement and success of students.

The preceding general remarks about the traditional academic framework must be supplemented briefly by comments about the role of specific administrators. A provost or academic vice-president cannot overview all the operations in the many units of the university; but he or she does have a responsibility to monitor these operations through contacts and reports from deans, chairpersons, and others. Evidence should be sought from counselors, residence hall personnel, and occasionally from students themselves as to how these groups view the operations and effectiveness of academic units. Institutional research offices ought occasionally to engage in studies directed to these ends, rather than being occupied solely with budgetary problems. Presidents and vice-presidents are likely to find that conspiracies exist to keep some difficulties and malfunctioning from their knowledge. Lower-level administrators usually believe that their modes of operation are appropriate, but they may be unaware of problems or, knowing of them, be incompetent to deal with them. Any administrator who depends on one channel for information about each unit will have a very biased view of what goes on in the institution.

The academic vice-president should regularly determine to what extent and how the several major academic units of the campus reinforce each other. Departments tend to operate largely in terms of their own immediate concerns and convenience. Deans can observe how various departments within their particular college interact. But deans are preoccupied with their own units and may not be very much concerned about planned interactions, cooperation, and services for other units in other colleges.

The natural preoccupation of departments with their own

immediate problems becomes a hazard to institutional unity and operation because administrators at higher levels frequently delegate too much of their authority to departments. Casual reviews of departmental actions by administrators and faculty committees readily become a rubber-stamp approval of actions not fully understood. I have seen several situations in which departments dropped courses that were regularly taken by students in other majors with no discussion or prior notification. I have seen the content of particular courses changed to suit the views of a new instructor or department chairman without clearance of the coordinators of the program for which the course was primarily designed. There are three administrative or management problems here. One is the necessity for lower echelons of administration and management to recognize that they operate in the interests of the total institution. Therefore, proposals for program modification should be brought to the awareness of other units in the university with opportunity for comment. A second problem is that disagreements and conflicts about course alterations may arise, requiring that the next echelon of administrative or committee review raise a certain series of questions or systematically explore reactions over the entire institution before taking any action on the recommendation. A third problem is that recommendations from units are too frequently made to the next higher level without any indication of the range of issues considered or the rationale justifying the final recommendation. This situation makes it impossible for others to review recommendations with any understanding, especially when budgetary considerations are involved.

The complexity of university organization results in some difficult situations. Courses are offered jointly by departments or by departments and institutes or centers. Faculty members cross the various lines in performance of their functions. There is a tendency for effective faculty service to units or for functions other than their salary line appointment to be overlooked or deliberately ignored. Recommendations in these situations require that special efforts be made by administrators to determine their equity and validity. Differential views of units and individuals with regard to the several academic functions of instruction, research, and public service frequently lead to inequities. I believe that the concept of research should be expanded to include scholarly activity; and that scholarly activity should be an expected aspect of good instruction even at the undergraduate level. I would also include advising, career counseling, and placement as an important academic function on a par with teaching and other functions. Faculty members deserve to know what the qualifications are for promotion, tenure, and salary increases. These should be specified with some care, and there should be assurance that the treatment of each individual is equitable in reference to the information placed before him or her. It is impossible to apply uniform standards on these matters across an institution. Any attempt to do so is likely to result in detailed rules, such as counting the pages of publication in recognized research journals. This is not very much different from counting the number of students taught. In neither case do we know quality; nor do we have any implication as to long-run significance of the activity. Nevertheless, there must be some common criteria and administrative responsibility in interpreting and applying them. The chairperson who exercises no discrimination only throws responsibility on others. That chairperson may gain temporary credibility as a good guy and a sound judge of performance, but he will be rightfully seen, in the long run, as irresponsible and perhaps incompetent. Especially, it is important to clarify the combinations of criteria used. Will recognition be given for excellence in performing one major academic function or will excellence be required in two? Will the individual who published a significant research article or a book within the past year be granted priority over others in recognition, or will productivity be regarded on an accumulative basis over a longer span of time?

Student Personnel Services

The student personnel function has existed for many years. In an early form, it was recognized through the designation of a dean of men and a dean of women, titles still found in some institutions. These titles came into being before there was any formal training for student personnel work. Professors of French were fairly common choices for deans of women, presumably on some vague cultural grounds. Not infrequently, an athletic background was a basis for choice of a dean of men. Such individuals were often seen by presidents and academic deans as mainstays of morality and decorum. The advent of formal student personnel programs headed by deans of students or vice-presidents for student affairs has been largely a development since around 1950. A committee on administration of student personnel work appointed by the American Council on Education in 1958 included all of the following as part of a student personnel assignment: admission, registration and records, housing and food service, counseling, health service, activities, financial aids, placement, discipline, special clinics for remedial work, religious activities, marriage counseling, and foreign students' activities. Orientation, veterans' advisory services, student paper, athletics, and evaluation and research have been included in some statements about student personnel work. Some of the early statements on student personnel work seized upon all activities not specifically assigned to the departments, colleges, and academic vice-presidents. There was implicit in much of the discussion a feeling that many of the difficulties that students ran into resulted because the academic demands placed upon students in courses and programs were unduly heavy, too narrowly conceived, and attended with insufficient concern about the welfare and aspirations of the student.

It seems obvious in retrospect that many of the responsibilities once included as part of a student personnel assignment are vitally related to the academic program and that they must be fulfilled by individuals involved in the academic program and responsible to the top academic officer. Admission, registration and records, remedial services, and some aspects of counseling clearly fall in this category. For the remaining activities, effectiveness and academic relevance depend on the student personnel administrator and the nature of the charge given by the president. Presidents are frequently confused as to the purposes of student personnel services. Many presidents have felt that the role of this unit was to devise and maintain reasonable controls on student behavior, provide safeguards on morals, and immediately get rid of homosexuals, pregnant women, and any others whose behavior might reflect adversely on the institution. Student activities have also been regarded as a means to keep students busy in ways of little concern to the faculty and administration. Hence student activities have duplicated or competed with faculty-developed services and programs of instruction. For these various reasons, student personnel programs have never been very highly regarded by faculty members.

I have found few student personnel programs that have been successful in meeting student needs in such manner as to satisfy the administration and the faculty that student personnel activities provide essential academic experience for students. It is of more than passing interest that the recent emphasis on lifelong education and on part-time students ignores much of what has been involved in the student personnel area. It is also of personal significance to reflect that in my own experiences as an undergraduate I was too busy to waste time with those activities then regarded as part of the student personnel program. Therefore, it is my conviction that every college or university should review in considerable detail all of the activities embraced within the student personnel program and determine the role that they should fulfill in contributing to personal development and to the academic program. I am certainly not advocating the elimination of the concept of student personnel work, nor am I suggesting that a dean or vice-president of student services is inappropriate. I am asserting that in an academic institution we must be chary of wasting money on activities that are diversionary, duplicative, or competitive in regard to the academic program. These services must demonstrate to the academic administrators and faculty the worth of the activities for which they are responsible.

Financial Administration

There are a number of different types of operations included in financial administration: accounting, auditing, preparation of financial reports, budgetary controls, and the receipt, management, and disbursement of funds. They are all essential to effective operations. Even so, there are some necessary limitations on the authority and responsibilities of the financial administration. Budgeted academic units will usually find it desirable to maintain their own accounts and check with monthly reports from the finance area. The academic segment of the institution must play a major role in defining the various expenditure categories and the operative policies and controls. Budgetary controls, to a large extent, should reflect the essential academic character of the institution, and expenditures from academic units should be approved by higher echelons of academic administration and management before being presented to financial officers.

Responsibilities for the physical plant, including operations and maintenance, are often placed in the financial administration, although the personnel may be essentially different in orientation from those found in the financial offices. Physical plant personnel must be conscious of the academic nature of the institution and operate under directives that make clear the need for this operation's support of the academic operation. Early in my own college teaching career, a physical plant employee appeared in my classroom to repair a radiator. When I remonstrated that this interfered with the conduct of the class, I was bluntly told that the orders made no allowance for instructor or student convenience. I found that no one less than the president could countermand this disregard of academic operations. Many facilities require special procedures with attendant difficulties in getting personnel to adjust. The appointment of an individual coordinating physical plant operation and maintenance should involve academic review and be made only if it is clear that the individual has a fundamental recognition of academic priorities and a willingness to manage operations in an appropriate manner.

Management of residence halls, food services, bookstores, student unions, and other auxiliary activities and services represents a special problem. They involve significant financial income and they are operated by nonacademics. Although every college or university recognizes that such activities and services have high significance for aiding or interfering with the formal academic program, few campuses avoid some continuing tension between the academic staff and the management-oriented people who control facilities and services. Scheduling of mealtimes, rules with regard to carrying food into recreational areas of residence halls, scheduling and quality of cleaning and decorating, and maintenance of security are examples of the many problems. Bookstores, with an eye to generating a profit, frequently take on the character of a general department store and arouse complaints from local merchants. Many of the problems caused here are a result of the expectancy that all of these operations will provide funds for occasional refurbishing and improvement of services and perhaps pay a rental charge for space. Some institutions even expect a profit to be diverted into support of the academic program.

The financial and operation officers usually have responsibility for selection and promotion of nonacademic personnel. I have found the trend in this direction desirable in some respects but undesirable in others. In my own early experiences, the nonacademic personnel serving in the academic area generally took as much interest and pride in their activities as did the academic personnel. Many of these persons put in hours well beyond the demands of duty and carried some academic roles, such as advisers to students, thereby acting as assistant deans or assistant chairpersons. They were part of the academic team. Unfortunately, many of these individuals were underpaid and had little opportunity for advancement. The current procedures for hiring such personnel and for promotion and salary increases tend to become so stereotyped that it is difficult to recognize devoted performance. It also becomes more difficult to take action on incompetency. A secretary, otherwise effective, who is unduly curt with students may be destructive of the academic operations but escape displacement on the grounds that the union-dictated personnel rules contain no statement of obligation to serve students or faculty.

The financial area naturally administers retirement and other staff benefits. Unfortunately, these operations become routinized and impersonal. Academic administrators should strive to maintain, even with retired personnel, a contact that evidences the concern of the institution and ensures that issues and questions raised by retirees are treated with respect and with equity and promptness.

Fund investment is a part of the financial operations that is usually shared with a board committee and frequently contracted for with some management firm. Especially when the sums are large, the knowledge, contacts, and time required for effective investment may not be available to the vice-president for finance and business or to any of the immediate aides. Furthermore, as recurring stories of misuse of funds demonstrate, this is an area where the president and the board must be vitally involved and must be buttressed by sufficient knowledge to react with insight to reports and raise appropriate questions. I have known some presidents with limited financial background who let the vice-president for finance handle all details and report directly to the board. In two cases, one of arrant dishonesty and the other of mismanagement, the president later claimed lack of knowledge and hence lack of responsibility for the situation. In fact, the president is fully responsible to the board for financial as well as other matters in the institution. Some boards designate the vice-president for finance as treasurer of the board and directly responsible to the board. With some individuals, this split of authority might work reasonably well, but it is loaded with peril and may cause a division within the institution that impacts upon the smallest academic unit and interferes with its performance. It cannot be asserted too strongly that the vice-president for business and finance should operate under the president and report to the board at the will and designation of the president, as does any other administrator or staff member.

Other Administrative and Management Functions

The size and complexity of an institution frequently dictates that a number of additional groups be headed by a vice-president. Public relations and information services are likely to require a separate recognition in the administrative structure. In some cases, the largest portion of these operations relates to the athletic activities of the institution. This is unfortunate, for athletic activities constitute a diversion from academic pursuits with many opportunities for both good and ill for the institution as a whole. The major concern of public relations and information services should be to interpret to the public, alumni, and supporters of the institution the activities in the instruction, research, and public service and to display items of significance in an interesting way so as to build respect for the institution.

Alumni relations and fund raising are frequently conjoined in an office of development, as it is recognized that the alumni may be a major source for fund raising. In smaller institutions, both these operations may be grouped together with public relations and information services into a single office. Unfortunately, much of alumni interest is with the athletic program. Indeed, it is quite possible that the success of alumni relationships and fund raising may depend upon the quality of the athletic program. Some years ago, a friend of mine became chancellor of an institution that was in dire financial need. He undertook to identify prominent alumni and friends and make contacts for gifts. In almost every case, he found that these individuals were unhappy with the athletic performance. He finally concluded that improvement in athletic performance was a prerequisite to successful fund raising. An administrator caught in such a situation can deplore but hardly ignore it.

Institutions with an extensive graduate program require funds for research. The competition for grants and contracts is such that, though the ultimate generation depends on the faculty, coordination is required by a special office, probably headed by a vice-president. Questions sometimes arise as to whether the graduate school operation should be part of the research office, part of the academic operation, or a dual operation. Since the faculty, through departments or institutes, is the arm for both research activity and graduate programs, duality in reporting is appropriate. One reason that some institutions have a composite administrative position as provost and vice-president for academic affairs is to recognize that other vice-presidents may, for some functions, be responsible to the provost.

Almost every institution of higher education will recognize these days the need to deal with various federal and often with several state agencies on matters of funds, on the availability of information, and on reviews of institutional fair employment practices. All of these functions are interrelated, so there must be full cooperation among the several administrators responsible. And all must also be interrelated with the more strictly academic units. One has only to take at random any one of the areas mentioned earlier and note the implications of that area for interaction with all the rest. For example, the development office, which includes alumni relations and fund raising, must be greatly interested in public relations and information services and is also rightly concerned about how the financial operation invests and uses funds. The development office needs also to know the major emphases of the academic, instructional, research, and public service programs and see that appropriate information is channeled to those alumni, friends, and others with whom fund raising is a possibility. The development office may become the channel whereby a particular academic need not covered by general fund sources can be met.

Levels, Titles, and Roles of Administrators

In recent years, even in small institutions, there has been an increase in the range and number of titles that carry an administrative or managerial implication. It is not surprising now to find, even in a relatively small liberal arts college, three to five or six vice-presidents. Academic affairs, financial affairs, and student personnel are probably the most common triple. Development or fund raising may be the fourth; and any one of the other functions mentioned earlier or combinations of them may justify additional vice-presidential titles. In large institutions, one may find vice-presidents for each of the areas already mentioned and, in addition to that, such further designations as vice-president for medical services, vice-president for management, and even vice-president for special assignments. Some of this title proliferation is due to the increasing incursion of external affairs into the operation of the institution. Part of it is due to the style of some presidents who prefer to disengage themselves from details and focus on the major decisions to be made about the institution. Another part of the problem arises out of a confusion between line staff (that is, staff in the direct line of authority with some delegation for decision making) and staff involving individuals who assist line administrators and may represent them in a variety of meetings but have no authority on their own. An assistant to a dean presumably has a different role than an assistant dean, although much depends upon the style of the dean. The range of special services, extending from various research or public service oriented institutes, offices, and centers to the development or remedial service area has generated extensive use of the titles *director* and *coordinator*. These are so confusingly used on some campuses that it is impossible to know the level and nature of the function involved. Residence halls have directors; departments have directors of graduate studies; business offices have directors of sectors of the operation. In addition, in larger institutions, there have been associate and assistant vice-presidents and associate and assistant directors with no relationship to the academic title, if any, held by an individual. I have proposed several times that the entire administrative structure of certain institutions should be reviewed and modified so that administrative titles would relate to some meaningful array of activities and responsibilities. Yet reflection on the matter indicates that ambiguity and obfuscation at times play a significant role in effective operation of an institution. Administrative reorganizations seem to be effective only as they conform to the predilections of the incumbents.

Management Problems and Responsibilities

Each area of administration or management has (or should have) specific functions and roles. Since the functions are interrelated, it is inevitable that the administrators must interact and cooperate. Obviously, the administrators should be selected with this in mind. Even so, a president may find, unless he holds regular meetings with his immediate staff for discussion of issues that cross the somewhat unclear lines dividing their responsibilities, that each will tend to extend his or her own area and even encroach upon others. Interaction and consultation take time. Unless the chief executive of a unit displays concern for such interunit cooperation, lower-level personnel are almost certain to avoid interaction with their counterparts in other administrative areas. The president and the head of the various units must set the example both for concern and for regular interaction and cooperation. They can then insist that associates and assistants are expected to do likewise. This expectation can be reinforced by insisting that new proposals reflect consultation and concurrence.

Every manager should be concerned with relating individual needs and institutional missions and goals. A vice-president for finance, by instituting a new procedure for fee collection based upon the accountability and convenience of his office, may inconvenience students and faculty members. Hasty action may also controvert the mission of the institution by presenting a poor model of how decisions are made and how procedures are determined so as to achieve the optimum combination of accountability, responsibility, accommodation to the individual, and effectiveness with regard to educational goals. Effective management in any enterprise, and certainly in the university, requires involvement of concerned and affected individuals in decisions. This involvement can be either active or passive. Active involvement is usually exemplified by group representation in committees or by discussions held prior to making decisions. Effective passive involvement is often achieved by interviewing individuals possibly affected by a decision so as to elicit their analyses and reactions. Surprisingly, in many institutions, decisions affecting significant numbers of people are made—often with the best of intent—without exploring the possible impact of the decision on those most directly concerned. Unanticipated and undesired outcomes are endemic in these circumstances.

Another management problem is that of identifying and resolving or, more frequently, living with conflict. In some of my earlier experiences as founder and director of a counseling center at Michigan State University, I learned that many personal problems were the outgrowth of irresolvable conflict.

Counseling might achieve little more than recognition of the fact that one must learn to live with this conflict. Frequently, however, counseling brought realization that undue priority had been attached to the problem. As other pleasant and satisfying prospects were addressed, the original problem and inherent conflict simply became less important. My own philosophy over the years has come to be that the uncertainties and problems in life make living worthwhile. The uncertainties that arise in academe and the conflicts they engender have always some value base. Conflicts arise out of attempts by administrators or faculty representing various units or disciplines to resolve a problem in terms of personal advantage, convenience, or other value commitments not easily distinguished from self-interest. The impact upon others affected by a proposal is often ignored. A proposal to assign credit for evening classes as part of the regular faculty load makes good sense for a public university, but it arouses strong opposition from those who resist evening classes and those who seek to augment their salaries by extra work. Such issues are unlikely ever to be resolved to the satisfaction of all concerned.

Another area with which managers and administrators must be concerned is that of relating unit goals and operations to institutional needs and resources. We have already emphasized that student and societal needs and institutional missions and goals should be related. This means that the unit goals and operations should be consistent with and contribute to institutional missions and goals. However, in the enthusiasm for program expansion and unit reputation and stature, faculty members, chairpersons, and individual administrators tend to ignore or misinterpret institutional priorities and needs and the limitations on resources available. The managerial aspect of administration requires that these priorities and limitations be held before the faculty constantly. Moreover, these priorities and limitations should be phrased in meaningful ways so as to demonstrate that they are not arbitrary administrative restrictions but significant institutional limitations imposed on philosophical, educational, and practical grounds, including lack of resources. It is also true that an academic unit may so narrowly interpret the unit's goals and needs that it fails to see social needs as institutional responsibilities to which it should attend. Academic units may also fail to recognize that attention to them could bring them additional resources that might even expand the range of possibilities within the narrower unit goals. For example, traditional academic units are reluctant to serve or even to consider the needs and potentials for lifelong education.

Leadership

Throughout this book, emphasis has been placed on the need for active management of an institution's resources, as opposed to the passive, bureaucratic caretaker type of administration that many faculty members seem to prefer. However, management in the sense of concern with details of academic operations and the promulgation and enforcement of rules and regulations about them makes no sense in the university. Management that would simply attempt to tell each of the units in the university how it must relate its resources to other units and to the university as a whole is not likely to arouse more than deep irritation and active opposition. What is required is leadership, and this leadership must come from individuals who know the university well, who know its particular problems and the type of personnel involved, and who can, at the same time, paint in highly specific terms the demands placed upon the university and the expectations in regard to it. Leadership of this sort is achieved through respect for the individual's knowledge and ability to analyze institutional problems, reinforced by the model of objectivity set by the individual in dealing with these problems.

Good leadership avoids the use of formal authority and of official power whenever possible. It requires that the individual immerse himself or herself in any problem sufficiently to understand its complications and the implications of various solutions before imposing the task or even the development of recommendations about it on an individual or committee. In the role of leader, the manager or administrator undertakes to establish mutual respect, trust, and confidence. He or she should avoid being boxed in by senior faculty members who have long served on various committees and quickly undertake to contain or resolve any issue by precedent and preference. The future of an institution of higher education rests upon its ability to involve individuals who are flexible, willing to look at alternatives, and capable of themselves developing leadership characteristics.

Effective leadership in an academic unit is evidenced in a variety of ways. When people are provided with leadership and stimulated to look at problems with some optimism that they can be resolved, there is present a degree of enthusiasm about examining the issues that concern the unit and its relationships with other units. Leadership stimulates concern with both ends and means and thereby avoids both the pointless philosophical arguments about ends and the more mundane complaints and expressions of preference with regard to means. Leadership is aimed at establishing constructive cooperation and compromise to achieve the optimum in means and ends rather than simply to gain acceptance of an idea by persuasion or by a retreat to generality or ambiguity. Effective leadership requires an openness to discussion of ideas, even when these seem rather farfetched. Honesty and frankness, properly clothed in tact, are essential. Accessibility is essential, although abuse of it must be prevented. The would-be leader who conveys to persons that he or she is seeking personal advancement and glory is not likely to receive support in academic institutions except from those few sycophants who see in the administrator's advancement prospects for their own. Effective leadership requires commitment to institutional advancement in performance of societal responsibilities and, by that continuing emphasis, tends to raise the focus and the concerns of faculty members to a more significant level of values. Those who seek leadership will do well to give credit to the ideas that they acquire from others, even though they may embroider these and interrelate them in a way that exceeds the original contribution. In crediting individuals for their suggestions, the leader demonstrates integrity, gains the support of those making the suggestions, and places others who are negatively inclined toward administration in the position of reacting to suggestions of colleagues rather than those of the administrator.

Some Advice to Administrators

I find it a curious but common situation that individuals who are, by their assignment, involved in wise use of resources are unable to plan the use of their own time. Their day is scheduled full of meetings and fifteen-minute appointments. They are frequently so preoccupied with the coming session or the preceding one that they do not listen well, and they may allow themselves to be so frequently interrupted by phone calls or secretarial interventions that the focus and flow of a discussion are completely disrupted. They have numerous assistants and secretaries to make arrangements but still become so involved in details that they waste the time of their aides. In this involvement with details, the administrator may find that he is not aware of developing crises. A good manager, using the eyes and ears of others as well as his own, should anticipate many problems and either prevent them or resolve them as they arise. It is important that the manager effectively balance in his various functions attention to processes and to substance in dealing with them. On many campuses, committees have so proliferated that several different committees become involved in almost any issue, so that decisions about assignments and responsibilities can take precedence over substance and the resolution of the issues involved. Managerial balancing requires reconsideration of the use of committees, attention to overlapping job assignments, and, particularly, development of staff members capable of accepting and fulfilling assignments with minimal administrative time involvement. Competent staff associates can effectively work with committees and individuals, achieving understanding of a problem and finding acceptable resolutions within a framework based upon knowledge of an administrator's views and values. Under these circumstances, the wise administrator who finds decisions and policies that are reasonably sound and acceptable (even though varying somewhat from his expectations) contents himself with a few copy editing comments to demonstrate that he has read, assimilated, and approved the document. The well-trained and tactful assistant may expedite this by pointing to any issues particularly deserving attention or by pointing out and apologizing for the incorrect punctuation or misspelled word on p. xx while leaving the pages themselves unmarked, thereby subtly discouraging detailed annotation and editing.

One of the pressing problems of all administrators is how to cope with faculty governance so as to demonstrate support of faculty involvement in governance while ensuring that personal participation in a host of committee meetings does not delay or negate decisions. Faculty governance is slow and deliberate and often both divisive and divertive. Too many individuals present slightly differing if not distinctive views. Some of what is intended as diverse tends only to divert. At times there are minorities (not solely of color or sex) who interject a definitely divisive note into meetings and refuse to be mollified by compromise. In this range of circumstances, the administrator who does not already have self-control must develop it to survive. Self-control is not simply a matter of holding one's temper. It involves recognizing asininity but refraining from commenting upon it. It also involves acceptance of responsibility for tactfully pointing out to various groups that resolution of these issues cannot wait forever and that the present discussion is hardly profitable and perhaps pointless. When issues lack clear resolutions, decisions will still be made.

One of the issues with regard to academic administration and management is the extent to which departmental and college executives serve on a rotating basis. Appointed or elected for a period of three to five years, some may be permitted to stay through a second term, while others regularly rotate. In my visits to institutions over a period of time, I have had the impression in some departments and colleges that the administrator's office is a segment of a revolving door, and that the section in view exhibits the current administrator who has no past performance to base actions upon and no future performance to be concerned about. Such a person approximates, in my judgment, a king or queeen of England who reigns but does not rule. However one regards the situation, this rotating pattern tends to leave many issues unresolved, makes it very difficult to get really able people in administrative positions, and virtually assures that significant changes in the unit involved will come about by force of external pressures rather than by foresight.

In my many contacts with administrators, I have been surprised, and sometimes dismayed, at how little some administrators knew about their own institutions. Asked about the number of majors enrolled in a department or the number of faculty members, some chairpersons have claimed ignorance and called the secretary or assistant for information. Similarly, some deans and presidents seem not to carry even the most rudimentary information about the institution in their minds, and a few have either been given false information or concoct it to serve their own ends. Any administrative officer who is trying to manage resources effectively needs reasonably exact information on the number of students and faculty involved in his or her units, the sources of these students and faculty members, the distribution of students by levels, the range of programs and some approximation of their size, the load of the faculty, and the quality of instruction provided in the institution. This list could be augmented considerably. For example, the size of the budget should certainly be included. The individual who does not do well in recalling statistics of this kind should develop a pocket memorandum book in which these figures are displayed and regularly updated. The administrator who can recall detailed statistics and quote them creates in faculty and students and in individuals outside the institution a confidence that this person knows what is going on in the institution and is ready to deal efficiently with its problems. The individual who has not such a good memory for statistics can create much the same reaction at appropriate points by commenting that he or she has just recently asked for up-to-date information on a number of aspects of the institution and is pleased to be able to report the following information on this point.

Summary

The major goals, objectives, and purposes of an institution of higher education are determined by its essential mission to society and to the particular unit or segment of society that provides support. The institution is accountable for the use of its resources to achieve these purposes and goals through its governing board, for which the president is the operating executive. To the president, then, and to the administrators at all levels who are responsible to the president, falls the task of managing resources in relationship to the avowed goals, but with the accompanying conviction that, in an institution devoted to the education and development of individuals, management requires extensive involvement of all individuals concerned. The individuals involved must, in turn, recognize the obligation of the institution to fulfill its responsibilities. But rather than preaching this repetitively to individuals, the administrator-manager is a leader who demonstrates through his or her own approach to issues the pattern of operation that conveys more forcefully than any words the essential nature of a college or university.

Suggestions for Further Reading

Balderston, F. E. *Managing Today's University*. San Francisco: Jossey-Bass, 1974.

Baldridge, J. V. (Ed.). *Academic Governance*. Berkeley, Calif.: McCutchan, 1971.

Blau, P. M. *The Organization of Academic Work*. New York: Wiley, 1973.

Clark, B., and Young, R. I. K. *Academic Power in the United States*. AAHE/ERIC Higher Education Research Report No. 3. Washington, D.C.: American Association for Higher Education, 1976.

Corson, J. J. *Governance of Colleges and Universities*. (Rev. ed.) New York: McGraw-Hill, 1975.

Knowles, A. S. (Ed.). *Handbook of College and University Administration*. Vol. 1. New York: McGraw-Hill, 1970.

Scott, R. A. *Lords, Squires, and Yeomen: Collegiate Middle Managers and Their Organization*. Washington, D.C.: American Association for Higher Education, 1978.

SIX

~~~~~~

Internal Organization and Conflicts of Interest

A few institutions of higher education have attempted to operate under an organizational pattern in which all personnel (faculty, clerical workers, maintenance personnel, students, and administrators) immediately associated with the institution were involved. From the few observations I have made of this unitary pattern, I would hypothesize that the attempt to operate in this manner can create some good will and rapport across subgroups in an institution, but that the very marked differences in concerns and areas of operation greatly limit the extent to which a united approach can be taken to resolving issues facing the institution. There are a few common interests of vital nature, such as salaries, benefits, and calendar, but even in these matters differences in concerns among various groups of employees within an institution may greatly limit the benefits derived from composite meetings. Depending upon the personality of the president, an annual state of the institution meeting and presidential report might be useful in cultivating awareness within subgroups of particular roles and obligations.

In most colleges and universities, one can readily discern about six distinctive groups differentiated by their institutional roles, titles, and basic assignments. These groups include: faculty, administration, secretarial-clerical staff, nonacademic administrative or professional staff (in business and financial operations and often in academic administrative offices of various levels), maintenance or custodial staff, and, finally, the students. One or more of these groups may be unionized, with the resulting tendency to place the various subgroups in more active competition with each other for acquiring a larger proportion of the resources and benefits available. The delineation and limitation on assigned tasks, usually associated with unionization, also pose some difficulties in achieving unity and rapport and full cooperation among the groups.

Since the major purpose of an academic institution is to provide education and related services, the faculty, which is the immediate means for providing these services, deserves first attention. It would seem that the faculty, as the prime subgroup, might display a unity symbolizing the nature and commitment of a college or university. One of the first issues that arise is that the faculty is separated into two or three major subgroups in reference to their disciplinary focuses and their commitment to research, teaching, or application of knowledge. The humanities and the sciences furnish one clear division within faculty; the liberal arts programs and the applied fields represent another. These cleavages are difficult to bridge. The majority of the faculty members find that their most immediate concerns and involvement in the institution are through their departments or colleges. In those institutions that also have a significant number of centers, institutes, and special services (of which the library may be regarded as one), the issue arises as to whether personnel involved in these operations, all of which are essentially academic, are members of the faculty by virtue of their involvement in these operations or whether faculty status comes only by departmental connections. Some institutions insist on the latter pattern, which imposes undue restrictions on the awarding of academic rank and tenure. In this pattern, it is often difficult to hire, in the academic service area, individuals of sufficient academic stature to carry out their assignments with full understanding of and commitment to their academic significance. For such persons, dependence upon academic disciplinary departments for rank, promotion, and salary is a hazard that they should not be required to face. The library has been noted as one particular example of this problem. Top-level library staff should be regarded and recognized as a part of the faculty. They should not depend upon the existence of a school of library administration for the acquiring of an academic title.

Despite the cleavages that break the faculty up into a number of distinctive subgroups, there exists generally an expectation that there will be a faculty organization running from the departments through the colleges to the university which will provide, through a senate or a committee structure, an opportunity for faculty at various levels to participate in the governance of the institution. This structure, in a sense, parallels the hierarchical administrative structure that moves downward through president, vice-presidents, deans, departmental chairpersons, and perhaps intermediate administrators. These competing structures can become very cumbersome in regard to the time of individuals involved and in the sense that certain issues may be dealt with in the two channels at various levels and in various ways. The necessity of referring matters from one group to another and the priorities involved with regard to jurisdiction or origination of issues can, particularly when accompanied by power-acquisitive individuals, provide a continuing threat to calm and rational deliberation.

Within the organizational structure there also exist separate groups in the areas of academic personnel, student personnel, finance, development, public service, and continuing education. It seems to me essential that top-level people in each of these administrative areas have some background of academic experience and some continuing academic association. I have been on several campuses in which the vice-president for finance or the business manager was an influential member of the department of economics or business. Similar situations exist with regard to chief student personnel officers and continuing education and extension. On the relatively small college campuses, it seems to me that this should be the accepted pattern. In larger institutions, it may not always be possible because of the differences in interests and competencies that are involved and because of the increasing complexity and ramifications of some aspects of these administrative responsibilities as institutions increase in size. Yet, in any institution, top-level appointments in any one of these administrative areas should not be made without some concern for the academic credentials and commitments of an individual, perhaps to the extent of having a few faculty members and administrators from relevant areas involved in the selection process.

The administrative organization has already been extensively discussed in Chapter Five. The immediately preceding remarks only emphasize the fact that the academic organization and structure must be based upon a commitment to the provision of educational opportunities and services and hence must, with due regard for accountability to the public, emphasize the responsibility of the entire institution in respect to its social service role.

The role of the clerical and secretarial staff of an educational institution is much more important than is realized in many institutions. Recognizing that the faculty of a college or university, through its professional expertise, is involved in a wide range of tasks and requires assistance to be effective, it follows (as most faculty members contend) that the provision of secretarial and clerical service to faculty is generally inadequate. The result is that many faculty members spend undue time on clerical matters and, even so, are often seemingly irresponsible or slothful in response when, in fact, they are being distracted from their major responsibilities by the necessity of dealing with details that might better be handled by assistants or aides. Clerical and secretarial personnel also provide a major line of contact with students. The attractiveness of a departmental major has frequently rested as much on the departmental secretary as on the departmental staff. Capable secretaries have relieved departmental chairpersons and faculty members of many time-requiring tasks and have often achieved for a department a reputation for efficiency and respect for individuals far superior to that which the departmental faculty would have acquired.

The maintenance or custodial staff plays a major role in the appearance of an institution both externally and internally. Visitors are favorably impressed by grounds and buildings that are well kept. The attitude of both faculty members and students is influenced by good housekeeping in the classrooms, laboratories, and residence halls. On some campuses, I have found that the maintenance and custodial staff maintain a close and cordial relationship with academic people and make a special effort to adjust to special needs and requests. On other campuses, the organization of this component of the operating force has become so bureaucratic that individual maintenance and custodial staff members receive their instructions and job assignments from a central spot and will not deviate from them unless prior contact and clearance have been established.

The last group of participants in the internal structure and organization is, on most campuses, by far the largest and in many ways the most important—the students. There is a tendency in all other sectors of the institution for individuals to plan their activities either ignoring students or imposing their own judgment of what is appropriate or best for students. Faculty members tend to do this with regard to the offering and planning of courses. Administrators tend to support this view by the expected delegation to departments and colleges of authority for planning courses, curricula, and academic requirements. Residence hall personnel and custodial staff obviously are faced with major problems in coordinating the operation of residence halls, in providing meal services, and in maintaining reasonable control over youthful exuberance which can lead to destructive and expensive action. Yet it seems at times that the understandable concerns about the excesses of a relatively small proportion of the student group lead to a set of attitudes and practices that precludes reasonable student involvement in the planning and evaluation of their educational programs. Perhaps the most serious aspect of this lack of student involvement is that many of the rules, restrictions, and procedures are imposed without due regard to the unique nature of an educational institution and the consistency of the rules and policies with the institutional mission. Administrators will do well to have individuals with an academic orientation involved in all phases of institutional operations. An alternative approach provides, from time to time, a self-study or faculty review committee empowered to look at all aspects of the campus operation.

Contrasting Views and Attitudes

The range of pursuits of faculty members—including varying emphases on instruction at the undergraduate or graduate level, research to either advance the discipline or to apply concepts and principles to technical or social problems, and various public service activities (such as consultation to business, industry, and government)—combine to divide the educational institution into subgroups with differing goals. The goals themselves, however, as well as the differences among them, are somewhat unclear. This is surely one reason why research activity productive of countable books or articles tends to supersede other performances in gaining recognition. But other than the tangible nature of publications, the actual impacts of them are essentially as intangible and unmeasurable as the performance of instruction or public service. No one really knows how much students in a particular course or program have learned or how effectively they apply whatever they have learned subsequent to completion of the course or program. With possibly a few exceptions in the technological area, no one ever really knows the benefits of public service activity or the extent to which the development and application of research findings yield tangible and useful results. Again, with few exceptions, no one really knows how many individuals read a book or research article and to what extent the future development of an area of knowledge is different because of its appearance. Furthermore, as has been pointed out earlier, professors tend to regard the institution of higher education as a means of supporting their own preferred activities in scholarship, research, and service. Just recently, a friend asked me how the university justified paying a salary to an artist who worked at home and sold the products of his efforts. This question implies a dichotomy that may not exist. The artist's composite effort is a cultural contribution to society. Both his reputation and his teaching are enhanced by the productivity at home.

The loyalty of many faculty members is to themselves and to their disciplines rather than to the institution that provides the salary and the resources to support their activities. I recall vividly the complete indifference of some junior faculty members to questions concerning the operation of the institution they served. This was a few years ago when research funds were more readily available. Nevertheless, an attitude of complete indifference to the institution and a willingness to move readily to any other institution offering more money and more research possibilities represents a point of view still widely prevalent. Thus the institution is made up of a number of special interest groups, and governance tends to take on the character of political maneuvering to serve these special interests rather than those of the total institution. Looking to state and federal legislatures, where individuals who are elected to serve the interests of groups of people or of political units are surrounded by lobbyists attempting to divert that obligation to their special interests, one gets the impression that, in the university, committees and governance bodies are made up of the lobbyists themselves. It is not surprising, then, that other sectors of a college or university have come to regard the institution as primarily a source of employment and one in which individuals can occupy their time in ways congenial to themselves, simultaneously using their position to promote ideas and schemes for personal or special group privileges.

Certain attitudes held by faculty members are readily observed or sensed by other members of the university community, thereby contributing further to the elimination of any sense of collaboration and unity in a common cause. Neither teaching nor administration is rated very highly by many faculty members. These views affect their students, clerical aides, and other associates. Some faculty members avoid students, and others who enjoy contacts with students still view them in a somewhat condescending way and see them as the primary beneficiary of this interaction. The faculty, as a group, tend to impose faculty conceptions upon students and are irritated when students question these impositions. The irritation is often abetted by the lack of a sound rationale and by personal prejudices or preferences. As an extension of this general attitude toward students, there is a tendency to use the recalcitrance or dishonesty of a few students as a basis for restricting student independence and rejecting individualized curriculum planning. These views tend to support the sanctity of the courses and the curricula as defined by the faculty and underlie the general faculty expectancy of regular attendance in classes where the predictability of instructor behavior and the specifics of the lecture coverage is very high. Although faculty members generally support the imposition upon students of a series of rules to control behavior and preserve standards, there is a general antipathy to rules specifying faculty behavior and particularly to any procedures for enforcement of those rules. Academic freedom is overgeneralized to include the right to reject any demand or request if it runs counter to the preferences of the individual faculty member. It is entirely natural, then, that many professors resist the involvement of nonacademic personnel in any type of decision making, despite the fact that many of the major interests of the various groups would be identical if the social obligations and public service role were fully recognized.

A number of studies have attempted to determine the goal priorities of faculty members, administrators, and students. The validity of such studies is doubtful, I feel, because the various sectors of academia have usually not given a great deal of time to clarifying and ordering goals. Thus, when an array of goals is put in front of individuals to make decisions about priorities, my own suspicion is that these decisions are very much off-the-cuff judgments, with various individuals putting quite different interpretations upon the words and phrases placed before them. Yet there are certain consistent patterns in the results that make some sense. To a greater extent than many people might expect, administrators and faculty members tend to agree on goal priorities. Perhaps the major difference here is that administrators are more sensitive to the external obligations of the institution, and are more perceptive and more concerned about unjustified variations in interpretation of standards, in appraising faculty performance, and in the administration or management of various units. There is some virtue in having common procedures and principles and some uniformity in interpreting them across an institution. Yet there is a tendency, as Baldridge (1971b) and Gross and Grambsch (1968) have pointed out, for the top goals of faculty to focus on protection of academic freedom, increasing the prestige of the institution, and maintaining top quality in programs which the *faculty feels to be especially important.* These goals are oriented to securing and maintaining faculty status and they are, in a sense, only supportive of the essential goals of an educational institution rather than directly reflecting them.

The most disturbing aspect of this internal division of the college and university community is that it arises out of lack of understanding and of commitment to a clear set of goals and purposes that reflect the obligations and responsibilities of the institution to society. The various divisions within the faculty tend to arouse some competition for scarce resources among units and some suspicion that other sectors of the university staff, especially administration, are unreasonably expanded and paid at exorbitantly high rates. This, in turn, stimulates these other sectors to pursue their own aspirations independent of the academic purposes of the institution.

It seems to me we have a situation here in which higher education has been flaunted as the major means to the success of democratic government, whereas the actual performance of institutions of higher education exhibits such internal dissension and competition as to make questionable the ability of educational institutions to model the ideal performance of a democratic society or to educate people for effective participation in it. All educational administrators should be concerned about this and should be aware of the situation on their own campuses or portions thereof. When orienting newcomers to the staff of the institution, they should discuss these matters thoroughly and exhibit some of their concerns about the essential collaboration of all sectors of the campus in achieving a clarity of goals and a pattern of operation for resolving internal conflicts in a manner appropriate to a democratic society. A major continuing problem of that society is to provide an environment in which individuals are treated fairly and have opportunity for optimal development.

Suggestions for Further Reading

Angell, G. W., Kelly, E. P., Jr., and Associates. *Handbook of Faculty Bargaining: Asserting Administrative Leadership for Institutional Progress by Preparing for Bargaining, Negotiating, and Administering Contracts, and Improving the Bargaining Process.* San Francisco: Jossey-Bass, 1977.

Baldridge, J. V. *Power and Conflict in the University.* New York: Wiley, 1971.

Bayer, A. E. *Teaching Faculty in Academe.* Washington, D.C.: American Council on Education, 1973.

Dressel, P. L., Johnson, F. C., and Marcus, P. M. *The Confidence Crisis: An Analysis of University Departments.* San Francisco: Jossey-Bass, 1970.

Dykes, A. R. *Faculty Participation in Academic Decision Making.* Washington, D.C.: American Council on Education, 1968.

Klingelhofer, E., and Hollander, L. *Educational Characteristics and Needs of New Students: A Review of the Literature.* Berkeley: Center for Research and Development in Higher Education, University of California, 1973.

Lehrer, S. (Ed.). *Leaders, Teachers, and Learners in Academe: Partners in the Educational Process.* New York: Appleton-Century-Crofts, 1970.

Lipsett, S. M., and Ladd, E. C., Jr. *Professors, Unions, and American Higher Education.* Berkeley, Calif.: Carnegie Commission on Higher Education, 1973.

Miller, R. I. *Developing Programs for Faculty Evaluation: A Sourcebook for Higher Education.* San Francisco: Jossey-Bass, 1974.
Mortimer, K. P., and McConnell, T. R. *Sharing Authority Effectively: Participation, Interaction, and Discretion.* San Francisco: Jossey-Bass, 1978.

〜〜

SEVEN

Understanding External Influences, Mandates, and Controls

Colleges and universities, like the church which originally fostered their development, are granted certain privileges. This is true even in a democracy that seeks to separate church and state, because colleges and universities are regarded as serving the public interest. This view holds in respect to both private and public institutions. Indeed, that distinction between private and public universities becomes less and less meaningful over time. Private institutions are the beneficiaries of public funds, and a few private universities have more income from public fund sources than from all others. Similarly, public institutions have, to a considerable extent, moved into the category of state-assisted institutions in that, for many of them, funds from the federal government, foundations, and private sources (including endowment) exceed the state support, which has come to be

121

more narrowly regarded as support for the instructional program and for certain aspects of public service.

Despite the recent loss of status of universities in the public eye, they are still generally regarded as an essential component of society and are viewed as aiding individuals as well as contributing to the development and improvement of society. The doubts and consequent difficulties that have arisen about higher education in recent years are, in large part, the result of the perception that, although colleges and universities have served some segments of society, they may have done so at the expense of other segments, such as the poor, disadvantaged, and handicapped. This perception is valid to a degree. It arises out of several factors for which educational institutions are not entirely to blame. One is the long-held conviction of many persons that the nature of higher education, as far as instructional programs are concerned, requires that attention be devoted to what may be described as an elite group capable of benefiting from the programs. A second factor is that, aside from agricultural and home economics extension originally directed to individual farms and households by the land-grant institutions, much of the public service and applied research has been utilized by business and industry in the expansion of both operations and profits. Although society moved ahead technologically, the benefits were unevenly distributed and often seemed to be disproportionately acquired by those who least needed them. But perhaps the factor that has led to the greatest dissatisfaction, if not disgust, on the part of those best informed about higher education has been the tendency of the institutions, their faculties, and administrators to expand for their own purposes and to seek stature for the institutions and themselves with little regard to the actual needs of society. This has been more apparent in regional public institutions in the various states than in private institutions—at least until the advent of extensive public funding of research projects available to both types.

The increasing expectation of college attendance and the value placed upon it as a background for citizenship and careers resulted in the designation as universities of the teachers colleges and technical colleges of an earlier day, in anticipation by these institutions that they would become universities in the fullest sense with a wide range of programs and the addition of graduate studies, programs of research, and a number of professional schools. In this expansion, administrators, ably abetted by faculties, sought to compete with the major existing universities, both public and private, in seeking funds from all sources to develop competing programs. Legislators at the state and federal levels also ably abetted this development by seeking recognition and advancement of institutions in their own political domains and by heeding the insistent calls from aspiring institutions, underdeveloped institutions, and community colleges to share in the large sums made available for program expansion and research activity in higher education. The availability of these additional funds had two very significant effects, with the first almost immediately generating development of the second. The first effect was that the inflow of additional funds from public sources made it possible for institutions to regard their acceptance of these funds as serving the public interest. But the tendency of faculty members to reinterpret any particular charge in terms of their own interests and predilections led some of them to misconstrue this public interest as serving their own interests. This second effect opened numerous institutions to suspicion of misuse of funds. Many of these suspicions were well based. One of the most prevalent practices has perhaps not been criticized as much as it should have been. An early push of institutions was found in the demand for increasing the indirect costs or overhead component of grants and contracts. Instead of using these additional funds to cover actual indirect costs, institutions frequently plowed them back into new construction, increased faculty, and equipment, with the full expectation and intent that the result in cost increments would be carried by state support or other sources. State legislators and other officials soon became aware of this chicanery and forced an accounting for such funds and imposed limitations on how they might be used. Likewise, the federal government found that the projects themselves underwent mysterious changes which dictated much more in the way of monitoring and of exacting accountability than had been anticipated. It is, to say the least, somewhat devious for an institution to explore all possible ways of developing a basis for indirect costs and then elect to use the one yielding the largest amount; yet, by its own report, one major private university did exactly this. And it comes as no surprise that that university has been, for some time, under investigation with the threat of having to return large amounts of money. In recent years, state institutions have been far less culpable in this way than major private universities. The reason is amply clear. As state legislators became aware of this windfall, they demanded a deduction of the anticipated amount from the budget requests of institutions. Clearly, there was no point in seeking higher indirect cost rates that might engender more elaborate investigation by federal agencies when that amount would be deducted from state appropriations. Furthermore, a federal investigation demanding return of funds would thus become a case of double jeopardy.

Unquestionably, it is in the public interest for institutions of higher education to aid in the attainment of equity for minorities, women, and the disadvantaged. At the same time, governmental agencies that have become energetic in making demands upon institutions have greatly increased the costs of institutions in collecting data, in spending time with investigators, and in attending meetings for discussion and clarification of the demands. Furthermore, the additional costs involved for personnel and data systems have generally had to come out of the basic general fund appropriation of the institution, almost invariably at a loss to the academic budgets of the various departments and colleges. The costs attendant upon handling appeals within the institution and the legal aspects of appeals to courts have also added greatly to the operating expenses of institutions. Obviously, the indirect costs of some federal programs have had to be assimilated by institutions without even any recognition or concern by the agencies involved that these demands seriously hampered and could even destroy particular institutions.

In a sense, one can regard all these events as in the public interest. If, as indeed was the case, institutions were ignoring their obligations to certain segments of society, it is only reasonable that their attention should be called to it and demands made for improvement. But, in the process, the universities have, to a considerable extent, come to be regarded as agencies to provide immediate gratification to individuals with little regard as to what this may mean for the long-term viability of the institution and for its highly significant role in serving the people of the future. In a sense, the university in the past was a storehouse of accumulated knowledge constantly re-searched for insights that could lead to the improvement of society in the future. The university has been forced into the posture of the federal government, in which there are continuing attempts to meet all needs of the present without much thought as to the long-term implications. An overwhelming national debt has been a major factor in bringing an end to many nations in the past and we may be moving rapidly to the same fate. Arguing that it is only fair that those who benefit from something pay for it, we now expect people to borrow money to go to college; we also expect them to pay for years to come for the vast highway system. Thus, in many respects, rather than seeking to benefit the future society, we are placing a heavy mortgage on it. At the same time, despite all efforts on the part of environmentalists, we still destroy the underlying resources necessary for the continued existence of any nation and culture.

The university too has, to a considerable extent, accepted this presentism. Some years ago, despite the obvious inequities within the institution, many an institution succeeded in developing a total enterprise of faculty, secretarial and clerical help, buildings and grounds employees, and administration in a mutually satisfying experience of serving the community and educating young people. Personal satisfaction, social recognition, and trust were accepted as more than adequate recompense for the discrepancy in salaries from those achievable elsewhere. The institution of higher education, like the church, was seen by individuals as a vital element in society and one so important that individuals associated with it were expected to make some sacrifices to forward its ends. At present, it appears that most of the employees of institutions of higher education view the institution only as a means of providing immediate gratification and also ensuring that that gratification continues until the age of sixty-five or seventy. In a way this is not unreasonable. Employees of colleges and universities are men and women of superior educational attainment but, in all other aspects, not very much different from the rest of the population. Although the university purports, in much of its advertising, to have a beneficial long-term effect on society, its views and operations at any point in time represent, to a large extent, those existing in the society. And, in the nature of events, the American society and perhaps that of much of the world worries more about getting through the next few years than it does about the long-term future. The idea of self-sacrifice for the sake of a better world, once a prominent value among our leaders and even among parents as they looked at the future prospects for their children, is nearly nonexistent. Environmentalists (who often go to extremes) represent one of the few groups that remain to remind us that continued attempts to satisfy the voracious appetites of the immediate generation will impose severe limits, if not obliteration, on future ones.

Balancing Public Control and Institutional Integrity

Institutional concern for autonomy has, in many cases, completely ignored the social responsibility of the institution and the fact that its existence and support are based upon a widespread conviction that institutions of higher education serve the public interest. As suggested earlier, sight of the public interest has frequently been lost in the scramble of the institution and its faculty to enhance its own reputation and increase its range of programs to justify the designation as university. Serving the public interest requires institutional integrity and responsiveness to society. It also requires concern about quality; but with increasing funding, most institutions have demonstrated less concern about quality (which may require increased support of existing programs) and more about expanding into new programs. Likewise, the institutions have demonstrated less concern about integrity and more about acquisition of funds, almost regardless of whether these funds supported or interfered with the major commitments of the university. Thus, to a considerable extent, expansion of faculty and the acquiring of faculty with a research orientation have been used as evidence of concern with quality. It is true that there is a reasonable correspondence between quality of graduate instruction and the presence of a strong and research-oriented faculty. However, my observations yield grave doubts that improvement of the faculty in this sense brings any improvement in the undergraduate program, except possibly for undergraduates looking to graduate study. The more specialized the faculty and the stronger its orientation to research, the less interest there appears to be in offering undergraduate courses appropriate to a liberal education and therefore at least equally valuable to nonmajors as to majors, if not more so. One of the concomitants of increasing attention to research and graduate instruction is a reasonable expectation on the part of the faculty that the credit hour and course load of faculty members will be reduced to one or two courses. One might anticipate that teaching fewer hours would result in better education by allowing more time for preparation; but the reduction in teaching hours tends to contribute to an increased class size, which hardly encourages attention to individual students either in talking with them or in reviewing their work. Moreover, the increasing emphasis on research results in a very low priority for anything directly related to undergraduate teaching. It is both amusing and vexing to observe that institutions that twenty years ago were damning the use of graduate assistants for instructional purposes at the undergraduate level are now justifying the introduction of graduate programs as the basis for finding graduate assistants to teach freshman and sophomore courses. The supporting argument is that these people are younger, closer to the age of the students, and therefore likely to have better rapport with them.

There is a tendency to ignore the very reasonable and appropriate grounds upon which external agencies attempt to influence and control universities because this would admit a deficiency or neglect in serving the public interest. Rather, universities take the view that public control and influence are an unreasonable intervention into the university autonomy and a denial of the authority and competency of the faculty to make academic decisions. In truth, the external intervention is an expression of doubt that faculties generally are either competent or willing to make sound educational decisions that take into account the public interests and the needs of the students. I suggest that colleges and universities ought to recognize that the discontent and dissatisfaction with higher education at the very least indicates that the institutions have not demonstrated to the public that public interest has been sensitively served. This may be, in part, a matter of faulty communication. Institutions have for too many years tried to paint for public consumption a picture of operations and consequences that frequently had little relevance to the actual situation. Deficiencies and weaknesses have been carefully glossed over, and credit has been taken for things to which the institution contributed little. Indeed, communication has been faulty and it has also, to a considerable extent, been misleading if not actually false. In some cases, institutions have even made a virtue of a characteristic that betrays a bad program. For example, one liberal arts college on the West Coast boasts that only 25 percent of the students who enter complete a degree there, although actual data show 40 to 50 percent. The actual retention, which is more nearly the standard, is bad enough for a self-identified elitist college. The lower figure savors of deception and chicanery. Only as a college or university admits that both its communication and its programs have been deficient and undertakes to improve these is it likely to acquire a reputation for integrity and document its commitment to quality. In this connection, it is noteworthy that, in a number of cases, new presidents coming into state institutions who have gone before legislative committees and frankly admitted the deficiencies of their institutions and asked for additional funds to correct these have been generously treated. Too frequently, however, these presidents have found that their deans and faculty, although glad to have the additional funds, are quite unwilling to work on the basic issues, and thus the legislative generosity is once again met by deception. I understand the frustration of the foundation executive who commented to me that the foundation would no longer give any funds to institutions that wanted to make studies of problems, but only to institutions that had decided upon a possible and reasonable solution to the problem and were ready to put it into effect.

Accreditation

Accreditation in the United States is often referred to as a voluntary enterprise. This is only in part true. There was a time at which some respectable institutions, engaged in a program oriented to a special group, found it possible to ignore regional accreditation. In recent years, so many federal support programs and state fund-raising programs have required accreditation that even regional accreditation has become almost a necessity for continuing institutional operation. Regional accreditation, however, has little impact, except upon very weak institutions or on new institutions going through the candidate-for-accreditation stage. To some extent, an institution that is seeking to expand its range of operation may also be materially affected if reexamination for retention of accreditation is required. In recent years, the extensive development of nontraditional programs (both graduate and undergraduate) offered by already accredited institutions and the development of new nontraditional institutions offering a range of degrees have shown the weakness or sheer inability of the regional accrediting associations in dealing with quality. Operating on the general basis that examining teams are to be made up of people who are sympathetic to innovation, the teams tend to assume that weaknesses that are pointed out will be corrected and that philosophies of education based largely upon personal development will move toward acceptance of academic goals. One of the regional accrediting associations has approved thoroughly disreputable graduate programs and, by this act, has called into question its approach to accreditation and its conception of standards. Protection of the public is a major objective of accrediting. Domination in an accrediting association of a collegial approach, accompanied by an assumption of integrity within each institution, quickly destroys the effectiveness of accreditation in those cases in which it should be most incisive.

The specialized accrediting programs in the various professions and in the health sciences can and do havè a marked impact on institutions. Typically, the specialized accrediting associations are dominated by the faculties and the administration of professional schools. They hold to rather traditional conceptions of education and are, in many cases, as much concerned with status, prerogatives, and salary of faculty members as they are with program quality. Not infrequently, a report from a specialized accrediting association contains, in highly critical form, a list of the local concerns on which the dean and his faculty have not been able to get action. It is by no means unknown for the chairperson of the visiting team to ask the chief executive of the particular unit under review to provide a list of those concerns that he would like to have directed to the administration. When these concerns are coupled with the threat of probation or withdrawal of accreditation, most institutions make immediate moves to correct the difficulties. At times, it is uncertain whether this is external influence upon the institution or simply internal influence brought to bear upon the institution in a more forceful way.

The proliferation of accrediting associations, especially in the health sciences, creates problems for institutions. The total time consumption involved in preparing reports, in scheduling and meeting with campus visitors, and in appearing before review hearings is no longer a small item in institutional budgets. If one could be sure, as I and many others are not, that the demands these groups make upon institutions are justified by the resulting quality, that expense could be considered a rather small item in reference to purposes served. In some cases, in fact, it appears that the demands made are not entirely reasonable and are much more concerned with the specialized nature of a program such as business than with the service role that program might play in relationship to other units in the university. On balance, accreditation probably serves higher education by upholding some concepts of operational character assumed to be related to quality. But as accreditation has proliferated into so many specialized fields, it may be questioned whether the costs and the repeated assaults on the unity and integrity of the institution as a whole may not have become a debit more than a credit.

Because of the possibility that accreditation may inflict upon an institution unneeded and perhaps even undesirable changes, deans, academic vice-presidents, and presidents need to keep abreast of the accreditation process in their institutions. Each department or unit preparing for accreditation review should be required to include in its planning and data collection a representative of the chief academic officer of the institution. Data collected should agree with that collected by the central service responsible for this—the office of institutional research or other unit performing this function. The contents of the report and accompanying data should be reviewed and approved by the chief academic officer, and this person and/or the president should meet with the accreditation committees when they appear on the campus. Unique aspects of the program should be identified and justified at that time. Most accrediting groups find it very difficult to criticize an institution or sever its accreditation status if it can demonstrate that it operates on well-considered and effective principles. If the institution can show that it has seriously considered the structure and activities of the program and that it has evidence that these are attaining quality results, a program is unlikely to be censured. It is the gradual deterioration in programs unnoted, unrecognized, and therefore not evaluated that engenders the greatest doubts on the part of accreditation committees and agencies.

When accreditation reports are in hand, they should be reviewed by administrators at levels above the unit examined. Criticisms and demands from accrediting associations can readily be promoted by the units involved to the level of demands on the budget that are difficult to refuse. Alumni, employers, and others who are asked to support the criticisms and demands are likely to do so without much thought or even understanding. Not infrequently, actual or implied demands resulting from accreditation are unrealistic. Immediate review of them by the chief academic officer may result in refutation of criticisms and a request for further review, thereby enabling the institution to alleviate the public concerns that may be generated by newspaper articles and public statements of influential friends and alumni.

In the past, many presidents have treated accreditation reports as confidential matters, not only refusing to release them to the press but also withholding them from the faculty or commenting only on the favorable statements and ignoring the others. Such administrators were delinquent, even though the conduct was somewhat understandable. It is unfortunate that accreditation, as it started through the regional agencies, has been an effort heavily dominated by administrators, with the result that reports have glossed over administrative deficiencies. The stance has been that the report was rendered to the chief administrator, and it was at his or her option how much was released to other persons.

In the present day, state and federal laws dealing with confidentiality of records, on the one hand, and the right of the public to know, on the other, have, in many cases, made it clear that an accreditation report is a public document, and so it should be. In addition, there needs to be a resolution as to whether an accreditation report is to the chief administrative officer or to the governing board of an institution. In some cases, boards may come under criticism, and it would be far easier on a president if copies of such reports were addressed to the chairman of the board or to board members rather than passed on to them through the president's office, which then immediately becomes suspect as having encouraged the criticism. In many cases, an adequate accreditation review will include comments that relate to administration, and these ought to be immediately in the possession of the board. If, in addition, accreditation is to serve the public interest and generate public support or demand for the maintenance of quality in an institution, it should be a public document. This, in turn, would mean that accreditation reports would eliminate the sometimes idiosyncratic comments, criticisms, or demands of individual committee members and deal more with the totality of the operation of a program and the evidence of quality in relationship to the resources used.

Matching Costs and Benefits

External influences upon educational institutions come about in a multiplicity of ways. Some years ago, the president of Michigan State was faced in a budget review by an individual committee member who said very bluntly that the committee would not talk about budgetary needs of the institution until assurance was provided that a particular agricultural extension agent would be fired. Fortunately, other members of the committee recognized the unreasonableness of that demand, and the whole matter was glossed over without the necessity of a major battle on the issue of institutional autonomy. Had it been necessary, it seems that this would have been a case in which a fight for preservation of institutional autonomy should have been made, even at the risk of some immediate loss in respect to next year's budget. Long-term implications would justify that position. Sometimes such a situation is complicated by the fact that a demand is justified by the performance of the individual. Nevertheless, a demand presented in the wrong way and at the wrong time and place must be resisted.

Another instance of external influence is that of an institution that possessed a rather nondescript name. It also had severe financial problems because, in the process of changing its character, it had expanded programs far beyond the enrollment and income to justify them. When an individual proffered a deferred gift—originally stated as twenty or twenty-five million, available in ten years or so—the president and board of the institution seized upon this as a solution to the problem and changed the name of the institution to that of the donor, with consequences both unanticipated and undesirable. The announcement of the gift, which in itself was vastly exaggerated, resulted in an almost complete suspension of gifts from other sources. The donor's wife demanded a part in the administration of the institution. The ultimate result was that the institution very nearly disappeared. No money was ever received from the gift, and ultimately the gift itself had to be rejected. The original name was restored and, in effect, the institution started over again under a new administration. A more cautious approach on this matter could have yielded very different results. Clearly, the immediate benefits to the institution of this projected gift were essentially nonexistent, yet the whole pattern of announcement glorifying the giver and implying that the financial problems of the institution were now solved destroyed relationships with others. There are appropriate terms of opprobrium for individuals who can be bought, and they may well apply to institutions also. It should be noted, however, that the price and the intent of the buyer are also factors of some significance. The University of Chicago, on the one hand, was the result of a major Rockefeller gift, but there was little or no intervention into the administration of the institution. Stanford University, on the other hand, suffered for many years from the continuing intervention of the donor's wife.

External influences may be useful in mitigating and redirecting internal excesses. For example, faculty members and departments claiming professional expertise in their particular disciplines insist, to a large extent, that the teacher of a course or the department handling a major or program should have complete autonomy. In actuality, it must be recognized that many courses and programs are interrelated with other courses and programs and, therefore, that other faculty members and units have some rightful claim to involvement in any decision about the curriculum. Likewise, individuals and departments at times present unusual and unjustifiable demands in respect to degree credits, requirements, facilities, section size, and the like. Administrators can exert influence and enforce restraint on such expectations. They can, by raising issues, cause rethinking of programs. Finally, they can impose mandates and controls that provide for review and the determination of accountability for units. These actions constitute a form of external intervention into college and departmental matters, but no serious compromise of institutional autonomy and professional responsibility is involved. At another level, board members who are, to some extent, external to the institution, donors, legislators, state budget officers, and auditors have an obligation and responsibility to seek evidence that resources are well used. If, by checking teaching loads, an external legislative auditor finds that some individuals drawing full salary have no recorded load, are not on campus, and are not on sabbatical leave, the auditor has unearthed evidence that something in the university is out of control. Since there is not full accountability for use of resources, the whole operation becomes suspect. When credits exceed class sessions for most courses in a particular department, it is reasonable to ask what the students are doing to justify the extra credit and how much time the faculty member is expending in an unstructured interaction with individuals as they carry out this work. Lack of such evidence may be taken as an indication that a department is primarily concerned with inflating its credit hours to enhance its budget and that administrators are collaborators in this lack of integrity. Intervention yielding such evidence generates increased intervention.

Many of the current interventions into internal academic matters result from a lack of internal management evidenced in the absence of clear policies and principles and of controls to see that these are taken into account by each unit. In talking with administrative officers about some of these matters, I have heard several remark, as a kind of aside, that in some ways it has been a benefit to have members of the legislature and of the audit office raise questions on these various points, since this has provided the ground for instituting some control over departmental and college operations. In making such a remark, an administrator, probably without total recognition of the fact, has admitted that the institution itself cannot use autonomy responsibly; and it is exactly this that has resulted in the increasing external intervention into institutions.

Some years ago, a state university was offered a small amount of money if it would launch an undergraduate major program in mobile homes. The agreement was reached and the program was introduced. Fortunately, students were not attracted to the program, and the program itself, like many mobile homes, was so lacking in structure that it soon fell apart and was eliminated. Responsiveness to public demands has always to be responsibly related to broader concerns of public interest. In this case, some preliminary investigation would certainly have revealed that the aspiration of an embryonic industry to achieve recognition through a degree program was not justified by the existence of complicated new technology requiring special education.

Another type of external intervention into college and university programs appears when state legislatures or other state agencies impose, by law or regulation, a demand that particular courses be included in the degree requirements. I recall having to take a course in the history of Ohio. The course was a complete bore, and included some materials that were erroneous. In general, education requirements imposed on prospective teachers have been unreasonable because the deficiency that arouses the concern is seldom buttressed by sufficient substance to generate a respectable course. Colleges and universities generally have gone along meekly with these requirements. The explanation is, in part, that such regulations are ultimately supported and promulgated by individuals who have received degrees in these institutions and use state education departments very much like accreditation agencies to impose external demands that support their personal desires for recognition. Faculty imposition of general education requirements on students is of the same ilk.

Summary

These remarks on external influences and mandates and their effect upon institutions could be extended to include many other examples, demonstrating even more fully that outside intervention is often resisted when it should be welcomed as an indication of the ineffectiveness and irresponsibility of the institution and steps taken to repair the situation. The tendency to resist when there is a real basis for the demand can only be seen as irresponsible, unintelligent, or dishonest administration. The last is evident when the deficiency is recognized but the chosen operation is cover-up rather than acknowledgment and adjustment. In other cases, external influences are encouraged and welcomed simply because the institutional demands for resources and the administrators' desire for recognition by acquiring those resources results in a cessation or sidetracking of critical review to assess underlying values and ultimate consequences. Immediate gratification is always a strong motivation, but the attendant suspension of judgment as to long-term consequences is often deleterious.

Suggestions for Further Reading

Benezet, L. T., and Magnusson, F. W. (Eds.). *New Directions for Higher Education: Building Bridges to the Public,* no. 27. San Francisco: Jossey-Bass, 1979.

Carnegie Commission on Higher Education. *The More Effective Use of Resources: An Imperative for Higher Education.* New York: McGraw-Hill, 1972.

Commission on Non-Traditional Study. *Diversity by Design.* San Francisco: Jossey-Bass, 1973.

Dressel, P. L. (Ed.). *New Directions for Institutional Research: The Autonomy of Public Colleges,* no. 26. San Francisco: Jossey-Bass, 1980.

Glenny, L. A., Shea, J. R., Ruyle, J. H., and Freschi, K. H. *Presidents Confront Reality: From Edifice Complex to University Without Walls.* San Francisco: Jossey-Bass, 1976.

Gollattscheck, J. F., and others. *College Leadership for Community Renewal: Beyond Community-Based Education.* San Francisco: Jossey-Bass, 1976.

Lee, E. C., and Bowen, F. M. *Managing Multicampus Systems: Effective Administration in an Unsteady State.* San Francisco: Jossey-Bass, 1975.

EIGHT

~~~~~~

Meeting University Obligations and Administrative Responsibilities

A college or university exists to serve the needs of society both in the immediate present and in the future. In serving these needs, administrators and faculty, assisted by students, alumni, and influential leaders in society, mediated by the governing board, attempt to interpret immediate and prospective social needs and place priorities upon them. This process identifies those needs that the institution should and can meet and the consideration of the ways those needs can be met in relationship to the available resources. It is essential that the procedures for doing this, the values involved, and the accountability for use of resources and results be open to input and review by all concerned. The processes of determining needs, assigning priorities, and developing operating principles and procedures should be so conducted as to exemplify how decisions can be made and carried out effectively in a democratic organization.

138

Students learn as much about values and democratic processes by observing their operation as they do from the classroom. Indeed, they may learn more—certainly more than most faculty members or administrators realize. But the ethos of the institution as perceived by persons external to the institution also provides a powerful example to students who come from and shortly return to the larger society. Whatever goes on within the institution is, in one way or another, communicated to an external audience. No one really expects that either a church or a university operated by and serving human beings will achieve perfection, even if we assume agreement on what constitutes perfection. But it is a serious error to assume that an educational institution can present even a facade of perfection to the public when there is continuing internal dissension and uncertainty. The policies and practices of an institution, as well as its standards, must be equitable, reasonable, and justly applied. The mode of determination of these policies and procedures, the underlying rationale for them, and the understanding and acceptability of them by all sectors of the university may be as influential in determining the ethos of the institution as are the policies, operational procedures, and standards themselves. One of the primary points of concern in an educational institution is integrity in both its operations and its accomplishments. If the statement of mission, the policies and principles, and the value commitments of an institution include statements contradictory to its actual manner of operation, there must be nonfeasance (lack of performance by individuals connected with the institution), misfeasance (irresponsible performance resulting from carelessness, ignorance, or timidity), or malfeasance (a deliberate ignoring of stated principles and purposes and a diversion of institutional resources and activities to serve personal or special group purposes different from those to which the institution is presumably committed). Integrity requires recognition of institutional obligations and the assignment of administrative responsibilities for assuring that these obligations are fulfilled. This administration-management role also requires continuing reminders to the university staff members that they too must accept these obligations. Furthermore, irresponsibility at any level in recognizing obligations or performing in ways inconsistent with them requires critical review, remonstrance, and correction.

Obligations to Society

In this section, I propose to discuss the educational institution's obligations as these relate to the educational role. In each case, I assume that the total operation of the institution must be such as to exemplify and contribute to these obligations. This view contrasts markedly with the assumption made in many institutions that this responsibility rests with the faculty. The first obligation of an educational institution is to educate students in diverse ways depending upon individual abilities, interests, and societal needs. This statement justifies, in the minds of many faculty members, the demand that all college and university teachers be Ph.D.s in their appropriate disciplines. The assumption is that a Ph.D., in acquiring that degree, has been immersed in scholarship, research, and/or creative endeavor and is able to exemplify, interpet, and pass on to students a grasp of the essential knowledge and competencies of his or her field of expertise. In fact, as a student and then as a faculty member, evaluator, and observer on many campuses, I have been dismayed at the extent to which this obligation has been ignored in undergraduate programs by overemphasis on content coverage and by insistence upon memorization of unorganized factual material never assimilated into the thought or behavior of students. Undergraduates generally are not (and they should not be) expected to become scholars or researchers in the same sense as faculty members. It is irresponsible to plan courses and programs for the few who do and insist that they meet the needs of all. Teachers have an obligation to see that each student has some understanding of the nature of scholarship and of the research process in various fields. Each student should develop some capability for thinking and communicating about issues and problems of concern by analyzing and discussing them in reference to the concepts, principles, and modes of thought characteristic of several relevant disciplines. A few students probe even more deeply. Some do go on to graduate school, and the faculty tend to point to these individuals as evidence of effective performance. In my judgment, this is an erroneous claim, for many of these students would have achieved equally well in almost any educational institution.

A second obligation, essentially an extension of the first, is that education develop judgment and provide criteria and means of making judgments. Unfortunately, many professors are much more concerned that students learn the evaluation and judgment of authorities (including those of the professor) than that they learn to make increasingly well-based judgments of their own. Students who simply *re*cite those authorities already cited by the professor have developed conditioned responses, but they are not educated.

A third obligation of an educational institution is to cultivate in its own staff and in students an objectivity in the approach to issues. This objectivity does not rule out value judgments or personal opinions. The intent of education is that individuals recognize bias or prejudice for what it is—a judgment or conviction arrived at without either a full understanding of the nature of what is judged or of the relevant facts, principles, and their implications. Bias or prejudice may, as a result of the cultivation of objectivity, be transferred or transformed into an acknowledged and understood value preference.

A fourth obligation of an educational institution is that it remain current and timely. This does not mean that every book used must have been published within the past five years; it does imply a recognition that recent and current scholarship throws new light on the past. However, the current scene and the prospects for the future may make some ideas and artifacts of the past more immediately relevant and more significantly educational than some materials to which a particular Ph.D. has made major lifetime commitments in research and study. Many of the distinctions made by scholars make no difference to anyone else. Maintenance of currency means that courses and programs need recurrent overhaul and redesignation, or elimination to be replaced by something more appropriate to present needs.

A fifth obligation of an educational institution is that it develop and disseminate *new* ideas. There are at least three different ways in which new ideas are educationally significant. The first is associated with the identification of some concept, particle, or object never before recognized as distinctive. The biologist who identifies a *new* species of birds or plants has not actually found something new in the sense that it never previously existed. He has simply become aware of it and brings that awareness to others. He has introduced an existing entity into the realm of human recognition and possibly of human exploitation. A physicist who identifies a new particle and provides evidence of its existence has added to human knowledge. However, the physicist has not created anything thereby. The added knowledge may lead to new hypotheses and ultimately to facts and principles about the nature and origin of matter and life. Painters, poets, and musicians can and do create novel combinations of colors, tones, and words, exhibited in styles or forms strikingly different from those previously used.

In many cases, *new* ideas are simply the extension of existing ideas by deletion or addition of new components or concepts—a new way of looking at an object or idea (the second conception). Such value conceptions as freedom, equality, and equity have, at various times, been researched and elaborated upon in distinctive ways, thereby affecting social values and bringing about changes in legislation and judicial decisions. In mathematics, the exploration of the concept of continuity has resulted in a range of definitions derived, to a considerable extent, out of weakening the assumptions or conditions under which a function is considered continuous. New fields of mathematics have developed out of this approach. Such a concept as symmetry has been extended into many fields, with various ways of defining symmetry and with subsequent exploration of the impact of denial of various kinds of symmetry. The abstraction *continuity* was a human creation that added significantly to human comprehension and analytic power.

A third conception of a *new* idea is a very simple one often ignored in the educational processes. It is simply that an idea or object may be new to—that is, never before experienced by—a specific individual. An intelligent, thoughtful individual may also assimilate the idea in such a manner and with such relations that aspects of it are indeed novel and different from previous conceptions. The view that much of education requires interaction among people is surely a recognition of this. One can read a well-written book several times and each time have new perceptions and increased appreciation. Group discussion adds human interaction and nonverbal communication and provides the opportunity for repetition, modification, and enlargement that can enable each person of the group to depart with new ideas. One characteristic of great teachers is that each time they enthusiastically approached their content and subject matter from a somewhat different (a new) point of view, and from each class they emerged enriched by the distinctive perceptions derived from interactions with the students.

Although research has always been a search for new ideas, the dynamism of that search and *re*search can be destroyed by the narrow or microscopic ventures in which neither the researcher nor his students or faculty associates see the activities or results in relation to any significant issue or problem. All too frequently, the dynamism of research has not penetrated to the classroom wherein the professor (perhaps to save time for research) regularly indulges in a repetitive droning of the same lectures term after term. There are timeless ideas and monuments but, being timeless, they can and should be made timely. It is the obligation of the university and its professors to do so. A further obligation in the instructional realm is the development in students of a conviction that action should generally be preceded by thought, and that knowledge and reason, rather than unanalyzed opinion or notion, should become the bases for their beliefs and actions. Trite and repetitive presentation savors more of indoctrination than of reason because it exposes students to the results of thought without involving them in the process. Innovation and renovation are essential to maintain dynamism and provide stimulation for both teachers and students.

Innovation has been a major point of discussion in analyzing and reviewing educational institutions in the past twenty-five or thirty years. Unfortunately, but understandably, in a nation that has been committed to growth as a major value, innovation in institutions of higher education has also cultivated

growth and used growth as a major criterion for accomplishment. Increase in student body, in programs, in facilities, and,
above all, in budget have long been accepted as evidence of
presidential prowess and institutional achievement. Thereby institutions have become complicated and incoherent arrays of
units competing rather than cooperating with each other. Education tends to be a conservative enterprise in that existing units
and persons seek to conserve their existing status rather than to
reconsider it. Much of the university's operation is through departments with professors committed to continued specialization in works of the past. Many professors find little challenge
and even irritation and boredom in organizing new courses and
developing new curricula. In particular, they may resist an introduction to and assimilation of new communication modes that
might significantly improve the educational process. At the
graduate and research level, innovation is often demonstrated
by the development of new disciplines that grow out of the increasing amount of knowledge in segments of an earlier discipline or the identification and development of a concept or
principle previously embedded in a number of disciplines. Specialization is indeed a form of innovation, but a form that leads
to more departments, more courses, and more majors for undergraduates, rather than an innovation that organizes knowledge
in new and more relevant ways and adopts or adapts ideas and
technology to improve the educational process and diffuse its
results and applications to society.

The preceding discussion of obligations can be expanded
to include more specific statements dealing with research and
public service and with the modes and procedures used to fulfill
these various obligations. Accountability would require that an
institution produce evidence that it had fulfilled, in some measure, the various obligations stated. In fact, most institutions
have not produced evidence of successful performance on these
points and are unable to do so. Lacking such evidence, they
indicate the number of credit hours produced or the number of
graduates in the various areas. Course structures, class attendance, and instructional loads identify processes but tell nothing
about the nature of the learning processes nor the nature, quality, or amount of work demanded of students to acquire credit

in the course. Statements about institutional accomplishments should be outcome rather than process oriented. They should speak to characteristics of educated persons produced by attendance and application in a college or university.

In reviewing institutions, I have found that few departments maintain a file containing course outlines or syllabi, examinations, and requirements of papers, accompanied by a grade distribution and a statement of standards or procedures used in assigning a grade. One would assume that, if for no other purpose than to provide information to later instructors, such materials would be available for review by anyone seeking evidence of the experiences offered by a particular course. This deficiency reflects the general practice in the college or university of permitting instructors complete autonomy in handling a course. Such freedom is often abused. I recall a number of cases of instructors who failed every student in a course. Since the department had no procedure for reviewing instructor evaluations, an investigation was made only after students complained to a dean. Even then, the response from the department after investigation was that the instructor was fully justified. One may wonder if any instructor can ever fully justify failing every student in a sizable class. It seems obvious that the departmental chairperson was delinquent in not providing some means of reviewing instructional practices and evaluation techniques of each staff member. Such instances, when they do come to light, raise serious questions about the integrity of an institution and about its fairness in dealing with individuals. A college or university, to be effective, must have a considerable degree of autonomy, but any institution that extends autonomy to each unit and to each individual within the unit has an obligation to maintain review processes that locate and correct inequities. Otherwise, accountability and external controls are fully justified.

Earning Independence

Independence or autonomy is needed, but it cannot be expected that it will be automatically extended to any institution. New colleges and universities have found themselves under severe scrutiny by both friends and foes and, in recent years, by accrediting agencies and federal agencies that provide funds for encouraging institutional development. Institutions have to earn autonomy and they have to be able to demonstrate that that autonomy has been effectively used. This requires a number of types of evidence.

1. The institution should be able to demonstrate that it has performed well the various tasks that have been assigned to it. This reflects directly back to the various obligations stated in earlier paragraphs. By including the word *well*, the statement makes it apparent that more is required than merely evidence that some processes have gone on and that a number of individuals have completed those processes. Perfunctory performance is not enough. Examples are plentiful to indicate that college faculties, like other human beings, cannot be assumed to be fully responsible in the exercise of autonomy, and the institution that does not provide checks and balances can expect embarrassing situations that reflect adversely on the institution.

2. The institution should demonstrate the capability of self-governance carried out in a dignified and effective manner, as evidenced in the behavior and morale of its staff and students and in the clarity, equity, and applicability of its policies and procedural rules.

3. The institution should be orderly. This is reflected in a number of ways. The policies and procedural rules just mentioned are sound and can be understood, and the institution operates in an effective and organized way. This reflects an orderly institution because it operates efficiently with respect to self-determined policies. But an institution needs also to be orderly in respect to the expectations of the community in which it is located and the applicable municipal, state, and federal laws. Governing boards have been known to ignore or evade certain laws—for example, those with regard to open meetings. Faculty members and administrators in some institutions have exhibited contempt for traffic regulations and local mores, thereby contributing to a town-

gown division. Disruptive activities by students, whether as part of some radical or reactionary movement or as an exhibition of excess energy, may not only be destructive but may also tend to create the view that an institution is not seriously pursuing its major purposes.

4. Institutions in which administrators, faculty members, or students become heavily involved in partisan politics or public controversy may unwittingly bring retribution by diminishment of resources or by the imposition of controls with no other purpose than to restore the institution to the objectivity that it should maintain. It is one thing for faculty members, individually or as part of some partisan group, to take a stand on controversial issues; it is quite another to imply or demand that the institution take a particular position on divisive issues.

5. The institution should be able to demonstrate effective use of its resources. This is not simply a matter of accountability. Effective and efficient performance of the institution is essential to meet its obligations to students and society. And since resources are always less than institutions desire, demonstration of their effective use provides a basis for relating institutional programs and resources to the optimal attainment of the range of accepted purposes. Effective use of resources also provides the basis for demonstrating additional resource needs. Responsible use of resources is essential to acquire new sources of funding.

6. Institutions earn and justify independence by demonstrating that their programs are carried on effectively and provide those services dictated by their missions and roles. Particular units on a campus, such as departments, institutes, or colleges, are, with some exceptions, generally of little interest to those who provide the resources for the institution. It is usually a mistake to allow the search for resources to become too closely tied to particular programs or units, although a few major private universities seek to have "every tub on its own bottom." Critics of a particular unit may seize the opportunity to demand a cutback on resources, whereas those who favor the unit may move to earmark ex-

cessive resources for it at the expense of other parts of the institution. Within the institution, apparent favoritism toward one unit encourages ill will and competition. Moreover, emphasis on obtaining resources by specific units confuses the organization of an institution with the functions that it performs and the needs that it meets. These needs and functions justify its existence and should be the basis for requesting support, rather than the name of the unit or the personalities dominating it.

7. Inevitably, at the stage of assignment of resources, assumptions are made as to how these resources will be used and what results will be obtained. But unless there is a follow-up evaluation, resources may be unwisely and ineffectively used. Faculty members who dominate particular units may have preferred ways of operating that do not support and are even inimical to the achievement of declared goals and objectives. As circumstances change and institutions innovate, there is a constant problem of optimizing the use of resources so as best to reach a specified end under existing conditions. An institution demonstrates responsible use of its autonomy only when it looks to the outcomes of its programs and makes successive resource allocations to units on the basis of the importance of those outcomes and the success of the units in achieving them.

Questionable Practices

Either irresponsibility or the lack of principles and guidelines such as those just discussed permits the development and continuance of questionable practices. Several examples illustrate the point.

The scheduling of classes to suit faculty convenience is an example of a practice that frequently causes scheduling problems for students and makes it difficult to use classroom facilities efficiently. It may be unfair to lower-status faculty members who are assigned unreasonable teaching schedules either in time or in place. If, as in a few institutions, evening classes are part of the regular faculty load, the exemption of several professors from evening classes because of their dislike of them forces others to teach these classes. An individual who insists that all of his or her classes be scheduled before noon may be justified if the afternoons are fully devoted to research or other professional activities. If, however, that individual spends the afternoons on the golf course or selling real estate (I have noted both at various times), such scheduling is unfair to others and will, in time, reflect upon the adequacy of management in the university. If, under a rule or policy requiring faculty teaching assignments to be spread equitably over the hours and days of the week, an individual accepts a 4:00 P.M. class but immediately after registration moves it to an earlier hour to suit his personal convenience, some counteraction should be taken. Administrators sometimes may be forced to take direct means of observation on such matters. A tour of a classroom/laboratory facility to note how many spaces are unused in the late afternoon compared with a schedule of classes is a quick way to determine whether unwarranted and unofficial shifting of class meetings for the convenience of the instructor is a common practice.

Another example of a practice very irritating to students is that of balancing sections by temporary closures during the registration procedure. It is appropriate that a department attempt to balance enrollments over sections, but some hours and instructors are likely to be more popular than others. If sections become full and are closed and remain closed, the order of registration becomes the primary factor in determining whether an individual gets a preferred section. This will cause some difficulties. If sections are arbitrarily closed to allow others to catch up, late-comers may enroll while enrollment is denied to those previously scheduled for registration. Most students so afflicted will regard this as unfair. However, these remarks should not be interpreted as indicating that students should always have schedules to suit their own whims. Even the schedules of athletes conform to the whims of coaches. Some flexibility in dealing with working students, commuting students, athletes, and the like is both reasonable and necessary. Full use of facilities requires that both students and faculty members accept schedules not fully in accord with personal preferences.

Another type of questionable practice relates to major and degree requirements. Over time, the increasing amount of knowledge and the number of disciplines and courses available require that changes be made. This is especially true in undergraduate professional or quasi-professional programs, such as engineering, business, nursing, home economics, and agriculture. Some of the new materials required can be folded into existing courses; some appear to require new courses and increases in requirements. In either case, any change in programs or requirements should involve a complete program review. By eliminating less important or outdated materials and integrating old and new materials, it is usually possible to update a program without increasing requirements. Yet I have seen degree requirements increase over a span of years by 10 to 20 percent while the program was still called a four-year degree program. If, as in some fields (veterinary medicine, for example), it has been found necessary to increase the undergraduate preparation in the sciences and specify a baccalaureate for entry to the professional program, the new set of requirements is clearly a forthright and defensible upgrading of the profession. Expansion of credit and course requirements without complete study and justification is unfair to students. Either a heavier load and lower quality of work or an extension of the period of schooling results. The decision may also be unfair to other units in the university, and to those who support the university, by requiring an increasing proportion of the available resources.

A related unjustifiable practice is seen when departments and colleges unable to increase the total degree requirements decide to reduce or eliminate general or liberal education requirements. The history of undergraduate technical and professional programs demonstrates this very well. Early programs in the late nineteenth century included large segments of the classical or liberal education of that day but gradually eliminated this over time to accommodate the expanding array of courses in the field. Throughout much of the history of general education, dating from the 1930s or 1940s to the present time, all undergraduate programs have stressed inclusion of some liberal or general education. I have seen general education programs of such low quality that departments or colleges were fully justified in seeking relief from them. The signs indicative of a needed change in general education course definitions and instructional practices were clear, but they were ignored by the general education faculty. Secure in the institutional requirement and in the mistaken conception of that autonomy and academic freedom, the faculty felt justified in their right to define the requirement. Administrators should take action in such circumstances. There remains the possibility that a liberally educated professional faculty can provide a more meaningful and relevant general education to its students than would be achieved by distribution or core requirements for all students. But whatever practice is encouraged or permitted, continuing review by an administrator external to and above that unit is essential. Another practice that I find questionable is that of arbitrarily increasing the number of credits required for any interdisciplinary major. The rationale is that interdisciplinary majors lack depth. This may well be true. That this weakness can be corrected by adding one or two courses beyond departmental major requirements borders on the absurd.

As faculties have become larger and increasingly discipline and department oriented, professional expertise on many educational matters (such as course offerings, instructional practices, standards, and personnel) depends more on maturity, experience, and the humanitarian commitment of service to individuals and society than on disciplinary expertise. Acquiescence to faculty insistence that matters of curriculum, faculty appointment, promotion, and the like should be delegated to the department is at the root of many of the problems faced in higher education today. It has become necessary, on every campus, to review critically recommendations for promotions, granting of tenure, and new positions to assure some reasonable semblance of equity. Departments can be unduly rigid or unreasonably flexible, depending upon the circumstances of the units and the personalities involved. I was told some twenty years ago by an administrator at Harvard that, by institutional policy, every tenure position involved a national search. Junior faculty members at Harvard might be considered, but rarely would a junior faculty member be promoted to a tenure position. The administrator added that this was made a university policy to prevent some departments from taking the easy way out by filling vacancies with their own junior faculty members.

External accountability to those who support the university and a reasonable amount of institutional autonomy require that administrators and managers exact from those within the university recognition of their obligations and responsible performance of them. I shall use two other examples to underline my point. During the 1960s, some faculty members were as active in revolting against the university as were the students. I recall one individual, hired by a department on my own campus, who insisted on living in the immediate community of an institution where he had done his graduate work. He became a commuting professor from a distance of seventy to seventy-five miles and insisted that his schedule be arranged so that he need not be present every day. He soon made evident a highly nontraditional approach to education by announcing that anyone who enrolled in his course would be assured an A. His rationale was that anyone who enrolled must certainly be interested in doing some reading and work. Accepting this as an operating assumption, he would forgo class sessions and automatically report A's at the end of the quarter. This naturally brought the individual a considerable following of students. Ultimately, of course, the question of tenure came up for this individual. In a quandary because of the multiplicity of demands from various sources, the department finally sent through a recommendation for tenure in the official channels but privately sent the dean a letter signed by most of the department members asking the dean to deny the recommendation. This and other examples observed over a number of years have convinced me that when really tough decisions have to be made, the initiative and responsibility rest with the administrator. Faculty governance performs well only when the issues do not require immediate action and when the general policies or principles are being discussed rather than specific decisions demanded. If, going up the hierarchy, the buck (marker indicating next dealer in poker) stops at an administrator's desk, decisions about money may well rest there on the way down.

One final example will be that of grading. The general inflation of grades in the last decade was undoubtedly, in great part, a reaction of the faculty to student demand for more relevance in courses, more freedom in selection of courses, and a greater flexibility in what students were permitted to do (or not do) to pass the course. Nevertheless, in a broader sense, the fluctuation of grades over a period of time only reflects the lack of clarity on requirements and *reasonable* standards. Some years ago, when many colleges were able to select their students carefully, presidents and deans told faculties at fall orientation that the incoming group of students was the best ever. A common response to this, verified by my review of grades at that time, was that the faculty grades for this group of students were considerably lower than they had been in the past. Presumably, the reason was that better students should mean higher standards, and higher standards are reflected by more failures. Following this reasoning, the best institution should limit its admissions to a few top high school graduates and then fail all of them. The moral is obvious. Academic administrators who want to be fair to students and demonstrate their own sense of responsibility to the public must keep track, in one manner or another, of grading practices and insist likewise that academic administrators under them do the same. It should be policy in any department that unusual grade distributions be reviewed with the department chairperson or other senior faculty member of the department before being recorded. I recall one chairman of a mathematics department (where unrealistically rigorous grading is often a problem) who remarked that, after establishing the practice that unusual grade distributions would be reviewed, he conducted the review by engaging in a rambling talk with the instructor, closing with the comment that he presumed the instructor had good reason for the unusual grade distribution. His summarizing comment was that, after a quarter or two of such interviews, he had no further problem with unreasonable grading distributions. It is somewhat unclear how the chairman's long rambling talks improved student performance.

Subjective Judgments Versus Routine Decisions

Some of the immediately preceding examples indicate the difficulties and the probable inequities that result when individual faculty members or units within an institution operate without any guidance or control from administrative levels, where there is (or should be) some awareness of institutional obligations and responsibilities. Administrators must keep certain values and issues before the faculty rather than resigning full control to them. For example, an attendance rule stating that a student who is absent from a specific percentage of classes must be failed ignores the issue of whether the student has acquired from the course and his own study a satisfactory mastery of course objectives. The rule is punitive rather than productive. I recall such a student who made A's on all examinations in a course, including the final. The instructor, irritated by the recurring absences, invoked the failure rule based upon attendance, despite his prior announcement that grades depended solely upon examination performance. The student, equally irritated and also a mature, highly intellectual individual, dropped out of college. The dean who refused to intervene should have been kicked out!

Attempts to enforce upon the faculty such policies as giving examinations, holding reasonably close to preferred grade distributions, filing course outlines or syllabi, or appropriate professional behavior in conduct of classes generate in faculty members a frame of mind and a set of irritations that jeopardize their own acceptance of professional responsibility in fulfillment of their obligations. An undue number of rules and regulations, or even the development on the part of an individual of a rigid habit pattern, tends to place efficiency ahead of humanity. In the face of differences in individuals and changing goals and values, it is essential that the institution, in its role as a model of decision making, recognize individuality and allow for unforeseen contingencies. Most rules and regulations specify either behavior intended to become habitual or the characteristics of a situation in which it is expected that a specified response will always be given. Many such rules arise out of specific cases rather than common events. The instructor irritated by late-comers who establishes the rule that lecture hall doors will be locked as he begins his lecture may have resolved his own frustration, but at the expense of ignoring contingencies that may cause even the most conscientious student to be late. The faculty reaction to a dean or president who applies the same policy at faculty meetings is predictable. A more flexible decision, using the classroom example, would involve discussing the problem with the students and attempting to resolve it by accommodations on both sides. For example, statement of a policy that all late-comers will use a particular door at the rear and seat themselves in a back row as noiselessly and unobtrusively as possible would ease much of the problem. A still more innovative solution might start by questioning the value of the traditional lecture approach requiring that large numbers be brought together in the same room at the same time. Quite possibly the essence of the lecture and demonstration could be provided to students in other ways. This illustration was deliberately selected to suggest that many rules and decisions result from a commitment to a traditional practice or a personal prejudice that is difficult to change. Reflection in similar vein on the pointlessness of many faculty meetings might be instructive.

It is not appropriate for a college or university to accommodate to all the idiosyncrasies and desires of a wide range of students. It is equally true that institutions that attempt to meet the educational needs of a wide range of individuals ought not to insist that every student adjust to the whims or prejudices of individual faculty members or departments. Higher education needs to move from rigorous enforcement of routine rules and regulations without regard for individual problems or unforeseen contingencies to recognition that individual circumstances and unforeseen factors may require an adaptive statement of policy.

Difficulties in enforcing policies may indicate that the policies are based upon some invalid or unrealistic assessment of circumstances and that a whole new approach needs to be explored and developed. In working with a number of professional schools, I have realized the difficulties of faculty members in developing policies and procedures suitable to the preparation of professionals. The pressures of the first year of medical school, for example, frequently result in student behaviors that are irritating to the faculty and inappropriate for persons entering the profession. Finding that some lecturers—particularly visiting lecturers—may not be very stimulating and generally repeat materials already recorded in books and notes, students simply do not appear. Administrators and faculty are thereby irritated and embarrassed, especially when prominent outside lecturers are involved. Should attendance be required?

Because of the large amount of material to be assimilated, medical students sometimes use devious means to avoid or to fulfill requirements. Rules devised to control these practices are inimical to the acquiring of the professional responsibilities and commitments that the program should develop. For example, one medical school operates under the policy that only pass-fail reporting is permitted, and another policy states that attendance at formal classes is optional. However, there is an unwritten policy that each department and, to a considerable extent, each professor is autonomous on these matters. Thus there is a great deal of variation in rules and in the rigidity of interpretation from one course to another. Many of the rules devised to control the undesirable behavior of a few students come to be regarded as unreasonable and inappropriate by responsible students. Can self-reliant, responsible, and ethical practitioners be developed in a program that assumes irresponsibility and lack of integrity?

Because of these inconsistencies and the tensions generated by them, constructive approaches to identification and resolution of such problems or issues are lacking. The ideal deliberation would be a completely objective comparison and contrast of various conceptions of philosophy and practice. This is difficult because many individuals with strong preferences can neither develop nor appreciate and assimilate a completely objective statement when presented. The tendency, then, is to find individuals who disparage the existing system and push for a preferred alternative. Junior faculty members desiring a change may become pitted against senior faculty members self-viewed as maintaining standards by holding to a traditional practice that they neither understand nor can fully justify. Those individuals dissatisfied with an existing system tend to view administrative actions directed to making the system work as attempts to perpetuate the existing pattern. They may be right, but they should recognize also that much of the chaotic pattern of present policies and practices has resulted from piecemeal changes of the past. Only a careful and detailed analysis of basic program purposes and objectives, followed by a statement of policies and examples based upon a consistent philosophical point of view, will be effective in displacing these incoherent and inconsistent historical policy accretions. To accomplish this, administrators at appropriate levels must so direct and coordinate activities over time that basic issues will continually be faced and resolved in the light of overall purposes and objectives. Problems that involve programs and issues that concern policy formulation are never fully resolved. New circumstances arise and new individuals appear. Participants in the study of issues tend to return to the isolation of their offices and resume traditional views and practices because these require less effort and coincide with customs, biases, and prejudices of the immediate unit.

Administrators have major responsibilities for encouraging continuous attention to those policies and practices that are indicative of basic value commitments and that provide the bases whereby students and individuals external to the institution make their judgments about the institution. Administrative weaknesses that have to be overcome are both numerous and well known. Some blame for the inadequate performance of administrators must be placed upon boards of trustees in that they do not require or engage in systematic evaluation of administrators. Most trustees know relatively little about their institution. Lacking either a president who seeks trustee involvement or a chairperson who demands it, boards tend to act routinely upon materials brought to them or to engage in petty investigations or discussions of particular complaints. They are unlikely to demand that university goals, purposes, and mission be stated and related to a set of policies and practices ensuring that the operation of each segment of the university is consistent with its overall commitment.

Some administrators are ill prepared to assume administration and management roles. They may have served in faculty
positions so long that they are indoctrinated with the view that
the faculty and the basic disciplinary departments should be
granted complete autonomy. If so, they ignore essential administrative responsibilities. If the new administrator accepts personal responsibility for an administrative overload of paper
work, committee sessions, external reporting, and appeal
mechanisms, he or she will have no time to think deeply on any
issue. An overload of busy work can readily become an excuse
for delaying an attack on major issues. This delay is ultimately
the source of much of the discontent and ineffective operation
of institutions. Though faculty members see centralization of
authority as a major weakness and push for delegation, it may
well be that administrators are so preoccupied with issues generated from lower levels that those lower levels achieve full
autonomy because no one has time to engage in critical review
of them. Faculty councils and senates include individuals who
have been highly critical of administrative roles and tend to
push governance structures and committees into formulation of
detailed rules, mechanisms, and elaborate procedural safeguards
of faculty members rather than into the appropriate role of advice, counsel, and collaboration with administrators in formulating policies for the institutional operation. At times, the administrative structure itself, because of personalities or because of
an interlacing of horizontal and vertical coordinating and administrative units, generates such confusion that no one is sure
who is in charge. I recall one dean in a major university who
told me that he had reached the point where originals of any
statement were sent to three different administrators because
neither he nor the administrators were sure where responsibility
and authority were placed. An inadequate communication system sometimes generates part of this administrative chaos but is
also a result of it. By acquiring knowledge, one is able to impress and influence others and thereby to acquire power. Thus
the intent of open communication to inform individuals and
seek their reactions and cooperation may come to be perverted
by some recipients to the use of information for enhancement

of personal status. Only when information is completely open and subject to scrutiny and interpretation by those holding differing value commitments does it become possible to relate it to the obligations of the university and the decisions required to fulfill them.

Too many administrators want to be loved. They do well if they are respected as administrators, but they are not then likely to be loved by the faculty. Too many administrators enjoy the title, salary, and social prerogatives but wish to avoid the difficulties involved. Regular rotation encourages a *locum tenens* attitude—a passing through with little knowledge of the past and no responsibilities for the future. More, rather than less, rotation is required to get rid of incompetents expeditiously, but when an administrator demonstrates responsibility and effective performance, it would be far better to retain that individual for a lengthy term than to continue the rotation policy.

Suggestions for Further Reading

Glenny, L. A., Berdahl, R., Palola, E., and Paltridge, G. *Coordinating Higher Education for the '70s.* Berkeley: Center for Research and Development in Higher Education, University of California, 1971.

Hefferlin, JB L. *Dynamics of Academic Reform.* San Francisco: Jossey-Bass, 1969.

Hofstadter, R., and Hardy, C. D. *The Development and Scope of Higher Education in the United States.* New York: Columbia University Press, 1952.

Jencks, C., and Riesman, D. *The Academic Revolution.* Garden City, N.Y.: Doubleday, 1968.

Mayhew, L. B. *Surviving the Eighties: Strategies and Procedures for Solving Fiscal and Enrollment Problems.* San Francisco: Jossey-Bass, 1979.

Selznick, P. *Leadership in Administration.* New York: Harper & Row, 1957.

Wegener, C. *Liberal Education and the Modern University.* Chicago: University of Chicago Press, 1978.

NINE

~~~~~~

Facing Up to Crucial Problems and Issues

Almost any issue can be crucial for someone, although in the broader perspective of institutional concerns it may appear to be insignificant. For example, whether or not an individual gets promoted or receives tenure at a certain time may be a crucial issue for the individual, and the dissatisfaction of the person not promoted may require many hours of time on the part of those who have to deal with the appeal. Although it is, in one sense, crucial that the appeal procedure be effectively handled and display full regard for the concerns of the individual, as well as recognition of the obligation to maintain equity for the faculty and quality within the institution, the issue itself can hardly be regarded as a crucial one for administrators or for the institution as a whole. However, appeal to the courts and judicial reversal of an institutional tenure, promotion, or salary decision does become crucial by questioning institutional integrity and threatening its autonomy.

Many of the concerns of importance to individuals and

units of the university have been discussed in other chapters. The point of this chapter is to try to identify a few major recurring issues that call for clarity and consistency in analysis and resolution. Each embraces a multiplicity of specifics, and the number and range of variables require that judgments be rendered rather than a rule applied.

Institutional Mission

One major recurring concern in the university is that of its mission, purpose, and scope. Even where these have been stated by a board or coordinating commission, there remains considerable ambiguity within that statement, and administrators at all levels are likely to be recurringly confronted with suggestions or requests, both internal and external, to provide new courses, services, or programs that are not obviously consistent with the institutional mission, level, and scope. Since such additions constitute one of the prime ways in which an individual gains some recognition from colleagues and from external agencies or individuals who support the program, one can expect, no matter how clear a mission statement may be, that new programs will be proposed. In fact, that is as it should be. One of the worst things an institution can do is to let a formal statement of mission and program operate as a straitjacket to prevent any additions or significant modifications. The university must keep up to date with changing social, economic, and technological requirements. Much of this renovation can be done by revising existing programs and course offerings. However, the tendency in the past years of expanding institutions and increasing budgets has been to add new levels and programs. So much of the human resources and dollars available has been assigned to program expansion that program revision to achieve quality or maintain currency has been overlooked. In these circumstances, it is a major administrative responsibility to keep before faculty the joint considerations that, although there are limitations on the range of programs that the institution can provide, there is a need to review existing programs to seek improvement and increased relevance and to reinforce and strengthen these programs with closely related ones that are within the scope of the present institutional mission. Pursuance of this path offers the opportunity to generate continuing discussion about institutional obligations based upon a firm understanding of social needs and the availability of resources. Such discussion should emphasize that, within the limits of its mission, the institution has both the autonomy and the responsibility to look for ways to improve performance and make it more relevant to changing external demands. Institutional missions themselves are subject to change to utilize changing institutional capability and social needs.

Balance in Institutional Purposes

The original American college emphasized the instruction of undergraduates. Later, an idea imported from Germany led to the creation of a number of institutions whose major emphasis was on research. With the advent of the land-grant institutions, public service became a major focus of every institution of higher education, although small liberal arts colleges, private universities, and major public service institutions differ markedly in the nature and amount of their public service. It is tempting to talk about the balance and harmony among the three major functions (instruction, research, and service) of the institution, but there are, in fact, no good criteria to determine just what this balance is or should be. There is ample evidence that the balance varies greatly from one institution to another, depending upon the clientele and fund sources. Yet it is equally obvious, in reviewing the history of federal support of research in the last twenty years, that sudden infusion of large sums of money can bring about an imbalance in an institution that threatens the quality of other programs—usually the undergraduate instructional programs. Faculty members who are involved in and enjoy some limited amount of public service activity may also withdraw from it if they can find funds to support their own research. But even without the availability of additional funds specifically earmarked for research, new departmental chairpersons or deans may find ways to manipulate the budget and faculty loads in such manner as to increase the emphasis on research. This can be done by reducing teaching loads or increasing class size, or simply by making clear to a faculty that instructional time should be reduced to the minimum in order to focus on other more significant activity. Sensitive administrators at any level can detect these shifts by examining data on teaching load and class size or by being attentive when students complain that they are unable to find faculty members or to receive help outside of class. Faculty members who are not directly involved in research are likely to make their frustrations known when recommendations for promotion and salary increases emphasize these other factors. It is also quite possible that an imbalance will be found in respect to public service. In one instance, in a department that encouraged individuals to make themselves available for speeches around the state, persons vied with one another as to how many times they were able to give the same speech to different audiences.

The administrator also has to be sensitive to external comments and criticism with regard to the institutional emphases and particularly to any changes in them. It is inappropriate to impose a pattern in which essentially the same percentage of each faculty member's time is relegated to certain functions. Instruction, research, and public service activities, as well as some involvement in governance of the institution, can be very well interrelated by some professors to the benefit of their scholarly efforts and that of their students. It behooves administrators at all levels within an institution to be sensitive to this balance, to discuss it with the faculty, particularly new appointees, and to scan such items of information as faculty load reports, section size, and faculty travel to determine whether, individually or collectively, that balance is shifting.

Balance in Educational Objectives

Most institutions have a statement of objectives representing the expectations of the faculty as to what the students will gain from their educational programs. Colleges and departments usually have similar statements, but with a great deal of variation from one to another. There is little point generally in detailed review of these objectives. The real issue with regard to the objectives is the specification of some appropriate balance among goals of personal development, social development, and intellectual growth. In addition, the means of attainment and the evaluation of success are crucial. Objectives are merely pious expressions of ideals, meaningless until programs for their attainment and evaluation are operative. At various times, institutions, colleges, departments, and even individual faculty members have tended to become obsessed with particular objectives to the point of placing undue emphasis on these while neglecting others. All disciplines and programs share these fads, but with profound differences in orientation. It would be difficult to imagine a department of mathematics so concerned with development of citizenship and socialization that it would markedly reduce the disciplinary content and the expected level of competency of students in mathematical thinking. If this were to happen, almost certainly there would be immediate repercussions from other areas that require mathematics of their students. In the social sciences and the humanities, however, concern by a few professors about the personal development and growth of self-realization in students can become so important that the substantive contributions are virtually eliminated. Marked increase in enrollments in certain courses or with particular instructors involves at least the suggestion that affect has driven out content. The resulting high grades attract at least as many indifferent students as students who seek and benefit from the affective emphasis.

I believe that the major emphasis of higher education should be on development of the intellect. I base this upon two convictions: (1) that affective development and value orientation are not learned by lectures or classroom discussions but are, rather, developed over time as one becomes sensitive to values and aware of the interrelationships among values, actions, and consequences; and (2) that the vast majority of college faculty members, while reasonably adequate scholars in their own particular disciplines, provide neither the models nor the know-how to grade the affective development of students. An experience in college over a period of time should and does have significant impact on a person's interests, values, and convictions. The college should attempt to make students consciously aware of the fact that this is happening, that the institution is concerned about it, but that ultimately the individual must take full responsibility for his or her values and character. Some professors and departments place their disciplinary emphasis ahead of individual interests and are unwilling to make what they consider compromises in their standards with regard to students whose interests and abilities are not in the discipline itself but rather in its applications and value implications. Such programs are as culpable as those that discard intellectual emphasis in favor of personality development. These professors, in their preoccupation with their disciplines, have abdicated their responsibilities as teachers. By their emphases, they encourage avoidance of the discipline by students, they endanger the personal development of students in their courses, and therefore they fail in their obligations to society.

The imbalance between acquiring knowledge, on the one hand, and the ability to use it, on the other, is an imbalance between theory and practice. This imbalance may show up in any of the three major functions of the institution: instruction, research, or service. The failure to deal with real problems is apt to become immediately apparent in the public service area, for the theoretician will hardly talk to individuals in terms of their specific problems, and he may not even pick the appropriate theories that relate to the problems at hand. In the classroom, unfortunately, students are, to a considerable extent, at the mercy of the instructor. There is a tendency across all areas of knowledge for some professors to feel that any approach to knowledge that involves ulterior purposes becomes essentially a technical educational experience rather than one of sound scientific or liberal education. In fact, this concern reveals two things. First, the professor is unaware or unwilling to admit that, in his own case, the knowledge of the discipline serves a very practical purpose by enabling him to earn his living as a teacher or researcher. Second, the professor has probably not had experience in applying his knowledge in the real world or he would have found that the experience of relating knowledge to reality added significantly to the understanding of its meaning and applicability. Faculty members, preoccupied with their own chores, are often not sensitive to these problems of curricular and instructional emphases across the campus. They are also chary of criticizing their fellows. Administrators are in a different role. They obtain reactions from students, parents, and others, and they should continually seek for evidence of an imbalance in emphasis on educational objectives in certain courses or departments. Maintaining or restoring balance here, as in connection with the functions of instruction, research, and public service, is not something accomplished by direction. Indeed, one might say, with considerable truth, that it is accomplished only by indirection. The administrator may appropriately put himself or herself on record with regard to these matters and may suggest to specific subadministrators that monitoring and regular review are needed. Various standing or ad hoc committees on these issues can be asked to look at the problem across a unit or within particular units. And, finally, with some support by policy statements from various sources, the reward system for faculty can incorporate statements that keep them aware that a balance in programs and in teaching emphases is regarded as important.

Changing Values

Much of the commitment to higher education has been based upon the valuing of knowledge—a belief that the more individuals know, the wiser the decision they *can* make. A strong pragmatic case can also be made for the worth of education in the development of technology and culture. Education, too, has been seen as the route to achievement of social status and economic security. In this country, we have vacillated over the years between commitment to institutions of higher education for the development of an elite upon whom major responsibilities would devolve for the governance and progress of the country, and a conviction that equity and equal opportunity require that almost everyone have opportunity for acquiring a baccalaureate degree. The development of the land-grant institutions in the latter part of the nineteenth century, and the community colleges in the twentieth, stemmed from this belief that education is advantageous to everyone as a means to a more satisfying life, more responsible citizenship, and increased self-satisfaction, and also contributes significantly to society.

Sociologists and others who have looked at pervasive value commitments in this country have suggested that there are certain continuing so-called national values embraced in the concepts of democracy, individualism, equality, and human perfectibility. This is an interesting set of concepts worthy of consideration. The term *democracy* implies that all individuals have the possibility of making some contribution to governance and to the character of society. The very concept of democracy implies that individual differences must be recognized and respected. Respect implies a certain sense of equality. Perhaps the most idealistic of the quarternity of concepts is that of human perfectibility. In question is whether this conception envisages an angelic perfection to which all individuals can progress, whether perfection involves some integration and unity in the total array of qualities and characteristics of each individual, or whether, indeed, perfectibility involves both individuals and society. It is no surprise that conceptions of these values have varied among individuals and over time and place. Those who have written about values in this context have identified a classic set of more specific values, a transitional set, and a current set which in itself is now perhaps transitional and to be replaced by something even more current arising out of the crises, national and international, of recent years. One of the so-called classic values was a belief in the work-success ethic—a belief that by hard work, coupled with integrity, success could be assured. The Horatio Alger stories were oversimplified contributions to this view, and their large sale at one time indicates the attraction that view held. The traditional value gradually replacing the work-success ethic and the individualistic drive to get ahead has been identified as sociability and emphasis on the mutual respect and interaction among people. An even more current conception has been that of social responsibility, evidenced by the fervent appeals and attempts of individuals and groups to impose upon society their own concepts of those restrictions and obligations that evidence social responsibility. Consistent with the work-success ethic, another classic value was a future-time orientation. Education, in particular, could be viewed as a necessary set of experiences for future success. In part, the future-time orientation was an outgrowth of the development of a new country and a conviction that each decade could see marked progress. It was also a reaction against emphasis on the past and on the acquiring of knowledge for its own sake. Yet, at the same time, it decried the emphasis upon education as an immediate benefit and emphasized deferred gratification. The transitional value growing out of this, however, placed emphasis upon the present. Individuals should see some immediate gain out of educational experiences and be able also to view them in relevance to issues of the present day. Yet this transitional value of presentism was still focused, to a considerable extent, on acquiring understanding rather than engaging in action. The next stage, particularly emphasized in the student activism of the late sixties, but to some extent continuing into the present day, is the demand that education not only deal in a relevant way with the issues of the day but also provide for, and even encourage, students and educational institutions to become involved in correcting social inequities immediately. This demand fails to recognize that an educational institution harbors many and differing views and that any organization dependent upon society for support deviates from prevalent majority views at the risk of losing respect and support.

The classic emphasis on the independence of individuals was related both to the work-success ethic and the self-sufficiency displayed by the western movement of the early pioneers. However, it has long been recognized that complete independence of individuals is an impossibility. Inevitably, independence asserted by some individuals causes the dependence of others. And so the transitional value was a move toward group conformity, which has moved again, in recent years, to a conception of a personal authenticity and the advent of various kinds of therapeutic, activist, and idealistic ventures in which the demand for personal authenticity becomes in itself a kind of group conformity.

The so-called puritan morality has been replaced by a moral relativism which has led gradually to the rejection of any generally accepted values or absolutes. As it becomes apparent that those who would stand for anything actually stand for nothing, there has been a resurgence of a demand for moral commitment.

It matters not so much whether the immediately preceding discussion is true or not. One can certainly make a case for these several value conceptions among certain groups of people at certain times. The issue of what proportion of the people at any particular time assent to a particular pattern of values and whether there is any natural sequence of development is relatively unimportant. The problem for the educational institution is that there are those who still believe in the work-success ethic, have a future-time orientation, have a strong belief in personal independence, and retain a commitment to puritan morality. In a society in which an increasing number of people seek immediate gratification and repudiate the values and patterns of the existing society, there are those who would impose their own value commitments by means which, in themselves, deny democracy. Problem solutions acceptable to all or even to a majority of persons are difficult to find. Within an institution of higher education, there exist among faculty members, students, administrators, and board members differing value commitments, all perhaps deriving from the same basic set of sacred national values and therefore giving rise to a belief on the part of each individual or group that theirs is indeed the right view. To a considerable extent, differences in these commitments are reflected among the disciplines. In the present day, they are also reflected among individuals and groups who have been denied equal opportunity and the advantages of higher education in the past and who therefore regard the institution itself as a conspirator in perpetuating inequity. Perhaps without intending to do so or recognizing the event, these same groups would turn the institutional resources and opportunities to the immediate advantage of themselves and their associates without regard for the special role of an educational institution in society.

The problem of inequity is a pervasive one that shows up in many ways. In one instance, pressures placed on one department to add immediately a minority representative in a special field resulted in the appointment of a young woman still working on her dissertation for a degree. Her work was in the particular field desired but was being done in a second-line university. When the department denied tenure several years later, on the grounds that the dissertation was still not complete and that the individual had not made the contributions expected in development of certain areas, the individual appealed. An outside investigating group heavily criticized the department for not extending to the individual appropriate help and for not reducing her load to permit completion of the degree. Clearly, there are a number of conflicting values in this situation. One may well wonder whether the insistence that the institution be used as a means of alleviating the disabilities and grievances of individuals and groups may not destroy the essential nature of the institution itself. Obviously, there is no easy answer to this difficulty. The answer does not lie in complying with all demands, even if this were possible, nor in denying them. The administrative role is a difficult one. It cannot assume that lower levels have balanced all the conflicts and resolved them in a satisfactory manner for individuals and the institution. It must be assumed, too, that various units in an institution will deal with situations in various ways. Some avoid difficulties by taking the easy route; others, committed to a hard line, may inflict inequities on individuals. The goal of the administrator should be to maintain scrutiny, review, and appropriate and adequate means within the institution to deal with these conflicts. To the extent that an institution of higher education finds itself forced into activities or decisions by interventions of courts or other governmental agencies, the institution makes evident to the public that it cannot operate itself on an equitable and effective basis. What can the institution, then, purport to offer either as an example to society or in the preparation of individuals for important roles in society that justifies the resources it claims?

Acceptable Alternatives

Individuals with strong value commitments, especially when they place one or two as preeminent over all others, are inclined to seek the best possible solution to any problem. If there exist a number of individuals or groups with somewhat different value priorities competing and even contradictory, several best solutions will be proposed. As pointed out in Chapter Four, however, the attempt to resolve a problem merely on the basis of finding an acceptable alternative may be no solution at all, either because it involves internal inconsistencies that make it ambiguous or noninterpretable in particular cases or because it has been pushed to such a high level of generalization that it provides no guidance whatsoever either to individuals who would perform responsibly or to those who have an obligation to observe and evaluate performance. For example, recurring discussions in institutions, and especially in some of the new ones founded in the last decade or so, have centered on the question of whether, and to what extent, rules regarding class attendance, grading, makeup of missed examinations, and the like should be imposed, or whether essentially complete freedom should be accorded to students without any formal grades to allow them the flexibility to pursue their own interests and to develop personal responsibility for their educational experience. There are many positions between these two extremes, and the inability to face up to and resolve the issues is very likely to lead to a situation in which each professor or department operates within its own frame of values, with the result that students are caught up in a series of inconsistent and frustrating educational experiences. Those individuals or departments that impose rigid requirements may actually detract from the significance of the educational experience in other courses that are more open and flexible. For this and other educational problems, there is no one best solution. If one intends to impose upon students patterns that force them to do their work each day, it may be that requiring the handing in of homework in each class or using the first ten or fifteen minutes for a brief quiz which is used to record a grade for the day would seem to be effective. But if one raises a question about developing pleasure and satisfaction in the acquisition of knowledge and encouraging personal responsibility for continuing one's education, that approach is quickly seen to be wanting. Nevertheless, the elimination of all requirements is certainly an invitation to pursue other interesting but less demanding and less valuable educational experiences. The ideal would be a pattern that imposes certain well-defined and fully interpreted requirements upon students but moves gradually to eliminate these as students demonstrate that they are able to take responsibility for their own education. Individuals who do not demonstrate that capacity would be terminated. Certainly this ought to be done in a professional school, but it is difficult to bring any faculty together to agree upon such a program and the specifics of how it will be interpreted and enforced. It will happen only if highly respected and competent administrators constantly remind both faculty and students that the interactions and significance of the entire program are an educational experience far more significant in its total impact than any of the separate courses. This goes further than merely seeking an acceptable solution. The solution must make sense and be practicable and functional in terms of the total educational program. Whether a proposed solution is workable depends largely upon how faculty and students respond. This, in turn, depends largely upon how rational and realistic the program is and how effectively it can be explained to students. Whether or not it is the best solution is of no concern so long as it works and achieves the goals specified initially. In fact, the workability of the solution depends on many other aspects of the program, and hence continuing review of the policies involved and of the other interacting phases of a program is essential. There are no best and no permanent solutions to any educational problem.

Class attendance is a recurring problem to which many solutions have been sought. I recall one institution in which all faculty members were required to report on attendance daily. An attendance officer and secretary collected all of these reports of absence and, when a student reached a certain number in any course or in total, he or she was called in for reprimand. An accumulation of a specified number of absences required deducting one credit from the student's total achieved at the end of a term. As might be expected, this did encourage class attendance, even in those cases in which instructor performance hardly justified it, but it also led to a variety of other practices.

A student who could not attend might arrange for somebody else to sit in his seat in a large lecture room. In fraternities, the freshman pledges were often delegated to fill the seats of full members. Since taking attendance in a large lecture would detract too much time from the lecture, student assistants were assigned to check attendance early so that individuals seated near the door could surreptitiously sneak out after attendance had been taken. Moving roll-taking to the latter part of the period permitted individuals to come into the class quite late and be certified as present. Despite the awareness of all of these subterfuges and the obvious indication that the rule was encouraging dishonesty, this policy continued for years. Many institutions can still find some residual practices within various educational units that really make no educational sense and, in many cases, encourage patterns of behavior contradictory to what higher education represents.

Productivity and Efficiency

One major problem in colleges and universities is what I have come to call the "add-on" syndrome. This syndrome is manifested by the creation of new units and the addition of new personnel to take care of a problem that usually is simply being inadequately handled by the existing staff. In some cases, these add-ons are forced by external demands. For example, special counseling for veterans and the expansion of financial aids, developmental programs, and equal opportunity offices all represent, in part, a forced response. Colleges add counseling staff because they find that faculty advising is poor. They add vocational counselors and expand the placement office because they find that the academic departments and their faculties are variously uninterested, incompetent, or indifferent in aiding students on such matters. Remedial services in writing, reading, speech, and arithmetic are commonplace, and courses or units devoted to helping students with study habits are widely found. Generally, the departments most vitally concerned lack either the interest or the ability to provide these services, so new units are created and special personnel hired. All too frequently, the mere existence of the unit, rather than evidence that it accomplishes the purposes in mind, leads to perpetuation of the unit even though it fails to solve the basic problems. Expenses increase, overall productivity falls, and the institution operates inefficiently. There are several basic problems here. First is the general ineffectiveness of developmental or remedial services isolated from the degree programs of an institution. Students permitted to enroll in courses find that most of their time must be spent with these courses if they are to get through them. Thus remedial work suffers. Second, it is difficult to maintain any interest in remedial work because it brings back vivid memories of bad educational experiences of earlier years. Often the immediate experience does not seem essentially relevant to what is required in credit courses. Third, it is also difficult to find teachers capable of arousing the motivation of students who have had prior educational deficiencies or difficulties. Perhaps the key problem, however, is that the departmental faculties take no responsibility for these deficiencies, comment negatively on them before students, and fail to teach their courses in such a way that the basic competencies involved are demanded for success in the courses.

The add-on syndrome frequently results in new units that are in themselves not effective. Their addition indicates an unwillingness within the institutional faculty to face up to their responsibility to the students admitted. Ultimately, the costs go up and the quality of education goes down as inadequately prepared students continue through the program. The integrity of the whole enterprise suffers. These add-on units are ineffective for several reasons. Their placement in an institution is often a handicap. They are not fully acceptable to either students or faculty. Frequently they attract inferior personnel. Neither the personnel involved nor the students find their efforts interrelated with and supported by the central academic units composing the institution. Even when departments or basic disciplinary units attempt to solve additional problems through institutes, centers, or special programs that are outside the existing structure, these add-ons invariably increase costs and destroy the unity of the institution. Furthermore, they may screen off most of the faculty from the realities that the institution and society face. This is not to say that such add-ons should not be permitted or that they serve no purpose. It is, however, probable that any approach to a significant problem that relieves the central faculty of an institution from making adaptations in their program and providing faculty to deal with it is likely to be ineffective.

Observation of many of these new units in various institutions around the country indicates several other problems that are apt to arise. Many such units are initiated with outside support; but, in time, the institution must take over these enterprises if they are to continue. The units themselves seek inclusion in the general fund budget of the institution, and each unit, in order to establish itself within the structure of the institution, attempts to take on additional academic obligations. For a time, individuals involved in these service units may be willing to teach courses elsewhere in the university to provide an academic connection for themselves. Eventually, they are likely to wish to give credit for their own remedial courses or teach a few courses of their own and take on some graduate students or provide a group of courses for an undergraduate emphasis. And as this develops, each such unit wants to control its own appointments, provide tenure, and take on all of the advantageous aspects of the departmental-college-academic connections. It would be unwise to rule out the possibility of any units outside of the traditional academic structures. However, the purpose of these units should be clear, their charter should be for a definite span of time, and the scheduled reviews should take into account not only what the unit does but also how it fits into and contributes to the total program of the institution. In justifying the continuance of such units, the benefits accruing to the institution should be weighed against the financial obligations incurred. In many cases, once the area of a special unit has been charted, its activities can be instated into the traditional structure and carried on with greater advantage than as separate items.

Power and Conflict

It is unfortunate in an educational institution if its administrators feel that the ideal situation is accord and complete unanimity. The goal of the democratic society is not to achieve unanimity and consequent uniformity but rather to develop and share a few common convictions that provide the binding for the society and, beyond that, to allow, and even encourage, a great deal of individuality. The college and university, as the educational institutions training people for participation in such a society, may be expected to, and indeed should, reflect that aspiration. A dedication to seeking the truth and a recognition that research is never completed represent the major common commitments of the institution of higher education. Administrators should insist on, and should themselves set the example for, that continuing research and likewise for full revelation of the truth as it is known at a moment in time. Over my years in institutional research, I have found numerous individuals who, for one reason or another, modified data for public consumption and refused, until confronted with threats of replacement, to provide facts on the programs they operated. Evaluators in institutions of higher education frequently find that criticism is rejected, that convictions rather than facts are the basis for continuing program operation, and that this stance reflects the desire to retain program control, resist change, and provide security. Like other people, academics tend to become committed to a particular belief or pattern of operation and resist evaluation and consideration of alternatives. To secure themselves from intrusion into their units, academics are hesitant about criticizing other units—at least in public. Those who hold the power are generally chary of using it to force critical review or to insist upon full accountability. Too many administrators refuse to acknowledge the existence of problems and paint a rosy picture hoping to convince themselves and others that everything is in excellent order. Other administrators recognize the problems, are willing to generate considerable discussion about them, but refuse to take a position on their resolution. In short, they resist decision making because they full well know that any decision will be unacceptable to some individuals. My own conviction is that administrators should seek for issues and for conflicts around these issues. They should recognize conflicts that already are in the open, and they should make clear to students, faculty, and the public that this is the expected state of affairs in a university in a pluralistic society. The constant search to expand knowledge and to provide better insights and solutions to social problems generates concerns in those satisfied with the status quo. The problem of the university is to find effective ways to cope with conflict and to demonstrate how to use power and authority in achieving resolutions of conflict or in setting up some pattern of exploration or experimentation that ultimately may produce evidence favoring one or more alternatives over others. Indeed, the essential process of acquiring, organizing, and interpreting knowledge generates a series of conflicts among scholars who come up with varying and inconsistent sets of data and equally varying and contradictory interpretations. The search for truth is a continuing conflict and its presence and its resolution are essential aspects of an institution's operation.

Crisis Management

A crisis has different meanings for different people in relationship to the importance of certain issues or the values that they hold. A truly serious crisis is one that threatens to destroy the essential nature of an institution or to end it. Many of the crisis situations in institutions that one reads about today have to do with falling enrollment, increasing costs, and consequent budget deficits. These crises bring demands for more careful academic planning and more rigorous budgeting. They require review of selection, appointment, and promotion of faculty, administrators, and service staff. They call for reexamination of priorities and possible elimination, among other things, of the clutter of add-ons, as discussed earlier. They involve, above everything else, a search for additional funds. Many elements of the current crisis situation were predictable. Some years ago, studies made at Michigan State University on the in-

creasing proportion of faculty on tenure, on program proliferation, and on enrollment and fund sources predicted difficulties
ahead and called for some plans to deal with them. This was
true in many other institutions, but there is a great reluctance
to change policies on the basis of warnings. The American Association of University Professors produced voluminous materials
pointing to the horrors involved in placing any limit on the percentage of professors on tenure. Yet ultimately, this has become
a necessity in many situations simply because, once a department has reached 100 percent on tenure, only retirements or
deaths can provide any remedy.

At various times, universities in the state of Michigan
have faced demands from the legislature that have been regarded as infringements on the autonomy of institutions and
have been taken to court. These were considered crisis situations and were, I think, to some extent, deliberately misinterpreted. In my reading of legislative and executive demands for
certain kinds of information and for controls over various aspects of the institution's operation, I found little more than a
statement of doubts as to whether correct information was
being provided and as to whether the institutions were effectively managing their operations in reference to providing quality education to the people of Michigan. In every such case that
I have seen in this state and elsewhere, there has been ample reason for expression of such doubts. A forthright response on
the part of the universities would have been to examine in detail
the internal operations of the institution and produce evidence
which certainly, in part, would have justified the voiced suspicions and demands. There is and there has been a crisis with regard to the autonomy of institutions, but not, as the institutions often suggest, because of unjustified intervention into
internal affairs. Rather, the crisis exists because institutions do
not demonstrate responsibility and thereby do not justify the
expectation of a high degree of autonomy in operation.

Many of the crises of institutions are of their own making. I was involved as a consultant in one institution that had
long been doing a respected job with a sound two-year program.
A new administrator understandably wished to make his mark

by moving the institution to a baccalaureate degree. The problem of enrollment in relationship to the number of majors involved in most programs was pointed out and, after lengthy discussion, a very economical and high-quality program was built for the last two years, with about two thirds of this as a required core. The program was well taught by the existing faculty, and my own interviews with the students involved indicated a high degree of satisfaction. However, the enrollment grew and new faculty were hired, with the requirement of a Ph.D. being imposed, and these individuals soon convinced some students that they ought to have majors in various fields. A new dean was imported who had neither understanding of nor respect for the kind of integrated program provided and who moved immediately to a departmental pattern with majors. The college had other problems too, but this attempt to move from the initial financially and educationally sound program into the traditional pattern of specialization had predictable consequences which, in considerable part, invoked some of the other problems. The college very nearly disappeared but has managed to survive several successive crises.

Despite the fact that many undesirable contingencies can be foreseen, changing demands for education, inflation, and other factors can bring to institutions crises that are not of their own making. My own observation is that few administrators who have been at an institution over a period of time with no serious problems can adjust to a crisis situation. Unwilling to recognize the development in its earlier stages, they are also incapable of dealing with it when it bursts into full bloom. Thus it is commonplace for new administrators to be brought in to manage crises. It is futile to expect that faculty members will come up with any solution, although they should be provided with a reasonable opportunity to do so. But an institution that is already in the red and losing students cannot afford to have faculty committees sitting around for months arguing about what is to be done. And one may be certain that they are not going to accept the rigorous actions necessary in eliminating programs, positions, and some fringe and luxury activities. Many faculty members are inclined to feel that there are funds hidden someplace unknown to them, that the total funds involved in administrative activities are excessive and could be markedly reduced, or that alumni, donors, and others could be roused to bring adequate support to the institution if only the administrators would do something about it. In general, faculty fail to realize the difficulties involved in fund raising, particularly in circumstances where funds are needed for operations rather than to erect monuments bearing the giver's name. There is a generally unfavorable reaction to support of a losing cause when reasonably healthy enterprises are asking for the same money to develop new activities bringing mutually beneficial recognition to the institution and the donor.

Perhaps the greatest difficulty in crisis management is to identify the one, two, or three most significant matters upon which energies must be concentrated. Increasing enrollment is likely to be one of these; and it may be very tempting to grab at some program—such as establishing classes for adults, initiating second-rate degree programs on military bases which will bring in considerable money to the institution, or launching other activities calculated to solve the immediate fund shortage —whether or not these ventures have any relationship to the essential character of the institution and will maintain its quality and reputation. Administrators geared to demonstrating their capability in assuring survival of the institution are all too likely to engage in dubious activities that threaten to destroy what they tried to save. Another difficulty in crisis management is that, once the major problems needing intensive attention have been identified, the very first sign of reversal may generate such a spirit of optimism on the part of the faculty, administration, and board that old habits are immediately reinstituted. I have seen several institutions that faced up to a difficult financial situation and then greeted an increase in enrollment in the next year as evidence that the problems were all resolved. Crises other than cataclysmic events, such as fires, tornados, and the like, do not descend upon an institution in one year, and they are not going to be corrected in one year. Even allowing three to four years for resolution of the crisis, patterns of management will have to be instituted and maintained that will ensure a balanced budget and continuing cooperation.

Much of the difficulty in crisis situations results from poor communication. Misstatements are made and correct statements are misinterpreted. Off-the-cuff statements made on the spur of the moment frequently convey something very different than intended. Thus individuals end up with greatly varying views of the issues, the factors involved, and the reasonable alternatives. When confidence and security are disturbed and mutual trust has disappeared, the restoration of completely open, forthright, and honest communication is likely to be the most crucial issue. Indeed, most crisis situations in colleges and universities result, in some part, from failure in some aspect of communication. Information has been ignored, misinterpreted, or held back from those who might have acted upon it.

Some Suggestions for Further Reading

Hostrop, R. W. *Managing Education for Results.* Homewood, Ill.: ETC Publications, 1973.

Lahti, R. E. *Innovative College Management: Implementing Proven Organizational Practice.* San Francisco: Jossey-Bass, 1973.

Mayhew, L. B. *Surviving the Eighties: Strategies and Procedures for Solving Fiscal and Enrollment Problems.* San Francisco: Jossey-Bass, 1979.

Palola, E. G., Lehmann, T., and Bleschke, W. R. *Higher Education by Design: The Sociology of Planning.* Berkeley: Center for Research and Development in Higher Education, University of California, 1970.

Palola, E. G., and Padgett, W. *Planning for Self Renewal: A New Approach to Planned Organizational Change.* Berkeley: Center for Research and Development in Higher Education, University of California, 1971.

Richman, B. M., and Farmer, R. N. *Leadership, Goals, and Power in Higher Education: A Contingency and Open-Systems Approach to Effective Management.* San Francisco: Jossey-Bass, 1974.

Rogers, E., and Shoemaker, F. F. *Communication of Innovations.* (2nd ed.) New York: Free Press, 1971.

TEN

~~~~~~

Evaluating Administrative Performance

The primary problem in evaluating administrators in higher education is defining administration. The related terms *leadership* and *management* provide some clues. Leadership has been characterized as knowing where to go, whereas management has been characterized as knowing how to get there. Leadership involves identifying and specifying goals; it tends to be idealistic, qualitative, and charismatic in nature. Leadership also tends to be unique; only one person at a time exercises the primary leadership in any particular activity. In contrast to leadership, management is directed to the achievement of goals, using analytical, quantitative, and pragmatic approaches. Generally, it is assumed that management is better defined than administration and that effective managers can be produced and exported.

Note: This chapter is a revised version of Paul L. Dressel, *Handbook of Academic Evaluation* (San Francisco: Jossey-Bass, 1976), chap. 16. It is included here because of its immediate relevance to higher education administration.

Management, being more objective and quantitative in nature than leadership, is more readily evaluated, and its efficiency and effectiveness are more easily demonstrated. These distinctions are of limited value in higher education, for it is not clear whether administration is leadership, management, or both.

Richman and Farmer (1974, pp. 13-16) assign to management such functions as decision making, creative problem solving, formulation of goals and priorities, reallocation of resources, negotiation, resolution of conflicts, dynamic or active leadership, diplomacy, statesmanship, and external relations. Administration, in contrast, is (by them) associated with routine decision making, implementation of goals, priorities, and strategies devised by others, and monitoring, direction, and control of internal operations. Administration is viewed as more adaptive, passive, and reactive than management.

These distinctions and the more passive roles assigned to administration certainly coincide with the preferences of many faculty members. But they also point directly to much of what is wrong with higher education. Both effective leadership and management are lacking within institutions, partly because of faculty independence and partly because boards and external coordinating or control agencies are making decisions, in the guise of policy statements, that gradually become so detailed that they allow no room for local interpretation or variance.

The terminology of administration in higher education cannot be equated with the terms used in business. In many large business enterprises in the United States, for example, the chairman of the board is the top executive officer of the organization, with the president second in line. In many corporations too, most of the board members are executives associated with the enterprise. The route of advancement goes through several echelons of associated or owned companies and ranks, with the culminating position being the board chairmanship. The chairman attends primarily to large policy issues, and the president is chief of operations. In contrast, the chairman of the board in higher education, unless he or she has unusual personal qualities and wields power and influence by virtue of other responsibilities, has only a symbolic role. Indeed, he or she may not even preside over board meetings, this task being reserved, in some cases, for the president as the chief executive officer of the institution. The president is appointed by the board and serves at the pleasure of the board. The president's powers and authority are delegated by the board, and such power and authority as are exercised by others within the university are informally extended (not formally delegated) by the board through the president to those individuals. Yet the major chores of higher education institutions are performed by faculty members who, to a much greater extent than the workers in a business, are autonomous both in what they do and how they do it. Some faculty members argue that the faculty is the university and that the faculty delegates certain prerogatives to the administrator largely to save faculty time for more important matters.

A second problem in evaluating administrators in higher education is delineating the power of administrators. In most cases, there are local boards for single institutions. There may also be a board for each of several groups of institutions (systems), and possibly another statewide coordinating or control board across all systems. Obviously, the role of an administrator is delimited by the nature of this hierarchy. There are chief executives on campus, executives of one sort or another at each of the system levels, and executives at the top of the system. In Wisconsin (as in several other states), there is a single comprehensive state system of higher education, with one board over all institutions, a chief executive officer designated as president, and a staff consisting of vice-presidents and other aides in a central office. Chancellor, a title used in some states for the chief executive of the state system, designates the chief officer on campus.

Assigned responsibilities and power differ from one system to another. Campus executives have somewhat different amounts and kinds of authority, depending upon the nature of the institution and system in which they operate. System boards and local boards (which may be wholly advisory) have varying relationships to system and campus officers. On a campus, one finds beyond the presidents (or chancellors), vice-presidents, provosts, deans, directors, department chairpersons, and sundry other titled associates and assistants. Some of these administrators have line relationships: president, vice-president for academic affairs, deans, and chairpersons. Others, such as graduate deans, vice-presidents for research, and deans of undergraduate instruction, have functional responsibilities that cut horizontally across the line relationships. In a single state system in which the central office has second-line administrators charged with academic programs, with research, and with graduate education, administrators on each campus assigned to these areas operate under policies determined by the central office rather than by the chancellor. The life of a chief administrator on a campus when there are one or more levels of administration above is sometimes devoted to seeking those points at which he or she has authority or influence. Obviously, the evaluation of an administrative organization presents problems different from those associated with the evaluation of a specific administrator, but the evaluation of the administrator should relate to the particular functions assigned and the authority delegated to fulfill them.

The power and autonomy of administrators are limited by the many constituencies they have to satisfy. Not only the president but a dean of a college (agriculture or engineering, for example) or even a department chairperson may find that administrators at higher levels have to be satisfied and that other constituencies, including legislators and administrators of state and federal units, have an interest in what they do. Direct contact with foundations and the federal government by administrators and faculty members of various units may be important. With these various constituencies, many decisions in an institution—including adding programs, eliminating programs, putting a ceiling on enrollment in a major, or even hiring or firing a faculty member—can become issues of major proportions. In these circumstances, the sources of authority, power, and influence are multiple, and they exist both within and outside the institution. The internal and external contacts of some professors may be so potent that any action or decision they find unacceptable is reviewed and possibly negated or altered. Increasingly, students take an active interest in decisions made within an institution. They occasionally make major attempts to influence policy on what would usually be minor matters, such as where certain supplies are purchased or in what companies the funds of the institution are invested. In almost all universities, power and authority are vested in a board of trustees, but influential legislators can exert more power through their influence on appropriations than can members of the board. Power and authority on a university campus, no matter how clearly delegated, are effective only when acceptable to those at whom they are directed.

Every educational institution has a statement of purposes. It may have a self-devised or an assigned institutional role in the region or area. Each institution also probably has one or more statements of objectives that purport to describe the expected results of the activities in the educational programs. But within a university, many programs exist, varying from liberal education to technical and semiprofessional programs at the undergraduate level; from discipline based to highly practical graduate professional degrees; from research, both pure and applied, to a variety of service programs. Thus there are differences in objectives, in the values sought, and especially in the priorities attached to them. Moreover, academics do not particularly prize agreement. Indeed, they thrive on differences and sometimes on distinctions that make no difference; they are inclined to analyze and to engage in dialogue to gain even a slight modification of policies. Administrators with definitive educational philosophies find that attempts to promote their views arouse strong opposition from sectors of the campus holding contrasting points of view, especially if they appear to be intervening in matters regarded as faculty prerogatives. In state systems, each institution is usually assigned a role that determines or emerges from a statement of purposes, mission, and scope. Such limitations become a definite hazard for the administrator. If he does not try to get approval for new programs desired by the faculty, he loses their regard. If he tries and fails, he gains nothing with the faculty and may have jeopardized relations with the state coordinating agent. The individual who wins several rounds threatens the system balance and is likely to move or be moved to other pastures.

A third problem in evaluating higher education administration is that there are no clear and generally accepted criteria of success. Every administrator and faculty member talks about quality. Every institution, according to its own descriptions, provides high-quality programs. Lacking either locally or generally acceptable criteria of success, each institution and program lays claim to excellence, and the great rallying cry in opposing a reduction in financial support is that such reduction will erode quality. Quality is always threatened, but never destroyed, by financial reductions—at least in official publications. It is also true (though never publicly admitted) that the quality of undergraduate programs has at times been undermined by financial increments that have permitted institutions to embark upon graduate and research programs. The inability to measure quality seldom bothers faculty members, who are convinced that they know what it is and that they are engaged in producing it. The administrator who would propose changes to improve quality is venturing at once on sacred ground and into quicksand, for the suggestion of the need for improvement implies less than fully acceptable quality.

A fourth problem for evaluators of higher education administration is that administrators often purposely communicate in ambiguous ways. Administrators at every level deal with several different constituencies, and the communications addressed to one are often carefully contrived to appeal to that particular group. In higher education, as elsewhere, the tendency is to tell people what someone thinks they want to hear or ought to believe rather than the truth. And, of course, some events and conditions in any university cannot and should not be publicized. It is also a curious characteristic of the university, which contains a collection of more highly educated people than any other social institution, that the problems of communication are complicated by the tendency of some individuals to withhold information as a means to power, while an excessive stream of communication by others clogs the channels and is ignored. Communications also tend to be misinterpreted and overinterpreted because of ambiguity in the original phrasing or because the academic mind is always looking for undercurrents, hidden motivations, and implications. Professors who avoid involvement in committee work want to know what problems are being discussed and what points of view are being promoted along with the associated rationale before decisions are made. When they hear only of the decisions, they feel put upon. But if students and faculty are to be informed of all the discussions and invited to assist in policy formulation, communication breaks down, discussions proceed without conclusions, and decisions that ultimately emerge are so long delayed that their significance is buried under the preceding torrent of words and papers. Even then, some individualistic professors do not feel bound by the actions of their colleagues. The democratically inclined administrator can reap a harvest of ill will, both internally and externally, by attempting to enforce policies developed by faculty committees and approved by a majority of those appearing at a senate or faculty meeting. General, vague, and ambiguous communication is thus used to preserve a semblance of administration performance without risking confrontation.

Organizational Patterns

The evaluation of administrative effectiveness must be based, to some extent, upon the organizational model that characterizes a particular institution. Several models have been developed for or applied to institutions of higher education; none fully applies to any one institution.

The Weberian bureaucratic model involves a hierarchical or ladderlike structure in which commands or orders move from top to bottom and are carried out at each level by individuals with delegated authority operating in well-defined jurisdictions or areas of responsibility. In this ladderlike (or scalar) structure, each individual is ranked or graded with respect to every other individual. The importance of the functions and of the responsibilities assigned to individuals presumably corresponds to their authority. The activities of individuals at various levels in the bureaucracy are both prescribed and limited by the authority delegated. The decentralization of authority within defined limits would seem to promote both efficiency and effectiveness.

However, many issues or problems requiring action do not fit neatly within a level and may even fall in several of the parallel vertical hierarchies that arise out of specialization of function. The bureaucratic structure often handles such matters ineffectively because no one person dares assume the authority for a decision and no one wishes to compromise or denigrate his or her own authority by negotiation with others. Such items rest long on desks, occasionally being shunted from one to another with no noticeable progress. Functional operations also cut across the several hierarchies at various levels. A graduate school dean, for example, without either faculty or budget, must attempt to coordinate, monitor, or review graduate programs across academic units, research programs, perhaps residence halls, and other units where graduate students may be employed. Research coordinators have similar problems, although separately identifiable research funds may enhance their authority. Coordinating groups collected around offices at various levels may become large and develop specializations that further obscure the hierarchical bureaucratic structure.

Viewed from a psychological or social psychological perspective, the bureaucratic structure tends to be ineffective because of its negative impacts upon individuals (whether within the structure or thwarted by it) and their attempts to resist passively or retaliate actively. In a university, where what might seem to be the lowest echelon in the bureaucracy—the faculty—is made up of highly self-directed individuals engaging in a wide range of specialized functions, the negative impact of the bureaucratic model on individuals is its greatest defect. From a human relations perspective, the needs of each individual for self-actualization and a measure of success are not met by a bureaucracy. Personal values and aspirations are sacrificed. Interpersonal relations and group interactions arouse tensions that destroy morale and decrease productivity. Conflict, whether caused by personalities or principles, tends to become accentuated by jealousies bred by concern about preservation of bureaucratic prerogatives. The human relations approach to alleviation of these difficulties gives primary consideration to "human values." The hope is that conflict will be reduced or eliminated, mutual trust and confidence created, and the needs of individuals integrated with those of the organization. Authority and responsibility would be shared. It is further expected that tensions would be reduced, each individual would experience satisfaction and psychological success, morale would be raised, and productivity increased. The preferred means for the achievement of this utopia are the removal of social and personal blocks to effective communication and the improvement of interpersonal relationships through sensitivity training, counseling, group therapy, use of expert consultants, and information feedback.

The importance of human relations cannot be questioned. Unfortunately, there is virtually no evidence that this approach is effective in increasing overall productivity—a fact that does not seem to concern those who enthusiastically support the human relations approach. It is not even certain that human relations would be improved, for some people cannot tolerate the approach (regarding it as both devious and artificial) and some react adversely to it. Furthermore, universities are not supported by society to the end that each person employed within the institution find personal fulfillment. The institutions have responsibilities to meet, and, without proposing that self-sacrifice for the good of the university and of society is the ideal, I think it still conceivable that many individual needs would be met and group conflicts lessened if the common social goals and obligations were enumerated and a unified effort made to achieve them. The administrative task in higher education is perhaps less that of encouraging the already rampant individuality and more that of enlisting that individuality in group and institutional efforts to meet institutional responsibilities.

Thus, neither the bureaucratic nor the human relations model applies to colleges and universities, although each contributes insights into some of the problems of governance. In essence, neither of these models applies because the major work of the institution is performed by faculty members who, individually and collectively in departments and colleges, possess task capabilities greatly exceeding the capabilities (both in performance and judgment) of persons in administrative positions.

And whereas in industry the research, development, production, sales, and service functions are clearly separate, in the university the departments and colleges and even individual professors carry out the equivalent of all of these. In addition, they have external professional careers and a role in institutional governance unparalleled in any other enterprise. Given this situation, there is and will be a diversity of goals and values. In many cases, the primary issue is not how to achieve goals but how to select among them or order them in a reasonable way in reference to available resources. This ordering must be done in such manner as to achieve acceptance by those responsible for accomplishing the goals.

The collegiality model, in its ideal sense, engages faculty and administration (though seldom students, board members, nonacademic staff, or the public) in rational dialogue to specify and clarify goals and the means of achieving them. This model has long been attractive, although it is no longer realistic in large institutions. In fact, it was seldom found even in the smaller but less heterogeneous institutions of an earlier era. The educational institution is both an instrument and a victim of social change. External pressures from various publics and internal pressures from students and special-interest groups have destroyed the applicability of the collegiality model. Were resources ample, as they have been in a few institutions, or were the various subunits financially self-sufficient, as a few are in some private institutions, then the benevolent-anarchy concept of organization, in which each sector of the university pursues its own interests almost divorced from other sectors or central administrators, might apply. In either the collegiality or anarchical model, the faculty plays a dominant role, and administrators are viewed more as facilitators or perhaps as managers who assist in carrying out policies and attaining specified goals agreed upon by the several faculties of the discrete colleges and departments. This view tends, when carefully analyzed, to end up close to the human relations emphasis—maximizing the satisfactions of the work force with no assurance, and with justified doubts as demonstrated by past history, that the faculty will fully recognize the social responsibilities of the institution.

If we turn from maximizing human values for those who

serve an institution to maximizing values for those served by the institution, then we must place primary concern on goal achievement by an institution rather than solely on its internal processes. In focusing on goal achievement, we recognize that, both internally and externally, the university has been heavily and rightfully criticized for placing its own development and that of its faculty ahead of its responsibilities to its students and to society. Accordingly, the institution itself requires at least alteration and renovation or innovation, if not a complete restructuring and revitalization. The erratic, competitive, and opportunistic development of institutions, based upon conceptions of excellence achieved by involvement in graduate programs and research, demonstrates that change governed by social responsibility must come from careful planning in which all views and needs (external as well as internal) are expressed and reconciled. Change is thus a political process in which conflicting views are to be expected. Power blocks and special-interest groups seek to advance their own values and goals, arguing either that these are best for everyone or that the fullest development of the institution requires that each unit be encouraged and supported to achieve its own goals. This contention is obviously not valid when resources are limited. They always are limited and there is always competition for them.

In this context, too, administrative authority is hampered by political pressures, bargaining, delaying tactics, and appeals to power sources outside the institution. External groups are invoked as a means of influencing internal policies and decisions. Decisions become negotiated compromises that fully satisfy no one and may even be inconsistent with announced institutional goals. Policy formulation, rather than policy execution, becomes the critical concern, and therefore the focus, of debate and conflict. The resulting compromises may also be so loaded with ambiguity as to be unenforceable. Moreover, those sectors of the faculty who lose in a compromise may not feel obligated to conform. Even though budget allocations are manipulated to enforce conformance, the impact may be negated by indifferent performance. In this circumstance, leaders who seek to define and implement large-scale organizational change consistent with stated values and goals must seek strategies and utilize persuasive powers to gain acceptance of new policies, rather·than simply exercise authority.

Administration in higher education cannot be an exercise of power. Within the university, many diverse groups, units, and individuals have access to board members, the legislature, and the public. The usual trappings of power in the form of coercion, penalties, rewards, and incentives are thus weakened. Furthermore, exercise of such powers is discouraged by the faculty who stand on principle even when to others the principle seems self-serving. Status and assigned authority go for naught if orders are neither acceptable to nor accepted by those to whom they are given. Prestige based on admiration, esteem, and respect or influence resulting from personal qualities, recognized expertise, or example becomes potent if possessed and wisely used by an administrator.

Even so, compromise (distasteful though it is to some) may become the only route to change. Compromise appears in various forms. One form gives to each of the contending elements something it dearly prizes. There is no consensus, no attempt to reach unanimity on issues. There is only recognition that every group gained something (if only the elimination of a sentence or paragraph), though not all it sought. In rapidly developing institutions during the 1950s and 1960s, many presidents were able to introduce innovations disliked by most of the faculty simply because the president, by increasing the stature of the institution, raising the salary scale, and bringing in graduate and research programs, provided so much that faculty members wanted that they were disinclined to oppose other changes that the president proposed. In a second form of compromise, sweeping changes are proposed that affect all and are bitterly opposed by many. Here the changes may be whittled down to a minimum acceptable to a majority, and consensus may be achieved only because some support the compromise to eliminate the controversy. Seldom does such compromise result in any major change. In a third form of compromise, protracted negotiations result in a give-and-take process of redefinition and refinement. This process may, in fact, end in a stronger and more rational alteration than was originally contemplated. Subtle continued pressure for change and further negotiation may move the initial compromise even further in a desirable direction.

The preceding discussion of governance patterns, policy formulation, and change is brief and therefore necessarily faulty in many respects. Nonetheless, it serves the present purpose, which is simply to indicate that effective administration in an educational institution is a complex task unlike administration in business or the military. The evaluation of administrators must, therefore, take into account the peculiar character of higher education governance, the specific nature of the particular institution, and the external pressures bearing on it.

Criteria of Administrative Performance

As Cohen and March (1974, chap. 4) suggest, not long ago the criteria for presidential (and institutional) success were relatively few, although not all were readily attainable. Primary among these criteria were continuing growth in programs, resources, students, faculty, salaries, and facilities; recognized high quality in students, faculty, and programs; a balanced budget; and respect exhibited for the president by the students, faculty, board, and community. If to this list could be added low teaching load, relatively fast promotions, early tenure, and strong support of research, both president and the institution were clearly successful and so regarded by the various university clienteles. In brief, if the goals and priorities of the university were achieved to an adequate degree and if the institution continued to grow in programs and resources, both internal and external clienteles tended to be satisfied. Success was obvious to all.

Upon closer examination, it is apparent that many of these criteria of success were much more the results of a particular period and the general American commitment to growth than of the qualities of presidential leadership. To be sure, the opportunities for growth and for funding had to be seized by an administrator, but they were there to be seized, and even the inactive, paper-shuffling, desk-tending administrator could probably point to the increased budget, enrollment, faculty, courses, and facilities over his term of office. The present and foreseeable future appear to require other criteria. Under current circumstances, job security (with or without tenure) has become one of the major criteria affecting morale and the faculty appraisal of administrative performance.

Criteria indicative of unsatisfactory administrative performance today are of two types. The first includes unfortunate attitudes or sheer incompetence on the part of the administrator. The second is reflected in the tendency to ignore or bypass the administrator. The academic vice-president and department chairpersons may tacitly agree to ignore an inept dean; even a president can become a figurehead. Some examples of poor attitudes on the part of an administrator are: expects a strong personal loyalty and support; cannot or will not tolerate lengthy discussion or dissent regarding his or her own ideas or extended controversy over any issue; ignores or bypasses others without clearance or explanation; depends overly much on the advice of a few immediate associates; basks in praise and does not differentiate between the university and himself or herself in accepting it; blames others for errors or weaknesses; does not encourage or assist able individuals to advance themselves either within the institution or by moving to another one. Such traits reflect a highly self-oriented approach to administration that arouses distrust and opposition. Sheer incompetence is reflected in inept actions and decisions or in absence of any actions or decisions.

The following are also signals of ineffective administration: overinvolvement of the board; inadequate or incorrect information; dissent and opposition in the institution; numerous complaints and criticisms from external sources; frequent and serious crises regarding both important and inconsequential issues; ambiguity, uncertainty, and confusion about rules, policies, and needed actions or decisions; conflicting statements or views issued to the press. These events and situations tend to characterize an administrator who avoids and attempts to cover up differences and controversies rather than face and resolve them.

Good administration is much more than an absence of negatives, however, and a more constructive positive approach is required. The concerns of presidents of universities extend to every aspect of operations, for they are ultimately responsible to the board for all of them. Moreover, their administrative staffs, the faculty, students, and the public, when contacting them regarding important issues, expect them to be knowledgeable and responsive. Yet the total range of operations certainly exceeds any one individual's cognizance or expertise, including, as it does, students, nonacademic employees, faculty members, board members, alumni, legislators, federal agency personnel, influential public figures, athletics, academic policies, programs and standards, graduate and undergraduate education, professional schools, extension, adult education, building and plant construction and maintenance, budget, management of financial resources, investment policy, and fund raising. Trust in and dependence upon associates are therefore essential characteristics of the administrator.

The composite of the desirable characteristics listed by various writers as essential for administrators, if seriously applied, would eliminate the species. These include: approachable, articulate, attractive (in appearance and personality), charismatic, confident, considerate, decisive, deliberate, emphatic, fair, firm, flexible, imaginative, persuasive, rational, reliable, sensitive, self-assured, sympathetic, tactful, and tolerant. In addition to this profusion of adjectives, such phrases as sense of humility, concern for quality, awareness and acknowledgment of personal and institutional weaknesses, inspires confidence, listens attentively, and morale builder appear repeatedly. An equally extensive list of roles and functions includes such diverse items as mediator, buffer, catalyst, unifier, synchronizer, synthesizer, and ameliorator of human conflicts. Designations involving a more active developmental role include: educational leader, both within and without the institution; promoter of change and adaptation; interpreter and spokesman for the institution; policy and goal formulator; enforcer of rules, standards, and policies; coordinator; organizer; and manager. Every list also notes the importance attached to the effectiveness and impressiveness of the manner in which the president presides over meetings.

The faculty tend to regard administration as a task too mean or routine to be undertaken by a scholar, yet they are also convinced that only a scholar can understand and serve scholars. Hence the requirements of an earned doctorate, service as a faculty member, and evidence of creative and published scholarship are usually added by faculty search committees. One such committee in a major university specified "no prior administrative experience" as a means of ensuring that a new academic vice-president would be faculty oriented. Minority and female members of a search committee will surely demand either evidence of accomplishment in hiring such personnel or promises of immediate action.

Former presidents and observers of administrators are also effusive in offering advice and providing specific injunctions to administrators. These, too, are diverse and easier to state than to heed. They include: develop and use the administrative and managerial talents of subordinates; delegate, support, and praise subordinates; avoid overreliance on immediate staff or associates who usually reflect presidential preconceptions; avoid favoritism, intimacies, and obligations or covert agreements; maintain distance, objectivity, and perspective on problems and controversies unless intervention is necessary; avoid confusion of office with self, and personal goals with institutional goals; listen attentively to (but do not necessarily accept and follow) advice and criticism from both supporters and antagonists; admit error and subsequently alter decisions and policies; operate by principle rather than by personality and assume that the opposition does the same (at least until otherwise demonstrated); maintain balance in attention to finance, the public, alumni, facilities, general administration, and academic programs; work to develop and maintain effective two-way communication internally and externally.

A broad inclusive definition of the president's role might run as follows: The president exercises overall leadership and direction, combining the interests, capabilities, and efforts of a diverse and sometimes discordant constituency and achieving a commitment by all individuals and groups to a set of general objectives for the institution without stifling individual or group fulfillment. This role requires defining, articulating, putting into operation, and coordinating goals and priorities that are acceptable, relevant, realistic, and attainable. With minor adaptation, this definition can also apply to vice-presidents, deans, and chairpersons.

This statement reads reasonably well but hides or obscures the points or areas of difficulty and conflict that have been noted by many writers on administration. A new president or administrator at any level has the choice of accepting and adapting to existing patterns and people or undertaking to alter one or both. Since a new administrator cannot quickly make a name by adopting the habits, goals, policies, and prejudices of predecessors, some changes are to be expected. Some changes that alter patterns of predecessors may be welcomed, but changes that tend to remake an institution in the new administrator's image may be resisted by a faculty that is generally conservative and dislikes change. Past practices have come to have moral legitimacy, even though procedural and instrumental values have actually displaced or replaced goals that embody the ultimate values to which the institution is committed. Deeply embedded contradictions and conflicts become sanctified by time, so that there is often a community consensus based upon a seeming, though misleading, unity of commitment to a set of goals and objectives that are variously ignored or so interpreted in practice as to justify whatever each individual and unit desires to do. Even when faculty members are receptive to discussion of change, their diversity in interests and the uncertainties and threats implied by change—combined with a faculty tendency to debate endlessly, edit and reedit in detail, and leave sufficient ambiguity for exercise of personal judgment—do not augur well for the speedy change required if an administrator is to receive credit.

The administrator must not avoid making needed changes simply because of faculty conservatism or recalcitrance. The noise made by a few does not necessarily express the views of the silent majority. The administrator may have accepted an obligation to make changes in the negotiations leading to appointment or may have become convinced that the changes are essential to institutional survival. It is also possible that the administrator's proposals for change have more to do with personal goals (survival, income, prestige, reputation, power, advancement) than with the good of the institution. Faculty members frequently, and with good reason, so suspect. Many individuals and groups, including the president and board members, tend— overtly or covertly, consciously or unconsciously—to divert the institution toward social revolution or to the support of personal or group ends, however disparate or inappropriate these may be. Even the revitalization and adaptation of an institution, which may involve less of radical change and more of recommitment to its traditional goals and program revision consistent with the current scene, evoke opposition because these moves question the worth of some practices and programs by suggesting the need for alteration or replacement. Redefinition of institutional identity can also evoke storms. Usually, such redefinition requires reexamination of a statement that has long existed and been ignored but is assumed to sanctify the status quo. Suggested changes are minutely scrutinized to read implications not intended and to arouse opposition based upon such implications.

Finally, administrators must be able to handle publicity. In approving publicity releases, in making personal statements, and in responding to questions, administrators must be aware that both friends and adversaries read or listen for words or phrases that challenge or can be interpreted as challenging the values or interests of some group. In addition, administrators who continually seek publicity for themselves rather than for their universities and colleagues soon evoke distrust and suspicion. Sensitive use of publicity can rally both internal and external support for needed change. Overuse of it can arouse opposition and encourage other institutions to mount competitive campaigns.

Reasons for Evaluation

Evaluation of the effectiveness of individual administrators must take into account numerous factors idiosyncratic to the institution (its traditions, goals, and priorities), the defined responsibilities and obligations of the office, the circumstances and conditions under which the administrator was hired, the expectations and views of the several constituencies that the institution depends upon or serves, and the administrator's perceptions of his or her tasks and responsibilities and of the goals of the institution. The focus of analysis here is on the office of a campus chief executive but can be readily adjusted to other administrators by taking into account factors unique to each level.

The goals and priorities of the administrator and of various constituencies do not necessarily coincide. Student demands only occasionally deal with basic educational issues or with fundamental policy matters. Faculty members give priority to their own welfare, security, and benefits, and, beyond that, to research, graduate instruction, and undergraduate instruction in that order. The federal government holds professional and graduate education and research as its primary concerns, whereas state government is more concerned with undergraduate education and the job market, except in such high-priority fields as medicine and law. Business and industry seek graduates in applied fields and also have some interest in practical research and in public service. Thus the administrator is caught in a difficult situation. Only in a period of rapid growth, when demands for new programs can be met or are deferred only temporarily, is there any prospect of receiving approbation from everyone. And only under these conditions do the administrator's goals and those of the various constituencies fully coincide.

When enrollment and resources are stable or decreasing, new programs and even continued employment of all personnel must be bought by eliminating or cutting back existing activities, some of which are surely cherished by some faculty members, alumni, board members, and others. At this point, voices never heard and never in accord before rise in righteous wrath and cast aspersions on the intelligence, motivations, and social responsibility of the decision maker. Even legislators or board members calling for reductions in spending join the cause. Administrators find that not only what they do (or attempt to do) but also how they approach the task is important. Moreover, those faculty members who insist upon participating in decisions when increments are available seldom participate in or accept responsibility for cutbacks or eliminations. The faculty ideal of administrators as facilitators of their efforts no longer applies. In fact, administrators who undertake program elimination rather than a general across-the-board cut may destroy themselves whether they succeed or fail in this intent.

A policy of evaluation of administrators at stated intervals for feedback and improvement is therefore essential; such a policy avoids the association of a demand for evaluation with crisis situations. This evaluation should be a joint review in which the administrator is deciding whether he or she desires to continue and others are deciding whether the administrator should do so. Once such a policy is instituted, each evaluation must cover the following points: (1) goal achievement—how the administrator's goals are developed and expressed, the affective and procedural aspects of his or her attempts to acquire support for or to achieve these goals, the extent of success in acquiring support for and achieving goals, the appropriateness of the goals; (2) personal characteristics as perceived by various individuals and groups both above and below in the administrative hierarchy; (3) the charge or the assigned tasks when the administrator assumed the position (some situations such as "sick" departments may require extreme measures and a high-handed approach); (4) the administrator's own perceptions and personal evaluation of the success of his or her efforts; (5) the approach of the administrator to decision making; (6) the extent to which the options and procedures of the administrator are limited by traditions, regulations, or lack of support from superiors in the hierarchy; (7) recognition that vastly different views of administration exist—some administrators do things efficiently, some simply get things done, some enable others to get things done, and some do only what others tell them to do.

Evaluators must recognize that their judgments may be based on erroneous assumptions, faulty or limited information, inappropriate goals or values, and emotion more than wisdom. Reliably assessed perceptions of people are still perceptions; they are not reality. Both the evaluator and the evaluated must be cognizant of this possibility and weigh it in recommending action or alteration. Accordingly, an evaluation of an administrator may lead to the conclusion that, because of faulty communication, what otherwise might be effective administration is generally misunderstood. Correction may involve both an evaluation of the evaluators and the development of an improved public relations and communication system.

Approaches to Evaluation

The evaluation of an administrator can involve several kinds of evidence. The development and use of objective and descriptive rating scales to which individuals react by checking an appropriate characterization are attractive to those who are oriented to statistics and norms. But norms here are virtually meaningless. An administrator, whatever the assignment, is unique, and his or her effectiveness or ineffectiveness depends on personal traits and capabilities and institutional characteristics. Unless reports of typical incidents that have given rise to a rater's reaction are included, the ratings are of no use in suggesting improvement.

There are several distinctive approaches to evaluation of administrators, although they correspond closely to those used for evaluation of faculty members or of any other position. The one most commonly used upon retirements, awards ceremonies, or death emphasizes outcomes. Typically, in the past, these litanies have noted greater growth in budget, students, faculty, programs, or facilities. Just what can replace these in the future is uncertain. Perhaps maintaining a balanced budget, increasing endowment funds, remodeling or replacement of buildings, and achieving a stable enrollment may be the most that can be hoped for. Claims to improvement of institutional reputation or programs are attractive but difficult to demonstrate for other than initially weak institutions.

Subjective appraisal of an administrator by various individuals and groups through procedures similar to those used by students in appraising instruction are useful if combined with other more objective evidence. Instruments for this purpose may focus on judgments of the administrator's accomplishments, as noted earlier, on personal traits such as trustworthiness, openness, approachability, ability to resolve problems, and sensitivity to individuals' concerns, or on the presence or absence of particular behaviors such as "confers with all concerned before taking action on an issue." Continuing self-evaluation is demonstrated by the administrators who follow up on decisions to determine their impacts and make decisions when necessary.

A complete evaluation of any administrator should include appraisals by both superior and subordinate administrators, students, nonacademic personnel, and individuals or units on or off campus with which the administrator or those within his or her area of responsibility must frequently interact or cooperate.

The procedures and the content of the evaluation should be shared with the person being evaluated in advance and somewhat modified, if needed, to achieve relevance and acceptance. Presentation and interpretation of the results should be made to the individual evaluated by a person acceptable to the administrator, but not a superior or subordinate. If the results are to be used in making a decision about the administrator, those responsible for the decision should first hear a similar presentation and interpretation.

Those who serve under an administrator are reasonably concerned that criticism can bring retribution if confidentiality is not assured, so the manner in which appraisals are collected and handled is critical. Interviews conducted by outside, unbiased evaluators or by senior professors or professors emeriti of unimpeachable integrity will evoke comments and specifics never obtained through checklists or written communications. The interviewers, in turn, should convey the substance of their findings informally to the administrator in oral form and later in written form. Following the initial oral statement and discussion with the individual, a discussion with the administrator's superior is desirable, with both the administrator and the evaluator present and actively involved. Copies of the final report should be given to the administrator and to his or her superior.

A brief feedback report to those participating in the evaluation is desirable so that they do not feel their comments have been ignored or covered up.

Evaluation of the president of an institution should be conducted by the board annually and quietly, with a senior member of the board interviewing each board member. The senior member can then summarize and present the views expressed to an executive session of the board, including the president but no other officers of the institution. At intervals of two or three years, a more penetrating evaluation should be made in which the views of other administrators, alumni, faculty members, students, and representatives of the general public are sought. This elaborate review of the president is more complicated than reviews of other administrators simply because of the extended constituency to which the president is visible. The president, with board support, will do well to initiate and sponsor the internal review through the checklist or interview format so that it is evident that his or her performance and judgments are not being secretly undermined by board probing. External reactions should probably be sought only from a few persons of integrity who have broad perceptions of the administrator's activities. These interviews can best be arranged by the board chairperson and conducted by a board member or a designated individual assigned to conduct the evaluation. Such reviews can and usually should be constructive experiences. More important, they can avoid the distasteful and disruptive confrontations that ensue when a crisis has arisen and differences have become deeply emotional and irresolvable.

Evaluation of the Board

A board that engages in evaluation of the president should also be willing to undergo evaluation. A president may engage in such evaluation in general terms by pointing to instances in which board actions or statements by individual board members have interfered with the president's own effectiveness. A board, however, should consider employment of an outside consultant of stature to sit in on a sequence of board meetings as an observer; to talk privately with individual board members, with administrative officers, and others as desirable; and ultimately to present to the board in executive session an appraisal of effectiveness and of the perceptions of others as to how they carry out their responsibilities.

The responsibilities of boards include the following: (1) selection, recurrent evaluation, and retention or termination of the president; (2) financial support and management; (3) public relations; (4) clarification of institutional purposes and goals and evaluation of success in achieving them; (5) awareness of conflicting views and probable consequences of action; (6) evaluation of board performance.

The following are criteria for evaluators of boards: (1) existence and quality of statements regarding the legal, social, moral, and educational responsibilities of the institution; (2) effective board membership and individual performance—selection of new members, attendance (individually and collectively), board size and frequency of meeting, participation and preparation of individuals, diversity in background and outlook and utilization of such diversity in discussions and assignments, levels of trustee knowledge (institution, higher education trends, social changes and needs), committee system (appropriateness and functioning), continuity and change; (3) recurrent delineation of major tasks to be accomplished—agenda and adherence to it, reasons for delays, maintenance of distinction between policies and specifics; (4) dynamics of discussions and decision making—leadership by chairperson, participation and roles of members, adequacy of background materials and analysis, participation of president and other administrators, extent of consensus in decisions, use of open meetings and closed briefing or discussion sessions, morale and achievement; (5) relation of board and of individual board members with various groups—president, faculty, students, special-interest groups, specific units (colleges, departments), external groups; (6) acceptability of board actions—to dissenting members, to internal institutional groups, to external groups.

As institutions differ markedly in the makeup and functioning of their boards, the preceding list and the particular procedures used need to be adapted to the local scene.

Summary

Administrators may be effective in a quiet, unobtrusive way that is neither obvious nor reportable. But they cannot expect to receive credit for that which is unknown. They can adopt a posture of austere, dignified noninvolvement, but when the institution is faced with serious problems, this posture cannot last. The alternative is active involvement in defining problems, goals, and alternatives, in seeking support for sound solutions, and in delineating and enforcing them. Administrators who are actively involved need to know how others are reacting to their efforts and how others perceive their accomplishments.

Many universities have caretakers and paper shufflers in the positions of deans and department chairpersons, for, under a rotation scheme, the wise chairperson or dean does not alienate those with whom he or she must shortly bed down again. This trend and the narrowing range of presidential influence require that the top level of administration in higher education be evaluated regularly and thoroughly. If effective performance and assumption of responsibility can be demonstrated, the tendency to reduce institutional autonomy may be stayed, and administration at all levels may be restored to an acknowledged stature that will again make possible innovation and leadership.

I have not undertaken in this chapter to specify any forms, checklists, or items for evaluation of an administrator. I have, however, presented an extensive range of traits, characteristics, and procedures that enter into such an evaluation. The criteria for board evaluation include numerous items that apply also in the evaluation of administration. It is my conviction that effective evaluation must start with a sensitive definition of what is to be evaluated relative to the scene of operation and the persons involved. And the administrator should have some input at this stage, for an evaluation that does not deal directly with his or her concerns will not be as well accepted or as helpful as it could be.

Suggestions for Further Reading

Dibden, A. J. (Ed.). *The Academic Deanship in American Colleges and Universities.* Carbondale: Southern Illinois University Press, 1968.

Dodds, H. W. *The Academic President—Educator or Caretaker?* New York: McGraw-Hill, 1962.

Dressel, P. L. *Handbook of Academic Evaluation: Assessing Institutional Effectiveness, Student Progress, and Professional Performance for Decision Making in Higher Education.* San Francisco: Jossey-Bass, 1976.

Irwin, J. T. (Ed.). *A Guide to Professional Development Opportunities for College and University Administrators.* Washington, D.C.: Academy for Educational Development and American Council on Education, 1975.

Kauffman, J. F. *The Selection of College and University Presidents.* Washington, D.C.: Association of American Colleges, 1974.

Millett, J. D. *The Multiple Roles of College and University Presidents.* Washington, D.C.: American Council on Education, 1976.

Salmen, S. *Duties of Administrators in Higher Education.* New York: Macmillan, 1971.

Stogdill, R. M. *Handbook of Leadership.* New York: Free Press, 1974.

RESOURCE A

~~~~~~

An Administrator's Bookshelf

In this volume, I have concentrated on presenting problems and issues and on identifying the values involved in them. I have largely avoided specific references but have suggested resources for further reading at the end of each chapter. The extensive volume bibliography also provides a wide range of works that enlarge upon topics discussed in the various chapters, as well as upon aspects of higher education largely ignored in those chapters.

I have listed few journal articles because these are usually difficult to locate and the essence of these articles is often included in works that are more easily placed and located on bookshelves at arm's length. There are, of course, some current materials that administrators will do well to follow. Over its relatively brief history, *Change Magazine* has dealt, in one way or another, with many of the major issues in American higher education. Its character may change under a recent change in publisher but, for the moment, it is worthwhile reading for every administrator. The *Chronicle of Higher Education* is a tabloid newspaper type of publication that also provides an up-to-date commentary on events both within higher education and in agencies or society generally that affect it. Both *Change* and the *Chronicle* provide lists of new publications and useful reviews of them. The *Chronicle* also provides an extensive list of vacancies. A nervous administrator may do well to scan these regularly and occasionally urge a friend to submit his or her name. Incidentally, I suspect that no aspect of higher education is more conducive to fabrication than the writing of a letter of recommendation for a grossly ineffective administrator. I attribute to this situation the many cases in which demonstrated incompetence is rewarded by promotion to higher administrative echelons.

Resource B immediately following lists a number of terms and concepts peculiar to the fields of administration and management. Some of these terms are discussed in the chapters, and the suggestions for further reading at the end of these chapters provide opportunity for further explanation. The volumes by Hostrop (1973) and Lahti (1973) are especially appropriate for exploration of this terminology.

It is important that the administrator have at hand certain resources that he or she can and will regularly use—an administrator's bookshelf, so to speak. Before making specific suggestions in regard to this bookshelf, I wish to enlarge upon the range of resources available to administrators.

One resource of administrators as they approach the responsibilities of their office is their own field of expertise. It is perhaps inevitable that an individual who has been educated in a particular discipline or who has had a number of years of experience in an activity or position, whether or not directly related to higher education, will explore the interrelationships between prior knowledge and experiences and those immediate to the new responsibilities. On the whole, this is appropriate, but an individual must exercise caution in how quickly and extensively the terminology of past experience is utilized in communication with faculty members and other institutional personnel. I recall one individual who announced within a few days of assuming a presidency that he would require a complete cost benefit analysis to be made before approaching the formulation of a budget request for the next year. For the faculty as a whole, this was an alarming statement; for those who knew something about the complications of higher education and the unsuccessful attempts to apply cost benefit analysis, the announcement was a clear indication of the administrator's lack of understanding of cost benefit analysis and of the complications of defining benefits in higher education. A lawyer president who uses legal terminology, whether in anticipation of appeal to the courts or to impress the students, faculty, and other employed personnel of the institution, may exhibit his ignorance of academic convictions and values and perhaps threaten or enrage the institutional staff by appearing to base personnel decisions on values foreign to the academic world. Apart from the personal field of expertise, there are individuals who repeatedly use words or phrases that grate harshly on academics. For example, the word *efficiency* goes over well with legislators and the general public, but the administrator who uses it in campus communications must realize that it has various connotations, most of which are resented in a college or university. Furthermore, the administrator who uses this word, if pressed for an exact meaning in the context of college and university operations, may find that he or she does not, in truth, know what it is. Every administrator should have immediately at hand on his desk or bookshelf an unabridged dictionary and a copy of Roget's *Thesaurus*. One who has not regularly used such resources will be surprised to find the range of meanings attached to some words and will, perhaps for the first time, acquire an insight into why administrative remarks, whether oral or written, are so often misconstrued.

The library also furnishes an extensive set of resources for the administrator. In a number of institutional accreditation visits, by specific question or otherwise, librarians have reported upon the extent to which they have dealt with administrative requests for assistance in preparing speeches, documents for distribution on campus, or articles, periodicals, and books having relevance to institutional or personal matters of interest to the administrator. Incidentally, the administrator who requests such assistance provides thereby some assurance to the librarian that the service is respected. Further respect for the service is evidenced when administrators promptly return materials forwarded by the library rather than retaining them interminably on their desks or personal bookshelves.

The administrator so fortunate as to have one or more aides, assistants, or administrative fellows should not hesitate to involve these individuals in bibliographical exploration or in interviewing or otherwise contacting individuals on and off campus who can provide insight into the nature of a problem. The appropriate activity and experience for such individuals is not always simply to sit in on a range of meetings or to read the extensive materials circulating on campus. Deliberations on issues require some prior preparation and should lead to further exploration. Anyone working in an administrative office in any role who comes to understand this will soon learn that problems are always more complicated than they seem to some persons and that hasty solutions only create more problems.

Faculty members have specific areas of expertise that, unfortunately, often tend to go unrecognized on a campus. I have known a number of professors, highly regarded as consultants on various types of problems by other institutions and by business and industry, who were ignored on their own campuses. This is not an uncommon story. It results, I surmise, from the fact that the strictly academic faculty regard individuals whose fields of expertise are practical as suspect. Their views are not regarded as representative of those appropriate to academe. Administrators, in turn, seem to hesitate to move outside of the constituted committee structure to request help from specific individuals or departments. Clearly, an administrator needs to exercise some caution in the extent to which he or she makes requests of specific individuals by taking into account both the characteristics of those individuals and the regard accorded them by other members of the faculty. Those persons who would attempt to use the administrative contact and confidence to their own ends should obviously be avoided. Furthermore, requests for assistance from individuals or departments or other units on a campus should be phrased so that they ask for help in clarifying the nature of a problem, the range of possible solutions, and the value implications of these, both on and off campus. When it is made evident that a specific recommendation or solution is not being solicited, the request will be seen as a search for insight and information and will encourage the individuals or units involved to educate themselves in the nature and extent of the problem rather than to become proponents of a solution. Offices of institutional research furnish special resources in this regard. In some cases, faculty publications already available will have relevance to a particular problem. The administrator seeking some way to show regard for publication should not overlook the fact that specific references to a faculty member's publication and particular points in it that are relevant to a current issue constitute more meaningful recognition than a note of commendation or an annual report of faculty publications.

Another way to get useful reactions from individuals, committees, or task forces is to forward an article or book requesting comments on the worth of the ideas therein and on the extent to which current practices and policies in the institution reflect or should reflect the points of view or values presented. A major consideration in directing materials to individuals in this way is that the accompanying communication should not imply that the administrator himself fully accepts the point of view presented or is attempting to curry support of it. The same approach is possible with members of the board, provided that the board chairperson is aware of and accepts the practice and that individual board members understand that the administrator (usually the president, in this case) is neither currying favor with a particular board member nor seeking to advance an idea that he or she wishes the board to approve.

There are numerous handbooks and source books available to the administrator who desires to have on a nearby bookshelf a ready reference that will quickly present the major issues and concepts of a particular aspect of the institution. All of the works discussed here are listed in the bibliography. The volume by Angell, Kelly, and Associates (1977) deals with many aspects of the negotiations and contracts involved in the bargaining process. The president and other academic administrators may not be (perhaps should not be) directly involved in the bargaining but, in one way or another, administrators do need to exert leadership. The volume by the American Alumni Council (1972) on educational fund raising, the report of the AAUP/ AAC Commission on Academic Tenure (1973), and the volume by King (1980) on benefit plans in higher education represent useful resource books. The handbook by Rowland (1977) provides an overview of fund raising, alumni relations, government relations, and publications as they relate to institutional management and advancement.

In the present day, many administrators are much concerned about and perhaps even extensively involved with enrollment matters. The source book by Willingham (1973) provides a guide to literature and information on access to higher education. Ihlanfeldt's (1980) volume on enrollments and tuition revenues, which emphasizes a marketing approach, should prove useful.

The two volumes by Smith and Karlesky (1980) deal with the state of academic research. Dressel (1976) provides an overview of the place and problems of evaluation in academic institutions. The Carnegie Commission on Higher Education has been responsible for the issuance of many books and reports on various aspects of higher education. The volume on governance (1973) discusses six priority problems in governance of higher education in the present day. Volumes on other aspects of higher education concerns include: Kaplin (1980), an overview of the law operative in affirmative action, collective bargaining, faculty tenure, and student loans; Delworth, Hanson, and Associates (1980), a handbook for student services personnel; and Wolotkievicz (1980), a handbook for administrators. All of these will provide useful insights.

The administrator who is strongly interested in innovative curricular and instructional practices will find many volumes dealing with innovation, but a reading of Levine (1980), which discusses some of the factors involved in the failure of innovation, may warn the administrator that changing policies or practices is unlikely to be effective if enthusiasm and acceptance are not forthcoming. The volume by Dressel (1980a) on evaluating and improving degree programs will be helpful.

The Knowles *Handbook of College and University Administration* (1970), in two volumes, provides insightful and thought-provoking essays on practically every aspect of operation of institutions of higher education. The issues presented in these essays are likely to be relevant for many years, although the particular practices and suggestions or recommendations may not be timely as circumstances change. The ten-volume *Encyclopedia of Education,* edited by Deighton (1971), and the ten-volume *International Encyclopedia of Higher Education,* edited by Knowles (1977), constitute two additional resources containing numerous articles on many facets of higher education and often with extensive further references.

The research reports of the ERIC Clearinghouse on Higher Education, available through the American Association for Higher Education, present relatively brief but generally useful overviews of the research and implications on a variety of higher education problems. For example, the reports of the years 1979 and 1980 include, among other topics: academic advising, evaluation and development of administrators, accreditation, and budgeting. The many publications of the National Center for Higher Education Management Systems (NCHEMS) cover in detail such matters as academic and program planning, institutional self-assessment, faculty evaluation, data collection and utilization, and student retention.

Obviously, the list of possible items for the administrator's bookshelf could be vastly expanded. Each administrator will have or develop special interests that will be reflected in the number of items acquired and used. Surely the shelf will expand over time. Yet I would prefer to see an administrator who regularly consults the resources listed here than one who attempts to develop a comprehensive library including many materials that remain unread and that have no impact on his or her thinking.

RESOURCE B

~~~~~~

Terms Used in Administration and Management

Accountability: Responsibility for achieving specified and measurable objectives by economical and justifiable use of resources.

Administration: Direction, organization, and execution of functions and activities, especially when purposes and objectives are imprecise or somewhat ambiguous.

Algorithm: A rule or procedure specifying the steps and their sequence for solving a problem.

Bureaucratic Model: A relatively authoritarian model based upon hierarchies and specific procedures, rules, and regulations.

Closed System: A self-contained and deterministic system primarily applicable to mechanistic situations. A bureaucracy tends to be a closed system.

Note: More detailed definitions of these terms are found in many sources. See, for example, R. W. Hostrop, *Managing Education for Results* (Homewood, Ill.: ETC Publications, 1973) and B. M. Richman and R. N. Farmer, *Leadership, Goals, and Power in Higher Education* (San Francisco: Jossey-Bass, 1974).

Collegial Model of Governance: A model based upon the notion of a collegium or utopian community of scholars which favors full participation in decision making, especially by the faculty.

Contingency Theory: A theory that the appropriate pattern of an organization is contingent upon the nature of the work to be done and upon the particular needs of the people involved.

Control: A procedure for enforcing administrative decisions and policies, used when there are indications that an action or order has been initiated that will violate policy.

Cost Accounting: A method of accounting used to establish the costs of the several elements or components of an activity or operation.

Cost Benefit Analysis: A process of examining and comparing alternative courses of action with respect to the cost in resources and the benefits attained.

Critical Path Method (CPM): An activity-oriented network representing relationships and durations of tasks of a project, used to plan, schedule, and execute the project efficiently. See *Program Evaluation and Review Technique.*

Cybernetics: A field of technology involving the comparative study of information-handling machines and the human nervous system in order to improve communication.

Decision Theory: See *Operations Research.*

Delphi Technique: A method of assessing group opinion through responses of individuals to successive questionnaires that collect ideas about goals and objectives, ranking and establishing the degree of consensus about them.

Efficiency: The achieving of objectives with the optimal combination of time, costs, and quality.

Feedback: Procedures built into a system that provide information comparing the actual performance with the planned performance.

Flow Chart: A pictorial description of a plan showing the interrelationships (network) of all required events.

Functions: The activities or processes developed to achieve basic purposes.

Game Theory: A simulation of competitive processes with established rules of play, mathematically determined strategies, a specified number of players, and stated end conditions with associated payoffs.

Heuristic Programming: A technique that utilizes guidelines or rules of thumb to limit the number of choices that must be evaluated, thereby simulating the human problem-solving process.

Information Theory: A mathematical theory or mode relating to the efficiency in transmission of information through a communications channel.

Input: Information fed into a computer or similar system. Administrative organizations are input-oriented organizations. Input organizations cannot demonstrate accountability because the structure militates against measurement of results.

Leadership: See *Management.*

Linear Programming: A set of procedures for optimizing objectives, profits, costs, or other measures of effectiveness in multi-variable problems in which the variables are subject to restraints.

Management: Planning, administration, and leadership involving decisions as to the most effective expenditure of manpower facilities, materials, and funds needed to achieve goals and objectives.

Management by Directives: A theory (bureaucratic in implications) that views the average person as lacking in ambition, disliking work, and avoiding responsibility.

Management-by-Exception (MBE): A procedure that alerts those "who need to know" when expectancies are not reached or are exceeded by a specified amount.

Management-by-Objectives (MBO): A systematic way of thinking about management that emphasizes the demonstrable, measurable achievement of goals.

Management-by-Participation: A theory (democratic in implications) that assumes that motivation, development potential, willingness to assume responsibility, and readiness to direct behavior toward organizational goals are present in everyone.

Management Information System (MIS): A system that provides management with timely and organized information needed for decisions.

Management Science: See *Operations Research.*

Mathematical Model: A model that characterizes a process, object, or concept in terms of mathematics, permitting relatively simple manipulation of variables to determine the results of a process, object, or concept in different situations.

Monte Carlo Method: A method based upon sampling methods to predict behavior such as course selections that will be made by students.

Objectives: See *Delphi Technique, Efficiency, Optimization, PERT, PPBS, System, Systems Approach.*

Open System: A dynamic system with multiple goals, involving individuals, constituencies, subunits, and subsystems having different values and objectives.

Operations Information: Information required for payroll, financial transactions, student records, and other clerical operations.

Operations Research (OR): The use of analytic methods adopted from mathematics, including such techniques as linear programming, probability theory, information theory, game theory, and Monte Carlo method, to provide management with a logical basis for making sound predictions and decisions.

Optimization: Strategy to maximize or optimize attainment of objectives.

Organized Anarchy: A system (or lack of it) characterized by ambiguity in purpose and goals, vacillation in participation, and inability to learn from experience, and hence lacking in clear measures of success and in accountability.

Output: Work done or amount produced by a person, computer, etc. Output-oriented systems require precise ranges of measures or defined results permitting demonstration of accountability.

PERT: See *Program Evaluation and Review Technique.*

Planning-Programming-Budgeting-System (PPBS): A method for costing program goals and objectives. PPBS focuses on the interrelations of goals and objectives, whereas PERT focuses on organization of steps and accomplishment of subobjectives.

Political Model: An open systems model (largely developed by Baldridge) that accepts conflict among competing internal and external groups and power blocks, focusing on goal setting and values and assuming that most decisions are negotiated compromises among these groups.

Priorities: Decisions regarding the relative importance of certain purposes, outcomes, and operations, indicative of the sequence in which the amounts of resources are assigned.

Program Budgeting: Preparation of a budget that reflects present and future costs of programs necessary to attain objectives.

Program Evaluation and Review Technique (PERT): A method used to organize, schedule, and evaluate progress of a complex project.

Programming: A method of optimizing goals by defining environmental factors, resource availability, and an appropriate choice of strategy among alternatives.

Purposes: Those general ends that justify the creation or existence of an institution, program, or specific functions.

Queuing Theory: A theory that deals particularly, though not exclusively, with people waiting in line and with minimizing the total costs of waiting and processing.

Simulation: The study of real problems or systems by use of analogous models based upon role playing, computer methods, or mathematical models.

Situation Theory: A unifying and somewhat eclectic theory of management that uses the best management principles known for specific situations rather than applying a single theory to all.

Statistical Decision: A decision based upon estimates of the probability of a particular sample or observed event. Alternatively, using Bayes Theorem (inverse probability), a decision as to the probable cause or circumstances generating an observed event.

System: An assemblage of components so designed and organized as to achieve a specified goal objective.

Systems Approach: A rational procedure for designing a system to attain specific objectives, including specification of objectives, definition of alternative approaches, selection of approaches, and development of a system and evaluation of its effectiveness.

Trade-Off: The weighing of alternative approaches to attain an objective, with the intent of selecting the "best" alternative on the basis of specified criteria.

Bibliography

AAUP/AAC Commission on Academic Tenure. *Faculty Tenure: A Report and Recommendations.* San Francisco: Jossey-Bass, 1973.

American Alumni Council. *Educational Fund Raising Manual.* Washington, D.C.: American Alumni Council, 1972.

Angell, G. W., Kelly, E. P., Jr., and Associates. *Handbook of Faculty Bargaining: Asserting Administrative Leadership for Institutional Progress by Preparing for Bargaining, Negotiating, and Administering Contracts, and Improving the Bargaining Process.* San Francisco: Jossey-Bass, 1977.

Baird, L. L., Hartnett, R. T., and Associates. *Understanding Student and Faculty Life: Using Campus Surveys to Improve Academic Decision Making.* San Francisco: Jossey-Bass, 1980.

Balderston, F. E. *Managing Today's University.* San Francisco: Jossey-Bass, 1974.

Baldridge, J. V. (Ed.). *Academic Governance.* Berkeley, Calif.: McCutchan, 1971a.

Baldridge, J. V. *Power and Conflict in the University.* New York: Wiley, 1971b.

Baldridge, J. V., and Deal, T. *Managing Change in Academic Organization.* Berkeley, Calif.: McCutchan, 1974.

221

Baldridge, J. V., and Tierney, M. L. *New Approaches to Management: Creating Practical Systems of Management Information and Management by Objectives.* San Francisco: Jossey-Bass, 1979.

Banfield, E. C. "Ends and Means in Planning." In S. Mailick (Ed.), *Concepts and Issues in Administrative Behavior.* Englewood Cliffs, N.J.: Prentice-Hall, 1962.

Bayer, A. E. *Teaching Faculty in Academe.* Washington, D.C.: American Council on Education, 1973.

Benezet, L. T., and Magnusson, F. W. (Eds.). *New Directions for Higher Education: Building Bridges to the Public,* no. 27. San Francisco: Jossey-Bass, 1979.

Bennis, W. G. *Organization Development: Its Nature, Origins, and Prospects.* Reading, Mass.: Addison-Wesley, 1969.

Berelson, B. *Content Analysis and Communication Research.* New York: Free Press, 1952.

Berlo, D. K. *The Process of Communication.* New York: Holt, Rinehart and Winston, 1960.

Blackburn, R. T. *Tenure: Aspects of Job Security on the Changing Campus.* Atlanta, Ga.: Southern Regional Education Board, 1972.

Blackwell, T. E. *College and University Administration.* New York: Center for Applied Research in Education, 1966.

Blake, R. H., and Haroldsen, E. O. *Taxonomy of Concepts in Communication.* New York: Hastings House, 1975.

Blau, P. M. *The Organization of Academic Work.* New York: Wiley, 1973.

Bowen, H. R., and Douglass, G. K. *Efficiency in Liberal Education: A Study of Comparative Instructional Costs for Different Ways of Organizing Teaching-Learning in a Liberal Arts College.* New York: McGraw-Hill, 1971.

Brann, J., and Emmet, T. A. (Eds.). *The Academic Department or Division Chairman: A Complex Role.* Detroit, Mich.: Balamp, 1972.

Brubacher, J. S. *Bases for Policy in Higher Education.* New York: McGraw-Hill, 1965.

Budig, G. A. *Dollars and Sense: Budgeting for Today's Campus.* Chicago: College and University Business Press, 1972.

Butler, N. M. *Across the Busy Years: Recollections and Reflections.* (2 vols.) New York: Scribner's, 1940.

Capen, S. P. *The Management of Universities.* Buffalo, N.Y.: Foster and Stewart, 1953.

Carnegie Commission on Higher Education. *The More Effective Use of Resources: An Imperative for Higher Education.* New York: McGraw-Hill, 1972.

Carnegie Commission on Higher Education. *Governance of Higher Education: Six Priority Problems.* New York: McGraw-Hill, 1973.

Caws, P., Ripley, S. D., and Ritterbush, P. C. (Eds.). *The Bankruptcy of Academic Policy.* Washington, D.C.: Acropolis Books, 1972.

Center for Research and Development in Higher Education. *State Budgeting for Higher Education: Data Digest.* Berkeley: Center for Research and Development in Higher Education, University of California, 1975.

Centra, J. A. *Faculty Development Practices in U.S. Colleges and Universities.* Princeton, N.J.: Educational Testing Service, 1976.

Cheit, E. F. *The New Depression in Higher Education.* New York: McGraw-Hill, 1971.

Cheit, E. F. *The New Depression in Higher Education: Two Years Later.* Berkeley, Calif.: Carnegie Commission on Higher Education, 1973.

Clark, B., and Young, R. I. K. *Academic Power in the United States.* AAHE/ERIC Higher Education Research Report No. 3. Washington, D.C.: American Association for Higher Education, 1976.

Cohen, M. D., and March, J. G. *Leadership and Ambiguity.* New York: McGraw-Hill, 1974.

Commission on Non-Traditional Study. *Diversity by Design.* San Francisco: Jossey-Bass, 1973.

Committee on Economic Development. *The Management and Financing of Colleges.* New York: Committee on Economic Development, 1973.

Cook, T. J. *Description, Analysis, and Evaluation of Principal Benefit Plans of Colleges and Universities in the United States.* New York: Columbia University Press, 1980.

Corson, J. J. *Governance of Colleges and Universities.* (Rev. ed.) New York: McGraw-Hill, 1975.

Cross, K. P. *Beyond the Open Door: New Students in Higher Education.* San Francisco: Jossey-Bass, 1971.

Day, E. E. "The Role of Administration in Higher Education." *Journal of Higher Education,* 1946, *17,* 339-343.

DeFleur, M. L. *Theories of Mass Communications.* New York: McKay, 1966.

Deighton, L. C. (Ed.). *The Encyclopedia of Education.* (10 vols.) New York: Macmillan and Free Press, 1971.

Delworth, U., Hanson, G. R., and Associates. *Student Services: A Handbook for the Profession.* San Francisco: Jossey-Bass, 1980.

Demerath, N. J., Stephens, R. W., and Taylor, R. R. *Power, Presidents, and Professors.* New York: Basic Books, 1967.

Dibden, A. J. (Ed.). *The Academic Deanship in American Colleges and Universities.* Carbondale: Southern Illinois University Press, 1968.

Dill, D. D. *Case Studies in University Governance.* Washington, D.C.: Association of State Universities and Land-Grant Colleges, 1971.

Dill, W. R. "Administrative Decision-Making." In S. Mailick (Ed.), *Concepts and Issues in Administrative Behavior.* Englewood Cliffs, N.J.: Prentice-Hall, 1962.

Dodds, H. W. *The Academic President—Educator or Caretaker?* New York: McGraw-Hill, 1962.

Doermann, H. *Crosscurrents in College Admissions.* New York: Teachers College Press, Columbia University, 1968.

Downs, A. *Inside Bureaucracy.* Boston: Little, Brown, 1967.

Dressel, P. L. *Handbook of Academic Evaluation: Assessing Institutional Effectiveness, Student Progress, and Professional Performance for Decision Making in Higher Education.* San Francisco: Jossey-Bass, 1976.

Dressel, P. L. *Improving Degree Programs: A Guide to Curriculum Development, Administration, and Review.* San Francisco: Jossey-Bass, 1980a.

Dressel, P. L. (Ed.). *New Directions for Institutional Research: The Autonomy of Public Colleges,* no. 26. San Francisco: Jossey-Bass, 1980b.

Dressel, P. L., Johnson, F. C., and Marcus, P. M. *The Confidence Crisis: An Analysis of University Departments.* San Francisco: Jossey-Bass, 1970.

Ducanis, A. J. "The Possible Uses of the Delphi Technique in I. R. Planning in Higher Education." In P. S. Wright (Ed.), *Institutional Research and Communication in Higher Education.* Proceedings of the 10th Annual Forum on Institutional Research sponsored by the Association for Institutional Research, 1970.

Duryea, E. D., Fish, R. S., and Associates. *Faculty Unions and Collective Bargaining.* San Francisco: Jossey-Bass, 1973.

Dykes, A. R. *Faculty Participation in Academic Decision Making.* Washington, D.C.: American Council on Education, 1968.

Eble, K. E. *The Art of Administration: A Guide for Academic Administrators.* San Francisco: Jossey-Bass, 1978.

Eliot, C. W. *University Administration.* Boston: Houghton Mifflin, 1908.

Epstein, L. D. *Governing the University: The Campus and the Public Interest.* San Francisco: Jossey-Bass, 1974.

Foote, C., Mayer, H., and Associates. *The Culture of the University—Governance and Education.* San Francisco: Jossey-Bass, 1968.

Gaff, J. G. *Toward Faculty Renewal: Advances in Faculty, Instructional, and Organizational Development.* San Francisco: Jossey-Bass, 1975.

Gilman, D. C. *The Launching of the University.* New York: Dodd, Mead, 1906.

Glenny, L. A., Berdahl, R., Palola, E., and Paltridge, G. *Coordinating Higher Education for the '70s.* Berkeley: Center for Research and Development in Higher Education, University of California, 1971.

Glenny, L. A., and Kidder, J. *State Tax Support of Higher Education Revenue Appropriation Trends and Patterns 1963–1973.* Report No. 47. Denver, Colo.: Education Commission of the States, 1974.

Glenny, L. A., Shea, J. R., Ruyle, J. H., and Freschi, K. H. *Presidents Confront Reality: From Edifice Complex to University Without Walls.* San Francisco: Jossey-Bass, 1976.

Goffman, E. *Behavior in Public Places.* London: Collier-Macmillan, 1963.

Gollattscheck, J. F., and others. *College Leadership for Community Renewal: Beyond Community-Based Education.* San Francisco: Jossey-Bass, 1976.

Gordon, F. E., and Strober, M. *Bringing Women into Management.* New York: McGraw-Hill, 1975.

Gore, W. J. "Decision-Making Research: Some Prospects and Limitations." In S. Mailick (Ed.), *Concepts and Issues in Administrative Behavior.* Englewood Cliffs, N.J.: Prentice-Hall, 1962.

Gould, J. W. *The Academic Deanship.* New York: Teachers College Press, Columbia University, 1964.

Gouldner, A. W. "Metaphysical Pathos and the Theory of Bureaucracy." In A. Etzioni (Ed.), *Complex Organizations.* New York: Holt, Rinehart and Winston, 1961.

Green, E. J. *Effective Planning.* Pittsburgh, Pa.: Planning Dynamics Company, 1975.

Greenleaf, R. K. *Servant Leadership.* New York: Paulist Press, 1977.

Gross, E., and Grambsch, P. V. *Academic Administrators and University Goals.* Washington, D.C.: American Council on Education, 1968.

Haney, W. V. "Serial Communication of Information in Organizations." In J. A. DeVito, *Communication Concepts and Processes.* Englewood Cliffs, N.J.: Prentice-Hall, 1971.

Harrison, R. P. "Other Ways of Packaging Information." In J. A. DeVito, *Communication Concepts and Processes.* Englewood Cliffs, N.J.: Prentice-Hall, 1971.

Heaton, C. P. (Ed.). *Management by Objectives in Higher Education.* Durham, N.C.: National Laboratory for Higher Education, 1975.

Hefferlin, JB L. *Dynamics of Academic Reform.* San Francisco: Jossey-Bass, 1969.

Heilbroner, R. L. *An Inquiry into the Human Prospect.* New York: Norton, 1974.

Helmer, O. *The Use of the Delphi Technique in Problems of Education Innovations,* P3499. Santa Monica, Calif.: Rand Corporation, 1966.

Hill, W. W., and French, W. L. "Perceptions of Power of Department Chairmen by Professors." *Administrative Science Quarterly,* 1967, *2,* 548-584.

Hodgkinson, H. L., and Meeth, L. R. (Eds.). *Power and Authority: Transformation of Campus Governance.* San Francisco: Jossey-Bass, 1971.

Hofstadter, R., and Hardy, C. D. *The Development and Scope of Higher Education in the United States.* New York: Columbia University Press, 1952.

Hostrop, R. W. *Managing Education for Results.* Homewood, Ill.: ETC Publications, 1973.

Huckfeldt, V. *Change in Higher Education Management.* Boulder, Colo.: National Center for Higher Education Management Systems, 1972.

Hudspeth, D. R. *A Long-Range Planning Tool for Education: The Focused Delphi.* Albany: New York State Education Department, 1970.

Hutchins, R. M. "The Administrator." *Journal of Higher Education,* 1946, *17,* 395-407.

Ihlanfeldt, W. *Achieving Optimal Enrollments and Tuition Revenues: A Guide to Modern Methods of Market Research, Student Recruitment, and Institutional Pricing.* San Francisco: Jossey-Bass, 1980.

Ikenberry, S. O. *The Changing Role of the College Presidency: Essays on Governance.* Washington, D.C.: American Association of State Colleges and Universities, 1974.

Irwin, J. T. (Ed.). *A Guide to Professional Development Opportunities for College and University Administrators.* Washington, D.C.: Academy for Educational Development and American Council on Education, 1975.

Jellema, W. W. (Ed.). *Efficient College Management.* San Francisco: Jossey-Bass, 1972.

Jencks, C., and Riesman, D. *The Academic Revolution.* Garden City, N.Y.: Doubleday, 1968.

Jonsen, R. W. *Small Liberal Arts Colleges: Diversity at the Crossroads.* Washington, D.C.: American Association for Higher Education, 1978.

Jordan, D. S. *The Voice of the Scholar.* San Francisco: Elder, 1903.

Kaplin, W. A. *The Law of Higher Education 1980.* San Francisco: Jossey-Bass, 1980.

Kauffman, J. F. *The Selection of College and University Presidents.* Washington, D.C.: Association of American Colleges, 1974.

Kemeny, J. A. *It's Different at Dartmouth: A Memoir.* Brattleboro, Vt.: Green Press, 1979.

Kieft, R. N., Armijo, F., and Bucklew, N. *A Handbook for Institutional Academic and Program Planning: From Idea to Implementation.* Boulder, Colo.: National Center for Higher Education Management Systems Publications, 1978.

King, F. P. *Benefit Plans in Higher Education.* New York: Teachers Insurance and Annuity Association-College Retirement Equity Fund, 1980.

Klingelhofer, E., and Hollander, L. *Educational Characteristics and Needs of New Students: A Review of the Literature.* Berkeley: Center for Research and Development in Higher Education, University of California, 1973.

Knowles, A. S. (Ed.). *Handbook of College and University Administration.* (2 vols.) New York: McGraw-Hill, 1970.

Knowles, A. S. (Ed.). *International Encyclopedia of Higher Education.* (10 vols.) San Francisco: Jossey-Bass, 1977.

Lahti, R. E. *Innovative College Management: Implementing Proven Organizational Practice.* San Francisco: Jossey-Bass, 1973.

Landau, M. "The Concept of Decision-Making in the 'Field' of Public Administration." In S. Mailick (Ed.), *Concepts and Issues in Administrative Behavior.* Englewood Cliffs, N.J.: Prentice-Hall, 1962.

Lawrence, B. G., and Sevice, A. L. *Quantitative Approaches to Higher Education Management.* Washington, D.C.: American Association for Higher Education, 1977.

Lawrence, P., and Lorsch, J. *Organization and Environment.* Homewood, Ill.: Irwin, 1969.

Lee, E. C., and Bowen, F. M. *Managing Multicampus Systems: Effective Administration in an Unsteady State.* San Francisco: Jossey-Bass, 1975.

Lehrer, S. (Ed.). *Leaders, Teachers, and Learners in Academe:*

Partners in the Educational Process. New York: Appleton-Century-Crofts, 1970.

Leslie, D. W. "The Status of the Department Chairmanship in University Organization." *AAUP Bulletin,* 1973, *59,* 419-426.

Leslie, L. L., and Miller, H. F., Jr. *Higher Education and the Steady State.* AAHE/ERIC Higher Education Research Report No. 4. Washington, D.C.: American Association for Higher Education, 1974.

Levine, A. *Why Innovation Fails: The Institutionalization and Termination of Innovation in Higher Education.* Albany: State University of New York Press, 1980.

Leys, W. A. R. "The Value Framework of Decision-Making." In S. Mailick (Ed.), *Concepts and Issues in Administrative Behavior.* Englewood Cliffs, N.J.: Prentice-Hall, 1962.

Lipsett, S. M., and Ladd, E. C., Jr. *Professors, Unions, and American Higher Education.* Berkeley, Calif.: Carnegie Commission on Higher Education, 1973.

Lowell, A. L. *What a University President Has Learned.* New York: Macmillan, 1938.

McGregor, D. *The Human Side of Enterprise.* New York: McGraw-Hill, 1960.

McHenry, D. E., and Associates. *Academic Departments: Problems, Variations, and Alternatives.* San Francisco: Jossey-Bass, 1977.

Mailick, S. (Ed.). *Concepts and Issues in Administrative Behavior.* Englewood Cliffs, N.J.: Prentice-Hall, 1962.

Mayhew, L. B. *Surviving the Eighties: Strategies and Procedures for Solving Fiscal and Enrollment Problems.* San Francisco: Jossey-Bass, 1979.

Medsker, L., and others. *Extending Opportunities for a College Degree: Practices, Problems, and Potentials.* Berkeley: Center for Research and Development in Higher Education, University of California, 1975.

Miller, R. I. *Evaluating Faculty Performance.* San Francisco: Jossey-Bass, 1972.

Miller, R. I. *Developing Programs for Faculty Evaluation: A Sourcebook for Higher Education.* San Francisco: Jossey-Bass, 1974.

Miller, R. I. *The Assessment of College Performance: A Handbook of Techniques and Measures for Institutional Self-Evaluation.* San Francisco: Jossey-Bass, 1979.

Millett, J. D. *Decision Making and Administration in Higher Education.* Kent, Ohio: Kent State University Press, 1968.

Millett, J. D. *The Multiple Roles of College and University Presidents.* Washington, D.C.: American Council on Education, 1976.

Millett, J. D. *Planning in Higher Education.* Washington, D.C.: Academy for Educational Development, 1977.

Millett, J. D. *New Structures of Campus Power: Success and Failures of Emerging Forms of Institutional Governance.* San Francisco: Jossey-Bass, 1978.

Mobberley, D. G., and Wicke, M. F. *The Deanship of the Liberal Arts College.* Nashville, Tenn.: Division of Higher Education, Methodist Board of Education, 1962.

Mortimer, K. P., and McConnell, T. R. *Sharing Authority Effectively: Participation, Interaction, and Discretion.* San Francisco: Jossey-Bass, 1978.

Orwig, M. D., Jones, P. K., and Lenning, O. T. *Enrollment Projection Models for Institutional Planning.* ACT Research Report No. 48. Iowa City, Iowa: American College Testing Program, 1972.

Palola, E. G., Lehmann, T., and Bleschke, W. R. *Higher Education by Design: The Sociology of Planning.* Berkeley: Center for Research and Development in Higher Education, University of California, 1970.

Palola, E. G., and Padgett, W. *Planning for Self Renewal: A New Approach to Planned Organizational Change.* Berkeley: Center for Research and Development in Higher Education, University of California, 1971.

Parsons, T., Platt, G. M., and others. *The American University.* Cambridge, Mass.: Harvard University Press, 1973.

Peters, R. S. *Ethics and Education.* Glenview, Ill.: Scott, Foresman, 1966.

Prator, R. *The College President.* Washington, D.C.: Center for Applied Research in Education, 1963.

Presthus, R. V. "Authority in Organizations." In S. Mailick

(Ed.), *Concepts and Issues in Administrative Behavior.* Englewood Cliffs, N.J.: Prentice-Hall, 1962.

Price, J. L. *Organizational Effectiveness: An Inventory of Propositions.* Homewood, Ill.: Irwin, 1968.

Raia, A. *Management by Objectives.* Glenview, Ill.: Scott, Foresman, 1974.

Rauh, M. *The Trusteeship of Colleges and Universities.* New York: McGraw-Hill, 1969.

Richman, B. M., and Farmer, R. N. *Leadership, Goals, and Power in Higher Education: A Contingency and Open-Systems Approach to Effective Management.* San Francisco: Jossey-Bass, 1974.

Riesman, D., Gusfield, J., and Gamson, Z. *Academic Values and Mass Education.* Garden City, N.Y.: Doubleday, 1970.

Rockey, E. H. *Communication in Organizations.* Cambridge, Mass.: Winthrop, 1977.

Rogers, E., and Shoemaker, F. F. *Communication of Innovations.* (2nd ed.) New York: Free Press, 1971.

Rourke, F. E., and Brooks, G. E. *The Managerial Revolution in Higher Education.* Baltimore, Md.: Johns Hopkins University Press, 1966.

Rowland, A. W. (Ed.). *Handbook of Institutional Advancement: A Practical Guide to College and University Relations, Fund Raising, Alumni Relations, Government Relations, Publications, and Executive Management for Continued Advancement.* San Francisco: Jossey-Bass, 1977.

Salmen, S. *Duties of Administrators in Higher Education.* New York: Macmillan, 1971.

Schmidt, G. P. *The Old Time College President.* New York: Columbia University Press, 1930.

Schramm, W. (Ed.). *The Process and Effects of Mass Communication.* Urbana: University of Illinois Press, 1954.

Schramm, W. "How Communication Works." In J. A. DeVito, *Communication Concepts and Processes.* Englewood Cliffs, N.J.: Prentice-Hall, 1971.

Scott, R. A. *Lords, Squires, and Yeomen: Collegiate Middle Managers and Their Organization.* Washington, D.C.: American Association for Higher Education, 1978.

Selznick, P. *Leadership in Administration.* New York: Harper & Row, 1957.

Shulman, C. H. *Private Colleges: Present Conditions and Future Prospects.* Washington, D.C.: American Association for Higher Education, 1974.

Shulman, C. H. *University Admissions: Dilemmas on Potential.* Washington, D.C.: American Association for Higher Education, 1977.

Simon, H. A. "The Decision Maker as Innovator." In S. Mailick (Ed.), *Concepts and Issues in Administrative Behavior.* Englewood Cliffs, N.J.: Prentice-Hall, 1962.

Smith, A. B. *Communication and Culture.* New York: Holt, Rinehart and Winston, 1966.

Smith, B. L. R., and Karlesky, J. J. *The State of Academic Science.* Vol. 1: *The Universities in the Nation's Research Effort;* Vol. 2: *Background Papers.* New Rochelle, N.Y.: Change Magazine Press, 1980.

Steiner, G. A. *Human Behavior.* New York: Harcourt Brace Jovanovich, 1964.

Stogdill, R. M. *Handbook of Leadership.* New York: Free Press, 1974.

Stoke, H. W. *The American College President.* New York: Harper & Row, 1959.

Stroup, H. *Bureaucracy in Higher Education.* New York: Free Press, 1966.

Tead, O. *The Art of Administration.* New York: McGraw-Hill, 1951.

Thwing, C. F. *College Administration.* New York: Appleton-Century-Crofts, 1900.

Thwing, C. F. *The College President.* New York: Macmillan, 1926.

Vardaman, G. T., Daltemen, C. C., and Vardaman, P. B. *Cutting Communications Costs and Increasing Impacts.* New York: Wiley, 1970.

Veysey, L. "Stability and Experiment in the American Undergraduate Curriculum." In C. Kaysen (Ed.), *Content and Context.* New York: McGraw-Hill, 1973.

Walker, D. E. *The Effective Administrator: A Practical Ap-*

proach to Problem Solving, Decision Making, and Campus Leadership. San Francisco: Jossey-Bass, 1979.

Walton, C. C., and Bolman, F. D. (Eds.). *Disorders in Higher Education.* Englewood Cliffs, N.J.: Prentice-Hall, 1979.

Wegener, C. *Liberal Education and the Modern University.* Chicago: University of Chicago Press, 1978.

Willingham, W. W. *The Source Book for Higher Education: A Critical Guide to Literature and Information on Access to Higher Education.* New York: College Entrance Examination Board, 1973.

Wolotkievicz, J. *The College Administrator's Handbook.* Boston: Allyn & Bacon, 1980.

Index

235